To Square with Genesis

Causal Statements and
Shamanic Ideas
in Wayãpí

To Square with Genesis

Causal Statements and Shamanic Ideas in Wayãpí

By Alan Tormaid Campbell

University of Iowa Press ψ Iowa City

International Standard Book Number 0–87745–248–2
Library of Congress Catalog Card Number 88–51972

University of Iowa Press, Iowa City 52242

Contents

Acknowledgements

To the memory of my mother
Jean Begg Campbell

A thousand thanks to Linda Jo Bartholomew, Calum Campbell, James Clifford, Leonard Findlay, Francis Huxley, Barrington Jones, Peter Rivière, David Shankland, Mary Tait, Lúcia van Velthem, and particularly to Christopher Fyfe, and Judith Okely. They suggested improvements to the manuscript. More importantly, they approached what I wrote with intelligent goodwill and gave me so much encouragement.

Fieldwork in Brazil was made possible by an SSRC grant directed by Peter Rivière at the Institute of Social Anthropology at Oxford. A later visit to Brazil was assisted by a grant from the Leverhulme Trust.

For kindness, hospitality, and help in Brazil I wish to thank Bruce Bushey, Celeste and Roberto da Matta, Dominique Gallois, Eurídice Lethbridge, Alcida Ramos, Marilda Rosado, Olímpio Serra, Peter Silverwood-Cope, and Ken Taylor. I would also like to thank the staff of the Museu Nacional in Rio de Janeiro, of the Museu Goeldi in Belém, of ICOMI in Santana and Serra do Navio, and, despite our disagreements, the FUNAI staff who helped so often, particularly those on the *frente de atração* in those difficult days: Fiorello, Paulo, Amérigo, Barcelá, Piauí, Toninho, and Maçaranduba.

And I'm due my friends in the forest so much more than thanks. When I think of what they gave me I am bereft of words. I love and admire them, and miss their company. The Wayãpí, like many other peoples in the Amazon area, face the prospect of seeing their great forests destroyed. They are threatened by government decrees that deprive them of their own lands, and by mineral companies and organizations that invade them. These forces devastate their environment, undermine their health and their autonomy, and put their very survival in question. I have written an academic book, and I hope readers will enjoy the academic debate. But no one should forget that at the back of this debate the most important issue we all have to face is that the peoples and forests of Amazônia are being destroyed by our world.

Phonetic Key

e = [e]
è = [ɛ]
o = [o]
ò = [ɔ]
' = glottal stop
ɨ indicates a vowel somewhere between [ɜ] and [φ], as in English 'bird' and French 'peu'.
ğ indicates a voiced [χ], after ɨ, e.g. ɨğ (water).
ë indicates a neutral, unstressed vowel, like the English schwa, [ə], found after terminal 'r', e.g. yarë (master).
ŭ is the nasalized [ʎ].
ˉ over other vowels indicates nasality.
Stress is indicated by underlining: anyimòrɨpa.
In the text, approximate Wayãpí pronunciation is indicated by placing the word between obliques, but words used frequently are given in an informal English convention and italicized thus: [yarë] and [mòyo] become *yarr* and *moyo*.

PICADA:
clearing a way

mi ritrovai per una selva oscura,
che la diritta via era smarrita

(I came to myself within a dark wood
Where the straight way was lost)
Dante, *Inferno* I, 2–3.

A *picada* in Brazilian Portuguese is a path that a hunter or traveller
makes when passing through untouched forest. Making a path in the
Amazon forest is not usually very difficult. Mostly the woods are
fairly open and if the eye does not register the relative size of the trees,
where the *angelins* and *sumaumas* of Amazônia make the most magnificent oaks and elms of Britain look like squat miniatures, the tropical forest can look as benign and beautiful as any patch of woodland in
the Home Counties. There can be strenuous stretches in clearing a
path but it seldom involves hacking one's way through a mass of
tangled lianas, as in the popular image. I have often followed a hunter
who seemed to be making his way absent-mindedly, cutting a slender
sapling now and again with one swing of his knife, or breaking and
bending the saplings with his hands, as the Indians always did in the
old days before they had knives or machetes. It marks the way so that
one does not get lost. 'My thoughts have left no track and I cannot find
the path again' (Thoreau 1937:202) reminds me how frightening it is,
when travelling alone in the forest, to lose the path.

This introductory chapter is meant to leave a few clues about the
way I've taken when writing about a particular group of people I met
in the Amazon woods. Over a spell of two years, between 1974 and
1976, I stayed with a people who call themselves Wayãpí. Up to that
time they were in an area of Northern Brazil that had not been
damaged by the intrusion of Brazilians or other foreigners, but which
was on the point of having a highway pushed through it. There were
150 Wayãpí living there. I visited them again in 1984 and found that
they had so far survived the worst effects of contact with outsiders,
and that in the intervening years just on 100 children had been born
and were living.

In writing about my stay with these people in a particular way I don't mean to assert that I've done anything particularly new. As ethnographies accumulate over the years, more and more writers begin by distancing themselves from the received approach, claiming some freshness in format or theme, but the work that follows usually sits comfortably within the familiar tradition. While staking my own claim, instead of asserting novelty it is more important to clarify what I have not done, since I find I have left behind a number of expectations associated with ethnographic work.

What follows is not an 'analysis' of 'material' gathered 'in the field'. I emphasize these words in warning-quotes for those who use them familiarly, so that when they look through this essay they will not be disappointed by its failure to satisfy their expectations. It is not intended as a compendium of 'ethnographic facts', and I am sure some readers will say it does not qualify as an 'ethnography' at all. The essay attempts to query the conditions of my encounter with those Wayãpí people. I look at certain puzzles and obscurities not with a view to clearing them up, for example finding a rationality behind what is apparently irrational, or finding hidden principles of order, but trying to find the conditions by which certain statements, certain habits and dispositions, certain liturgies, come to appear puzzling to us in the first place. As far as possible I want to move away from diagnostic statements: that they are such and such; that they do this and that; that they have this feature or that feature. In place of that I want to try a relational account where puzzles and mysteries are just as much a function of our predicament as of theirs. The questions appear in the form: why do we identify this or that as a puzzle?; why does this statement or that habit appear mysterious to us?; what lies between us and them?.

The central chapter looks at the problem of causal statements, both theirs and ours. This leads to looking at statements about causes of death and particularly to those practices we call shamanism. These examples lead to the following account of what lies between them and us. Firstly, I suggest a predicament in which we are working with certain kinds of distinctions and they are not. This seems to be a barrier that cannot be broken, like a protective cocoon which they can emerge from if they want to, but into which we cannot step. I use the particular example of the noun/verb distinction, the distinction between *onoma* and *rhema* established by Aristotle. In this case, wherever we turn to our language, 'the Stagirite o'erlooks each line', like the angel guarding the entrance to Eden, forbidding our return to a state where we do not see the distinction. Once the distinction is established, it is peculiarly difficult to emulsify it again.

Secondly, the noun/verb distinction in our habits of thought allows the proliferation of hypostases – things, categories, abstract entities – which we bestow haphazardly on ourselves and others in the form of names and diagnoses. (What actually makes a thief a thief and a boxer a boxer is that they *do* something.) Translating actions and qualities into substances (translating doing and having into being), may be all very well for us to get by with amongst ourselves, but we may be misunderstanding others if we lumber them with our odd, spurious, and superfluous things. Examples of how to confront this difficulty are found in the work of those translators I have looked at who are dealing with pre-Socratic Greek and classical Chinese texts. I suggest a parallel difficulty in translating from Wayãpí where, on the subject of shamanism for example, a statement such as 'The Wayãpí have shamans' is misleading and I suggest that we should try in this case to loosen up our categories of noun, adjective, and verb and learn to place more emphasis on the verb. In other words, there is no such *thing* as a shaman. People shamanize. They use a quality.

It is a serious matter to interfere with our distinctions.

> Hsun Tze, who lived about seventy years after Mencius, in his chapter on the *Rectification of Names*, repeats the recommendation found in the *Li Ki*, Book III, iv, 16, that those who introduce new terms or make unauthorized distinctions should be put to death.
>
> (Richards 1932:24–5)

What is referred to here in such extreme terms is the more usual way of interfering with distinctions, that is, introducing *new* terms and making ever finer discriminations. A great deal of the practice of our philosophy consists of doing so, and indeed the ability to make distinctions is used as a measure of how clever people are at philosophy. But I am suggesting a move in a different direction: looking at the peculiar demands made on our imagination when we are asked to give up our established distinctions.

The chapter on Wayãpí relationship terms, although appearing formal and esoteric, is a graphic, diagrammatic illustration of precisely this kind of exercise. It shows that once we find ourselves thinking in terms of duality, in this case a distinction of 'two lines', the formal contortions required to release this knot are surprisingly complicated. Unfortunately, although the example is so clear in its simple formality, it will be found forbidding, since it strays off into that awful desert marked 'kinship' on the old anthropological maps. There's hardly a path there; just footprints.

To balance this extremity, chapters 2 and 3 contain introductory descriptions of the tropical forest, an outline of Wayãpí history, and some ethnographic bits and pieces. These chapters describe the natural context of the questions asked, and readers unfamiliar with the Amazon woods may find the details useful. The main point of chapter 2 queries the way names and dates are used. Chapter 3 gives an account of how anthropological interests are pursued through the conditions of a comprehensive process of contact between Indians and the representatives of our civilization. But before getting to the

forest, I want to give an account of two areas that had to be negotiated. Here, at home, it turned out to be a particular diction. There, in
the woods, it was their language.

After returning to Britain from Brazil and settling into my old habits, I
became aware of a depressing paradox. While it was clear that the
previous two and a half years in Brazil had been such an important
period, both academically and privately, and while I found myself
drawn to tell the story, informally at any rate, with 'adjectival and
worse than supererogatory insistence' (as F. R. Leavis described the
language of *Heart of Darkness*), I found at the same time that attempts
to write something seemed like fiddling with inconsequential details.
While there was ample opportunity in conversation to emphasize
how intense it all had been, formally I found myself with nothing to
say worth the slightest attention.

The oppressive sense of having nothing to say resolved itself
through various stages. I had doubts about the quality of my fieldwork. Had I worked harder at the language, had I brought back hours
of tape-recordings and bundles of notebooks, then would not sheer
weight of detail have been the inspiration and would not the task be
only how best to *organize* and *arrange* it? Well, the conviction that I
could do better fieldwork were I to go back, that I could find richer
details, and that I could use the time there more fruitfully, was a
consequence of the expertise gained from having been there in the
first place. And it was therefore silly to turn that conviction into a
matter for regret. The problem was not the notebooks.

Perhaps the Wayãpí themselves were not a particularly interesting
people for an anthropological study. Perhaps had I found a thriving,
vigorous population, with elaborate rituals and a voluble cosmology,
preoccupied with articulating the principles of order that imbued
their world, then surely my writing would have had a momentum of
its own. What I found was a people who had lost an appalling number
of their community over the previous few decades and who talked
sadly and anxiously about the prospect of their extinction. One of the
· first phrases I learned was / wayãpi̠ õ-pa /, 'the Wayãpí are finished'.
There were 150 people left and I spent most of my time in one
settlement of 50 people. There were 12 adult men and 24 adult women
there, not all of them eager to converse at any length. Ethnograph-
ically there was nothing peculiar or novel. The material culture (pots,
baskets, feather-work, and so on) while wonderful enough for me,
was crude and rather shabby when compared with similar artefacts
that I had seen in museums and private collections. Their language
was one of the Tupi-Guaraní family, a group that includes some
particularly well-known languages. Their relationship terminology
was straightforward. They hunted and fished as anyone does in the
Brazilian interior, and their horticulture was based on manioc culti-

vation, again a commonplace for anyone who knows the area. The myths I heard were mostly no more than fragments of similar stories I had previously come across in much fuller form in other ethnographic documents. And as for rituals, large quantities of *caxirí* (manioc beer) were prepared every few weeks and everyone went on the spree. Occasionally, special preparations of costumes and artefacts were made for a spree, which was then named as a particular kind of dance. But there was a hesitancy in the proceedings, like people here these days trying to get through all the movements of an eightsome reel. How things should be done was only half-remembered, and there was a lot of giggling and light-hearted embarrassment, all resolved when everyone got drunk and stopped worrying about proper procedure.

It would be a *trahison des clercs* to start grading different peoples according to inherent qualities that reflect degrees of anthropological interest. But that betrayal is hinted at whenever anthropology encourages a desire for novelty by seeing the enterprise as the discovery and accumulation of new facts about unknown people, and by looking for ethnocartographic blanks to guarantee the student an area of original research. It's that wild surmise again, which silenced them all when Cortez (standing in for Balboa) first stared at the Pacific. In 1968, Claudio Villas Boas and his companions first saw the astonishing geometric patterns of the Kreen-Akarore gardens when they flew over the Peixoto de Azevedo area in Central Brazil searching for the villages of these isolated Indians. It was a sensational discovery, and through the excitement of the moment Claudio saw its implications. He is reported to have said: 'Never, never has there been anything like this. The anthropologists will run to see it' (Cowell 1976:108).

There is a genuine wonder in this kind of discovery, and I am sure that the curiosity encouraged by anthropology includes a desire to stand silent upon that peak in Darien. But pursuing novelty as an end in itself turns the activity into something vulgar and competitive. What Claudio had noticed was more than just an itch to gape at a new revelation. Those who can carry back some report of novelty can gain a certain status for themselves, hence those who become secretive about their unpublished fieldnotes and who guard their 'material' like the sulky dragon in *Beowulf* sitting on its treasure horde, protecting some ethnographic baubles which will be cashed in to make a reputation.

'Our tastes greatly alter.' I used to have a fanciful image of the kind of culture I would like to find – thriving, vigorous, elaborate, uncontaminated, and assertively unique. But such a picture is a counterfeit that no one should try to pass. Any such account of novelty reflects something about ourselves, not about that which we discover; or rather, it is a statement about our relationship to that which we discover. It is not *that out there* which is new; it is our encounter with it which is new. Furthermore, all of us have to take our first look into Chapman's Homer on our own. It can't be done by proxy. And what if our first look produces an unredeemably banal response? Would that say something about Chapman's Homer or would it say something about ourselves? The writer of the ethnography bears the responsibility for its quality. The people written about are innocent on that matter.

My writing was not being held up by anything in the nature of what I had done, nor by anything that concerned those I had stayed with. The difficulty was how to work within the vocabulary that everyone in the business was currently using. It was an idiom that talked easily of 'material' and 'analysis', of 'social structure' and 'system of thought', and the problem was not that the vocabulary was obscure and technical, but that it was so casual. Being a restricted vocabulary and being used throughout a particular corner of academia, it gave the appearance of referring to scrupulous, specialist activities, like 'recension' or 'parsing'. But it was not precise and careful. It was a lazy vocabulary.

DICTION

In this essay, apart from examples where they are repudiated, and apart from quotations, the following words will not be found:

analysis, model, structure, system, order, logic, symbol, ritual (used as an adjective);

transformation, mediation, opposition, conjunction, disjunction, inversion, metaphor / metonym (used as a distinction);

fact, theory, hypothesis, method, proof;

informant.

That list is not intended to be comprehensive, although the second block refers to a particular vogue called structuralism for which Claude Lévi-Strauss was responsible. Taken altogether these words are examples of a more extensive idioticon widely used in human studies. It is a working vocabulary that incorporates presuppositions I want to lay aside. I know that disparaging the words people use in their everyday vocabulary can be taken as exaggerated contumacy. It certainly provokes a more tetchy response than the more familiar kinds of thematic dispute. But the words and images people choose can give a clearer indication of assumptions and expectations than their attempts to elaborate these into what are called their theoretical positions. Correspondingly, giving up a word here and there can usefully clear away all sorts of tangled preconceptions.

The word 'fact', for example, reveals a peculiar obsession. As long as ethnography sees its job as furnishing facts about unknown peoples, the activity will remain prone to forget that 'indissoluble liaison between fact and value' (Ricoeur 1977:216), and to persevere

with a misplaced confidence that as long as the ethnographic material
is produced in sufficient quantity and arranged in a coherent way, it
will constitute a description whose significance is guaranteed. But
most ethnographic descriptions make very tedious reading for those
unacquainted with the area described, and although Edmund Leach
made this point so long ago (1954:227) the predicament is seen in the
same way more than thirty years later:

> For the lay person, such as myself, the main evidence of a
> problem is the simple fact that ethnographic writing tends to be
> surprisingly boring. How, one asks constantly, could such
> interesting people doing such interesting things produce such
> dull books? What did they have to do to themselves?(Pratt
> 1986:33)

The tedium of ethnographic writing is not considered a critical problem. It is accepted with a shrug as a necessary part of the business, like
bad weather in the British Isles. It is not considered appropriate to
query the significance of these reams of facts. They are immune from
questions of value and are left inert.

They are allowed to lie like that because questions about value have
been deflected into discussions of what is called 'theory'. It is here that
struggles about significance take place, where 'positions' are defended and refuted, where 'models' are assayed for their adequacy,
their conceptual clarity, or their consistency. But curiously, it is just
here that clarity and consistency, or the lack of these, do not manage
to explain the grounds on which one accepts or rejects a 'theory'. All
the decisions have been made before, amongst proclivities that arise
from murky areas of personal taste and temperament: ' . . . il n'est pas
de théorie qui ne soit un fragment, soigneusement préparé, de quel-
que autobiographie' (Valéry: see Righter 1977:126). Hence the locus of
discussion has been exquisitely misplaced.

With novelty value gone, what can be done with the inert facts? The
answer is to start arranging them. 'Arrange' in English is a curiously
modern word, not found in the Bible, Shakespeare, Milton's poetry,
nor Pope's work. Apart from its military sense of putting soldiers into
a rank, the first example of the sense of 'putting things into order' is
given by the *OED* as 1791 where James Boswell described green-
grocers 'arranging' their hampers. It is one of a list of words with
recently acquired senses, given by Waissman (1968:220), that includes 'category', 'classify', 'method', 'organize', and 'systematic', all
of which are put to strenuous use in anthropological writing. The
conditions of the arranging activity are made possible because of the
separation of fact from significance, as it is put in Lithgow's *Travayles*
of 1632, given as one of the earliest uses of 'organize' in this sense: 'I
Organize the Truth, you Allegate [sc. "allege"] the sense', or more
vividly in Ricoeur's laconic comment on 'structuralism', a fashion that
carried this activity to grotesque extremes: 'Vous sauvez le sens, mais

c'est le sens du non-sens, l'admirable arrangement syntactique d'un
discours qui ne dit rien . . . ' (Ricoeur in Lévi-Strauss 1963:653).

   Arranging structures is the senseless extremity of a more benign
and general search for *systems*. The simplest justification for this
interest in systems is that people's behaviour and the events that
surround their lives are not random affairs. And among the useful
guiding images that help articulate and develop this point of view are
Saussure's idea of *la langue* and Wittgenstein's idea of 'following a
rule'. These ideas, and many others like them, give body to the
intuition that underlying people's apparently arbitrary ways of doing
things and explaining things there are organizational patterns and
rules which, when discovered, show the initial appearance of arbitrariness to be illusory. From the organic analogy to the algebraics
of structuralism, from Radcliffe-Brown's image of the structure of
a scallop shell picked up on the beach to Lévi-Strauss's image
of an order of orders, although the exercises grow more sophisticated,
the guiding notions of system, structure, and order remain
untroubled.

   The following is a most genial summary of these preconceptions:

   A structural analysis deals first with the cultural categories in
   terms of which a given people organize their own experience. It
   then seeks to relate the rules of their society and the patterns of
   action observable within it to these ideas. Above all it seeks to
   determine what are the principles underlying this aggregate of
   ideas, rules and actions and relate them to each other in such a
   way as to show the crucial relationships in the society studied.
   Clearly the procedure is based on certain assumptions about the
   coherence of cultures. It is gratuitously polemical, however, to
   assume or insist that structural analysis must depart from the
   supposition that all cultures are utterly coherent. The only
   necessary assumption it makes is that there is at any given
   moment a systematic aspect to any culture which is worth study-
   ing. This is an assumption which I make and which I do not think
   requires any defence.   (Maybury-Lewis 1974: second page)

Systems, structures, models, logics, and organizational principles
clearly identify the preponderant direction of inquiry in ethnography
and anthropology, as a cursory glance at the vocabulary of recent
monographs will confirm. And it has been going on for a long time
elsewhere. However curiously modern Waissman's word-list may
be, the assumption of the systematic nature of what one is looking at
is as old as Anaximander's notion of *kosmos*:

   Anaximander's world is indeed a *kosmos*, a 'seemly array',
   governed by uniform periodicity, the cosmic opposites balanced
   within it, the whole structured symmetrically, and in proportions that conform to an intelligible arithmetical formula.
                                              (Mourelatos 1974:7)

Alternatives to this assumption also have a long and vigorous history:
> The Milesians ... supposed ... that the universe, being con-
> trolled by a supreme divinity worthy of the name, must necess-
> arily be a universe of order, of lawlike regularity, and of
> intellectually satisfying construction. To hold this belief inevi-
> tably inclines men to be naïvely optimistic and to underrate the
> subtlety of nature. Their constructions are doomed always to
> turn out crude by comparison with reality. As Pindar said, 'They
> pluck the fruit of wisdom when it is unripe', and with these
> words he dismissed the first century of Presocratic thought. The
> sneer, coming from Pindar, is no cheap one; but it applies if at all
> to the whole history of all sciences, not only to the first Presocrat-
> ics.   (Hussey 1972:16)

Hussey mentions that the book of Job is of the same period as Pindar,
but my point is not to relapse into resignation in the face of inscrutable
logics. The point is rather to put questions about the status of systems
and structures to one side and get on with something else. But, as part
of a more general move away from a diagnostic attitude, this involves
giving up other assumptions too: the easy currency of named collectivities; and the easy attribution of predicates to these names. Let me
look at these in turn.

Where demographic or linguistic boundaries so often cannot be
drawn with any certainty it is perverse that cosmological or ethical
notions which are often extremely elaborate should be tagged 'collective representations' and ascribed sometimes to large conglomer-
ations of people most of whom the reporter has never met.
(Purveyors of the intelligence are given the conspiratorial title of
'informants', compounding the notion that the ethnographer has
been clever enough to crack the code of these mysterious collective
habits of thought by befriending a spy who is privy to them.) Durkheim's elementary distinctions don't help here. What would a coherent and convincing account of our own collective thought look like? I
wonder if any responsible anthropologist would care to describe 'that
indescribable enchorial something which is British and not Nether-
landish' (OED 'enchorial'). If the boundaries cannot be drawn there,
then there is no reason to suppose that descriptions of the enchorial
somethings of others should hold our attention for long.

The use of names – the Nuer, the Azande, the Trobrianders, the
Bororo – to refer to others is the crucial device that releases those
potentials for engendering abstractions. The social diagnoses
couldn't be done without them. This question should be distinguished from the theme of those numerous studies that look at the
way people themselves conceptualize and maintain boundaries between themselves and others. The question here is how anthropologists use names to refer to discrete entities. The boundary, especially
when indigenous populations are large and widespread, may be

non-existent. The name may not even be the one those living there use of themselves. And even in the case of a very small group, such as the Wayãpí I knew, where several hundred miles of unpopulated forest and the span of a decade separated them from anybody else, one could still query what, exactly, constituted the boundary of that name. (The people I know are closely related to a group of 'French Wayãpí' living in French Guiana. This relationship is described later. There had been some intermarrying between the two.) But with the name set up like a honey-pot, the hypostases swarm around.

When a name and an attribute are coupled, an integument of peculiarity is thrown round the description. Even the simplest description of, say, 'the material culture of the Bororo' or 'Bororo ecology', is, by its nature, going to find it difficult to discriminate amongst (a) what might be peculiarly 'Bororo-ish' (perhaps body-paint designs, a form of dress, or the use of a plant not shared by others), (b) a widespread feature, not 'Bororo-ish' at all, shared by many other groups in the South American forest (bows and arrows, perhaps, or manioc cultivation), and (c) features which far from being 'Bororo-ish' are indications of relationships with others (practices learned, artefacts introduced from elsewhere). Certainly the illusions of peculiarity provided by descriptions of material culture or ecology do not mislead in any serious way. They can be so easily corrected. I remember the surprise, having been introduced to anthropology by way of the Nuer, of finding later that dozens and dozens of pastoral peoples in Africa not only have cattle but also elaborate cattle lexicons, cattle songs, cattle institutions, all just as pronounced as the Nuer. The peculiarity of the Nuer was not their cattle and cattle names but the anthropologist who visited them and the quality of what he wrote.

What happens, then, when we move on to 'the social structure of the Bororo' or 'Bororo cosmology'? And what happens when we move further to 'Bororo conceptions of time, of space, of the person', and to that catch-all phrase 'The Bororo believe that . . . ' where all sorts of epistemological and metaphysical hypostases are linked to the people named? The first step depends on the notion of 'system', implying boundedness, discreteness, separateness, and expressed through guiding suppositions like 'holism' and 'totality' The second step ('Bororo conceptions of time, etc.') is supported by the morbid presuppositions that there is an identifiable thing called 'a notion of time'; that we have one; that they have one; and that the two don't fit. Reading essays based on these presuppositions I simply do not believe that 'they', whoever they may be, have a different notion of time or space or of the person or of cause from 'us', whoever we may be, and I lay any further judgement aside having made three qualifications.

First, that the problem has been stated in the wrong way. Second, that were I able to question the evidence it would probably turn into a linguistic problem of how best to translate certain words, not one of lack of fit between certain concepts. Third, that there are probably no conditions under which the first two surmises could be taken any further since it is not a question of 'asking the ethnographer for further details' but of 'doing ethnography in a different way', that is, starting all over again asking different questions of the activity. I return to the 'illusion of difference' in the final section of Chapter 3.

To sum up; firstly, looking for systems is an attempt to tame congeries of unruly phenomena by simplifying them, reducing them, and bringing them into clusters of principles which are expressed in ever more formal, abstract, statements. In place of this I want to start from singular, isolated puzzles and go out from them, finding fortuitous connections that will expand the puzzle into something of ever increasing significance. Put crudely, it is a choice for writing interpretative glosses on instances of *parole* rather than looking for the rules of *langue*. The Wayãpí, all of them to some extent or another, were my friends during the time I stayed with them and though I cannot keep any direct contact with them they remain my familiars in a haunting way. When I ask 'what is it about these people and their way of life that puzzles me?' it would be silly to say that the pressing question that appears is 'what is it about these people's lives that is *systematic*?' The particular puzzles are always: 'what does this person mean by that statement?'; 'why is that way of doing things strange to me?'; 'what am I going to make of this person's explanation or that person's justification?' That their world is a 'seemly array' is obviously the case and I can see no question in that direction. The unseemly aspects of their lives, the epidemics and the erosion of their self-sufficiency, are a consequence of the impact that our civilization is having on them. No theory or hypothesis is required to explain these brutal facts.

Secondly, instead of diagnosis ('Amongst the Bororo . . . ', 'The Bororo believe that . . . '), I want to look at the relation between us and them, at the 'conditions whereby what we encounter says something to us' (see Gadamer 1976:9), at the possibilities and difficulties of mutual comprehension between me and the people I stayed with. If I emphasize that ethnographic interpretations of other peoples are founded on this relation, where the grounds of our interest in them are just as much part of the question as the peculiarities of what they say and what they do, this avoids, or at least tries to minimize, the obscuring effects of the conventional hypostasis that makes the people named in the title of the essay, the paper, or the book, into an object, susceptible of description and observation, so obliterating the 'us' side of the relation and turning the enterprise from a fluid, indeterminate effort of understanding towards a petrified lump of observed fact.

A consequence of this effort is to ask that an account should be ever more reluctant to attribute qualities and features to the people named in that encounter, since these qualities and attributes are likely to be, in a psychoanalytic metaphor, projections of our own perplexities, or, in a mathematical metaphor, in a functional relation to the intellectual fashions we are involved with. The statement 'the Bororo are matrilineal' is not so much a statement about the Bororo as a reflection at a particular time of a particular concern in anthropology. An essay on 'Bororo conception of space' is more precisely an essay about the notion of space worked out in the context of an encounter with the Bororo. It is simply wrong to claim that it is an 'analysis' of *their* notion of space.

CRITERIA

Diagnoses can be judged correct or incorrect. Obviously I would ask for other criteria. In the following passage A. R. Louch, having undermined the claim that fieldwork is a 'scientific' enterprise, leaves the reader with a choice:

> Consequently anthropology is only a collection of traveller's tales with no particular scientific significance, or else it is really theoretical after all, and anthropologists in the past, in their methodological naivety, have failed to formulate hypotheses with sufficient rigour to allow for observations or experiments which would support them in a decisive way.
>
> I shall argue for the first of these options, but without prejudice, that is, without the pejorative 'mere' or 'only' qualifying the terms. Travellers' tales can be, as much as scientific theories, contributions to human knowledge; they can be better or worse, more or less accurate. Moreover, they are not the first and random comments that some day will be organized into a scientific theory. They are sufficient unto themselves. The pattern of explanation in anthropology is not a poor approximation of the generalizing and experimental and predictive capacities of the methods of science, but moral explanation, within which instances may be judged more or less adequate.
>
> (Louch 1966:160–1)

I gladly accept this. I am going to put together some anecdotes (a word that originally meant 'things unpublished') and I hope that they are found to be of deeper implication than the more relaxed, informal kind of traveller's tales.

So far the contrast has been between diagnosis and interpretation, between on the one hand standing outside the encounter, cataloguing, looking for principles of order and relations of regularity; and on the other, standing within, accepting that the activity is participatory, that everything interesting in it is the result of processes of reciprocal understanding and misunderstanding between us and those we encounter. The point of the contrast is to make room

for expectations and assumptions and criteria of assessment that are
inhibited by current diction. As an example of how reluctantly such
space is given, consider the way the following distinction is
described.

Mary Douglas refers to 'one of the present crises in sociology'
which 'comes from the criticisms of phenomenologists'. She goes on:

> Consequently many scholars, sensitive to the criticism, have
> been tempted to give up striving for objectivity and to shift their
> own writing into a mystical mode, indulgent to their own sub-
> jectivity. Others, who would still like to try for objective compari-
> sons, find little alternative but to work on in the old framework of
> enquiry . . .   (Douglas 1980:11–12)

Mary Douglas offers a choice between science and phenomenology,
between the severity of objectivity and the indulgence of subjectivity.
But there is no choice there. Firstly, if the word 'phenomenology' is to
be used in a helpful way, examples should indicate just how the views
of Brentano, Husserl, or Schutz are being used, otherwise the word
becomes no more than a lazy term of suspicion like 'peculiar' or
'subversive'. Secondly, the more important point is that the contrast
between 'subjective' and 'objective' is a bogus distinction. 'Subjective', like 'impressionistic', is intended to indicate that the work
referred to lacks rigour, precision, control and 'scientific objectivity',
but I suspect that the reproachful implications of the term indicate no
more than that the work does not conform to the critic's expectations.
If something slips beyond the reach of received judgement it provokes uneasiness and suspicion.

Whenever I converse with someone or write something, my views
can be queried, commented on, accepted, challenged, or ignored. It is
only in offering my views that I can be said to have any in the first
place. And whatever the response, I have begun a process that
requires me to repeat them, modify them, find other ways of putting
them, reject them, look for something else to say, and so on. The idea
that my accounts and descriptions could be sealed in a solipsistic
context of subjective impressions, making it impossible for others to
comment on them or judge them, does not make sense (although this
is what Mary Douglas may have meant above by 'mystical'). Whether
the account is 'subjective' or 'objective' is neither here nor there. What
is required is a judgement as to whether on the one hand it might be
muddled, shallow, or wilfully eccentric, or on the other, that it might
be well-put, perceptive, and interesting. The values and standards
that inform such judgements are justified by example, by illustration,
and by analogy: by referring to other pieces of work that one is using
as a yardstick.

Christopher Ricks describes a parallel predicament:

> Language is the most vital instance of an undying human
> achievement: navigating between the rock Scylla and the whirl-

pool Charybdis. Scylla is the petrification of the obdurately mea-
surable, of objectivity, and of the cult which is not science but
scientism; the claim that everything which matters is a matter of
fact. Charybdis is the flux of the personal, of subjectivity, of
madness and solipsism; the claim that everything which matters
is a matter of opinion. Hideous alternatives . . .

The meaning of a word is not a matter of fact (which is why an
argument about it can't be settled by recourse to the dictionary),
and it is not a matter of opinion (which is why an argument about
it mustn't be unsettled by a refusal to have recourse to the
dictionary). The meaning of a word is a human agreement,
created within society but incapable of having meaning except to
and through individuals. We may find evidence for such agreements, but we can't find proof of them. A language is a body of
agreements. Some lapse; others change; new ones form.

(Ricks 1980:xi)

Making the appropriate changes, this describes the nature of an
ethnography. It is neither a matter of the obdurately objective fact nor
of the impressionistic subjective opinion. The value of an ethnography is established by the common drift of judgements made by
those who take part in the discipline. As tastes and interests alter, so
do the agreements.

Finding a way between the hideous alternatives requires an effort
against two forces, one that pulls towards eccentric obscurity, or
worse, ill-informed triviality, and another that pulls towards an easy
imitation of the vocabulary, the turns of phrase, the expository conventions, the lines of interest, already established in the discipline.
One is no more dangerous than the other. (There is no reason to assert
that writing a lightweight travel book is easier than producing a
vacuous structural analysis.) If it is easy to fall into the triviality of
self-absorption, it is also easy to follow an established way of doing
things with uncritical acceptance. The double effort is, therefore, on
the one hand to be sceptical of the conventions of the discipline and to
interrogate the tastes that underlie them, and on the other to elaborate as clearly as possible the inchoate interests that inform my
inquiry so that others will not be puzzled or disappointed when they
cannot find their own interests encouraged by what I present. I can't
presuppose a community of shared taste, nor assume that I can be
interesting in an original way. Hence this must be *une tentative*, like
saying one comes from a country that does not yet exist.

LANGUAGE

I cannot seriously suggest that discovering the meaning of the
Wayãpí word / maïɡwò / is an original contribution to knowledge, but
I remember the moment vividly. It was a wild surmise.

I had the word / maïɡwò / recorded in so many sentences but I could not place its significance. Out hunting with a companion, following spider monkeys, the two of us paused when we heard a shot in the distance. 'Who's that?' I asked. 'I don't know. Kuyuri, /maɨgwò/.' It was the word 'perhaps'. Of course it was. 'I don't know. Maybe it's Kuyuri.' I was so impatient after that to get the hunt over with, get back to the village, and check through the notes trying 'perhaps' in every instance of the troublesome word. It worked.

Discovering a way of saying 'perhaps' was a great step forward, as anyone who tries to communicate without using some kind of speculative construction like this will quickly find out. And there were many similar examples. Generally I found the discovery of what we might call adverbs and prepositions the most exciting since their sense is so elusive to demonstration.

Learning an unwritten language is a humbling job since it requires so much patience and so much sheer plod. There is none of the spectacular success of solving an obviously important problem through protracted concentration. The excitement is in solving tiny technicalities. The effort is not tense perseverance. One has to bear with a tediously pedestrian progress while being aware that one is inevitably going to be defeated by time running out. It is so different from learning a written language where the acquired skill makes the literature accessible and where the skill can be practised to some benefit even when there is no one to talk to in that language. There are no boundaries to that skill. But in the forest I felt threatened by a passing-bell, both in the sense that my own stay there had a deadline with little room for negotiation, and in the sense that their way of life was transitory and that once I had left, there might be nothing to come back to. I was trying to learn a language that I might never be able to practise again and in which only a handful of people in the outside world would have any interest.

I went through a bad period of depression in the middle stretch of my stay. It was aggravated by illness, by the misery of the rainy season, and by various crises in their lives. But it was around the sense of hopelessness with the language that the depression congealed. My impatience to become adept in the language was overtaken by the frightening sense of time running out, and that produced the despondency.

I felt that I had not been prepared for this dejection. The hints and suggestions I had gathered from friends before I set out had been immensely helpful but no one had talked much about linguistic difficulties. I remembered comments such as: 'If you find just one Indian at least you can start learning the language'; 'My preparations for the field are going well – I've even started learning the language'; 'It will take you about six months just to learn the language'. 'At least', 'even', and 'just', are the words that now seem so out of place. Edwin

Ardener (1971:xv) quotes a statement similar to my third example and he goes on to describe the problem vividly. I had read this passage before going, but I had not properly appreciated its significance. Thinking back, I can only remember one comment that put the problem well. It was from a friend who said laconically: 'By the end of a couple of years you should be following most of what's going on'. The informality of that statement is exquisitely accurate. Another writer, Charles Wagley, is more candid than most:

As the months went on I learned to speak Tapirapé, and I could understand what was said – after a fashion. I could ask almost any question in a rather simple way and I could understand most people when they spoke to me directly, but I was often faced with 'group encounters', and then I became lost. I always had the feeling that there was a linguistic haze between the Tapirapé and me.   (Wagley 1977:20)

'No man fully capable of his own language ever masters another' asserts Shaw in 'The Revolutionist's Handbook'. That is an eccentric overstatement, taking into account the work of Joseph Conrad, Vladimir Nabokov, and Samuel Beckett, or even Malinowski for that matter, but it does emphasize the impudence of the field-worker's claim to having 'learnt the language'. I would trust more the 'lean-jawed traveller of the "I-rapped-out-a-few-words-of-Swahili" type' (Ardener 1971:xv). Furthermore it is difficult to see how individual competence can be assessed. What counts as fluency in a foreign language seems to be a vague attribution of approval, rather like the way a person is described as 'able' in academic, political, and business circles. There are those who are exceptionally gifted in picking up languages just as there are those who have exceptional talents for music. There are also separate skills such as being able to do phonetic and phonological transcriptions and being able to spot grammatical principles, all of which may have very little to do with using the language effectively. I am not particularly gifted in any of these skills, and I get along with all the various aspects of language learning as best as I can by improvising amateurish techniques. I would expect this is what most people do, and it would be as well to admit that it is an unsatisfactory state of affairs.

It is an obvious and not very interesting point that technical training for those who are to encounter an unwritten language is inadequate in anthropology (in British anthropology at any rate). That aside, the more important point is to confront the 'linguistic haze' that lay between the Wayãpí and me as the limiting condition of the work I was trying to do. 'The limits of my fieldwork are the limits of my language.' No amount of inspired observation or tenacious participation will make up for or take me beyond those limits which my linguistic inadequacy imposes. Learning the language is not a preliminary obstacle that has to be overcome before proper fieldwork begins to fill the pages of the notebooks. Confronting the language constitutes the conditions whereby what I encounter is made intelligible to me; and the body of this essay shows how a number of puzzles centred on linguistic difficulties and on problems of adequate translation.

To put the limits in a clearer perspective, I sometimes think that I have had glimpses of what it looks like on the far side of them. Living in the forest soon became familiar, and just as I got used to the environment, so I got used to the people themselves. After some months, when I had learnt to some extent how to look after myself there and when daily life was no longer so mysterious, and as my proficiency in listening began to grow, I became aware occasionally that there was a great deal of imaginative life going on around me. It was all the more obscure because it was not particularly obtrusive. I don't mean observable habits such as birth precautions, which were easily explained in a relaxed way: 'We do it because the grandfather-people said this is the way it's done.' Nor this sort of thing:

> A young man called Tenetí whose wife had recently had a child used to accompany us when we went off to hunt. He could not kill anything but he liked to come along for the walk. The first time out when we came to a *sumauma,* one of the huge trees that contain / yarë / (masters, making it dangerous for a man observing birth precautions), I was pleased to find when I looked round that Tenetí had disappeared. I had been told that this was the thing to do and here was someone doing it. But after a few excursions, if I was at the head of the line with Tenetí some way behind, and I spotted a *sumauma* or an *angelim,* I would shout a warning back to him without a second thought and would expect him to disappear.

The strangeness went out of that kind of behaviour. It was the proper way to go about things. But moving away from action (from hunting, canoe-building, house-building, observing birth precautions) I became more aware of the beliefs of a detached imagination. When I cannot see what effect a belief has on action the matter becomes puzzling.

> Two of us are travelling, and there is a strange sound in the forest. 'That's Yurupari' (something demonic) I'm told. But is my companion deeply afraid where I am not? He is alert and listening for more clues but there are no signs of alarm. After a moment we move on and the incident is never mentioned again.
>
> There is an eclipse of the moon one night and we are all awakened by someone shouting: 'The moon is dying. The moon is dying.' Everyone gets up, the fires are made to blaze again, and people gather around their hearths talking excitedly. Kuyuri, on the far side of the village, lets off his shotgun, and Waiwai arrives at our hearth chuckling about that saying: 'It's good to

make a noise when the moon's dying. There's a huge mouse eating up the moon.' The talk goes on: 'This means we're all going to die.' After all this commotion the next day is just as usual and no one mentions the eclipse again unless I bring it up. The question is: how portentous is a portent? Or in general: how do they experience this belief?

Evans-Pritchard ends *Nuer Religion* (1956:322) with the suggestion that 'inner states' are not for the anthropologist to explore. I can happily ignore that suggestion, except to note that to go forward in that direction requires a sophisticated grasp of the language. It is the kind of question that lies beyond what I could do. I wonder if the famous valediction at the end of *Nuer Religion*, where the theologian is invited to take over from the social anthropologist, is not really a matter of linguistic limitations, where a fair grasp of the language is adequate for discussing 'exterior actions' but where a far greater fluency both in understanding others as well as expressing oneself is required to explore 'inner states'.

Self-expression, as part of achieving fluency in a language, is something I cannot remember reading much about in ethnographies. I read frequently that anthropologists were able to ask questions of their 'informants' in the natives' language, but I cannot easily find an example of this kind of work being described as a conversation, where anthropologists might be expected to be just as informative, creative, and forthcoming with their hosts as 'informants' are expected to be with them. It was in my attempts to express myself that I collided most heavily with the limits of what I could do.

Waiwai used to enjoy hearing me recite lists of Indian tribal names, starting with the ones he knew: 'Wayana, Aparai, Emerillon, Tiriyó' and going on to as many as I could remember. Since Waiwai used to repeat each name with relish this could easily keep a kind of conversation going for a very long time. One warm night, in the dark away from the fires, I sat with the men along a huge fallen tree trunk which ran through the village, and having been asked to give the list again, I went on afterwards to an account of the arrival of the European invaders and the tragedy that befell the Indians over the centuries, explaining that at one time there were only Indians in the forest. It was my first attempt to express myself at any sustained length in Wayãpí and I was pleased to find that I had managed to make myself understood. The next day one of my particuarly good friends explained that I had filled everyone with / ɨã-gɨɔ̀ / (sadness, longing, nostalgia). Why? Because talking of the past is always sad. A few nights later, in the same circumstances, I tried again. I have no note of the subject, only of the result . . . Having talked for some time, and aware that I was stumbling, I stopped. There were grunts and mutters. Then the same friend said something like: 'None of us can understand your words at all.' My attempts had been blethers to them, and that was all the more disappointing since I thought I had been doing quite well.

The ability to listen and pick up the broad outline of a conversation does come remarkably quickly. The ability to interrogate others with staccato questions is also quite easily acquired. But I think the best way of appreciating one's limits is to look at how fluently and effectively one expresses oneself, and a claim to be fluent in a language would be better related to that. Most people interested in academic work are familiar with the standards required to claim competence in another European language, and many will themselves be familiar with the feeling of being reasonably at home in another language. These are high standards of fluency, and there is no reason why anthropologists should be satisfied with less when they deal with unwritten languages. Whereas at the moment it is conventional both to expect and to claim that 'the anthropologist mastered the native language', it would be more balanced to say that both the expectation and the claim are unrealistic, and that the most accurate way of describing the ethnographic enterprise is to say that fieldworkers characteristically do *not* achieve much competence in the native language.

Judith Shapiro contrasts the interaction between the Yanomamo Indians and the missionaries on the mission post with the interaction among the Indians themselves. The first, she says: ' . . . has a flat, foreshortened quality, the product of mutual ignorance and consciously self-limiting patterns of conduct' (Shapiro 1972:34). She goes on to refer to Henry Roth's novel *Call It Sleep* which contrasts the richness of life and speech within a Jewish immigrant community in the United States and the 'forlorn clumsiness' which characterizes their dealings with outsiders in the larger world. If these descriptions were to characterize the interaction between anthropologists and their hosts it would be a despairing state of affairs. These difficulties were ameliorated for me because I lived with my friends in their houses, dressed as they did, ate as they did, and took as much part as I could in their daily activities. I'm sure I was not involved in the more serious results of mutual ignorance, where immigrants are abused and exploited by a hostile society, and where Indians are infantilized by missionaries and government officials, nevertheless Judith Shapiro's descriptions do indicate an important aspect of the fieldwork predicament. There was obviously a sense in which interaction between the Wayãpí and me involved us in consciously self-limiting patterns of conduct, and there was certainly clumsiness in our dealings although it was good-natured rather than forlorn. I could not express myself effortlessly in their language, and they in turn had to make peculiar efforts in trying to get something across to me.

My stay began and ended as a struggle with Wayãpí language. And with what purpose? To begin with, an interest in the language is itself respectable enough, and I found myself absorbed in it at an early stage. I was surprised at how quickly I could pick up the broad outline of many conversations. Partly, that was because they used to go over the same conversations so often. I listened to these conversations either in the early evening when the men gathered to sit around a fire prepared in the middle of the clearing, or later in the night when everyone was in their hammocks and a conversation would go on shouted across the village. The themes were often easy to pick up: what game was sighted that day; what the lightning means; what someone from the next village did and said the last time he visited; and so on. I had heard them many times before. As time went on I found my interest in these conversations becoming more and more refined. I wanted to find out exactly how these sentences worked and to be able to appreciate every connective, every morpheme, and every nuance of grammar. This cerebral phase of interest in Wayãpí language has never faded. Like an old-fashioned detective story, I am still trying to make discoveries from a few tantalizing clues.

I eventually succeeded to some extent in maintaining a less desperate feeling about language learning, accepting whatever I had learned as an achievement sufficient to that day. I was never going to 'learn the language' to a degree that I would find satisfactory. There were always going to be limits. And there was no guarantee that all the effort would lead to a discovery of any significance. (Perhaps there really was nothing else to talk about other than pigs and lightning and visitors.) Further, once I had left, I might never have the opportunity to return again, and to expand on what I had learned. And the Wayãpí themselves might soon disappear.

At the moment I know five people who are or who might be interested in learning Wayãpí with a view to using it. Added to that there will be a fair number who are familiar with related languages of Tupian stock, as well as linguists interested in the technicalities of Tupian languages. Outside that no one will be interested in the details of Wayãpí except to the extent that I can intrigue people with curios: that there are no morphologically indicated plurals; that there are numbers only from one to four; that words such as / tukan /, / pirãyë /, / yawarë /, / mani'ɨ /, / tapi'irë /, might sound familiar. (They are 'toucan', 'piranha' where / pira / means fish and / ayë / tooth, 'jaguar', 'manioc', and 'tapir'.) But the main justification for persevering with the fine details of language is that many of the problems and obscurities in anthropology begin and end with inadequate attempts at translation. When von den Steinen reports that the Bororo said they were macaws (parrots) I am perplexed that I shall never know *exactly* what was said nor how the discussion went. Evans-Pritchard properly sees the problem of interpreting 'twins as birds' inhering in the difficulties of the verb 'to be'. In my account of shamanism below, I suggest that the problem rests in the interpretation of a specific point of grammar. My clues are minuscule, and I could have made elementary errors, but if I am right on these particulars then the implications are worth following through.

THEORY AND METHOD?

The main theme I follow is querying our distinctions; looking at the way our distinctions stand between us and them. I am guided by no theory, just a few remarks from various writings, particularly from Godfrey Lienhardt's 'Modes of Thought' article (1954) and from Chapter 4 of his *Divinity and Experience* (1961). At various points he comments that our distinctions between, for example, literal and metaphorical, or between natural and supernatural, are inappropriate when describing the thought of others.

These remarks kept reappearing in other forms and in other disguises, as if I was being nagged or haunted by a single problem that was always being skirted and left unresolved. The question is: can we get beyond our distinctions, or rather can we get back through them again? Or does their either-or rigidity hold us so firmly that we are unable to follow the movements of what appear to be more supple forms of thought?

Just as there is no theory behind this, so there is no method. Sometimes it seems as if all my time with the Wayāpí has produced only a handful of images which I registered by accident in some casual moment. Those I have kept could so easily have gone unnoticed, and so much must have done so. So much ethnography dealing with the exegesis of belief and cosmology, religion and thought, turns around the explication of one or two metaphors. 'Twins are birds' and 'cucumbers are oxen' have leapt from Evans-Pritchard's work to inspire numerous debates and it would be easy to mark the history of anthropology by a trail of images like this from all over the world. Perhaps those few Bororo Indians who told Karl von den Steinen that they were macaws deserve credit for starting one of the best veins of the discipline. Theirs was one of the images that fascinated Lévy-Bruhl (1926:77) and, like 'twins are birds', it was taken up by many others (see Douglas 1980:17 and 125 note 3).

When Thoreau grew beans at Walden Pond it was not to sell them or to eat them (since he was a Pythagorean by nature). He grew them because he enjoyed the process of husbandry for its own sake: ' . . . as some must work in fields if only for the sake of tropes and expressions to serve a parable-maker one day' (Thoreau 1937:146).

IGARAPÉ:
names and things

To-day we have naming of parts
Henry Reed, 'Naming of Parts'

The Brazilian Tropical Forest covers an immense area. The best way of organizing a knowledge of the area is to learn from the maps the names of rivers and the names of a few ranges of hills. The names that appear most prominently in this account, and which can be found on the maps at the end of the book, are the following: The SERRA DO TUMUCUMAQUE, a low range of hills forming a watershed that divides Brazil from French Guiana (Cayenne) and Surinam. The OYA-POQUE RIVER rises in the Tumucumaque and is an official frontier between Brazil and French Guiana. It flows north-east into the Atlantic. The RIO AMAPARÍ and the RIO JARÍ both rise on the Brazilian side of the Tumucumaque. The Amaparí flows south-east into the Rio Araguarí which then finds its own way to the Atlantic. The Jarí runs southwards to join the Amazon roughly opposite the point where the Rio Xingú joins from the south. The Jarí is the last major tributary to come into the Amazon from the north and its course marks the boundary between the Territory of Amapá and the northern part of the State of Pará.

The Wayãpí I know live in that area on the Brazilian side of the Tumucumaque between the headwaters of the Amaparí and the Jarí.

Some other names which will help readers find their way area:

(1) The RIO CUC and its tributaries the Igarapé PIRAWIRI and the Igarapé KOROAPI.

(2) The RIO NIPUKÚ and its affluents the Igarapé AIMA and the Igarapé AROÁ. Both the Cuc and the Nipukú run into the Jarí.

(3) Over to the east, the Igarapé ONÇA and the RIO FELÍCIO run into the Amaparí.

Igarapé is a standard Brazilian-Portuguese word for a small river. It is a borrowing from the Tupi-Guaraní languages and, like an Anglo-Saxon kenning, means 'canoe-path'.

Finally FUNAI is an acronym for Fundação Nacional do Índio, the Brazilian government department charged with looking after Indian affairs.

From the early decades of this century until 1972 there is no record of any Indians living in the area between the Amaparí and the Jarí. Two authoritative surveys of Brazilian Indians by Brazilian anthropologists done in the 1950s (Galvão 1960 and Ribeiro 1977) both indicated that the Oyampí or Oianpik were extinct, although it was known that survivors of this once numerous group lived along the Oyapoque River in French Guiana (see below). The Wayãpí themselves tell of occasional contact with Brazilian hunters and frontiersmen but it is remarkable that their area should have been left undisturbed for so long given their situation. There are two approaches by riverways into the Wayãpí area: from the south up the JARÍ and its tributaries the Nipukú and the Aroá, and from the east up the AMAPARÍ and the Felício. Either approach takes the traveller past impressive outposts of our civilization: the 'Jarí Project' and ICOMI, the acronym standing for the name of a manganese mining enterprise.

The Jarí, like many of the northern tributaries of the Amazon, is difficult and dangerous to navigate by canoe on account of its numerous rapids and falls. Few venture upstream beyond its lower reaches, and to this day the river is almost empty of Brazilian settlers. But in the 1960s and 1970s the name became widely known throughout Brazil and throughout the world on account of the controversial 'Jarí Project' which then occupied one and a half million hectares (perhaps half to three-quarters of the area of Wales) at the mouth of the river. The project was conceived and run by an American, Daniel K. Ludwig 'who since the death of Paul Getty in 1976 is reckoned to be the richest man in the world' (Bourne 1978: 153). Descriptions of the enterprise seem to require superlatives:

> ... a meticulously planned and all-embracing development scheme which includes one of the world's largest forest plantations, a kaolin mine, record-breaking rice plantations, and water buffalo and cattle herds, all serviced by the world's largest merchant marine.   (Goodland and Irwin 1975: 114)

The Jarí Project created a world of its own at the mouth of the river, attracting some 8,000 people to the new company town of Montedourado and some 20,000 others to the nearby squatters' city of Barradão. It was a mysterious world in many ways. In 1976 the Governor of Amapá said he had very little idea of what the company was up to in his territory since his representatives could not at that time get on to the property (Bourne 1978: 156). The Jarí Project also brings together some of the ambiguous aspects of our civilization. Is it an example of vigorous industrial enterprise leading to development and progress? Or is it an example of the insidious activity of multinational companies which take their profits at the expense of human misery and ecological disaster?

When I first heard of Ludwig and the Jarí I was unaware of how close these questions were to home. While I was in Brazil, Daniel

K. Ludwig was planning to develop an oil refinery in Northern
Scotland, a few miles away from the village in Ross and Cromarty
where I was brought up. Like the Brazilian project, this plan
caused controversy and suspicion (Rosie 1978). I found it an
uncomfortable coincidence – as if the world were too much with
us.

At any rate, between Ludwig's project at the mouth of the Jarí and the
Wayãpí area there is a straight distance of roughly 150 miles.

Taking the way in to the Wayãpí from the east, the last place on the
Amaparí where there is Brazilian settlement is SERRA DO NAVIO.
Manganese was discovered there in 1946 and it is now a vast mining
complex run by ICOMI (Indústria e Comércio de Minérios S.A.). Until
recently, I believe, forty-nine per cent of the stock of this company
was held by Bethlehem Steel Inc., an important North American
organization. Travelling into the interior of Brazil, one expects to find
the trappings of our civilization dwindling away. It is therefore astonishing to arrive in Serra do Navio as a guest of the company and to
enjoy the trim comfort of the town – a social club with restaurant, bar,
swimming pool, and tennis courts; a supermarket, a cinema, and a
hospital, everything kept in the immaculate order of a quiet wealthy
suburb. Upstream there is nothing until the Wayãpí settlements.
Though there are only about fifty miles of forest between Serra do
Navio and the Wayãpí area, there was no official record of the existence of these Indians until 1972.

Going back to the southern approach, by way of the Rio Jarí,
roughly half way up, an affluent joins on its east bank. On
the inaccurate maps of the region which I had to use, where
rivers are suspiciously straight, the river is named Rio Maparí.
The Wayãpí have always known it as NIPUKÚ, that is, as 'grandfather–people said', /ini-p̧oko/ long hammock, and this indeed
is the name Diaz de Aguiar (1942) gives in his account of the work of
the Frontier Commission. In 1968 there was a Wayãpí settlement well
up towards the source of the Nipukú and in that year a group of
Brazilians arrived in one large motorized canoe. The Wayãpí had
always known that / karai-ko /(Brazilians) lived to the south and east
of their lands but no one then living at the Nipukú had seen any
of them before. The Brazilians explained that they were *companhia*
(Portguese 'company') and that they were interested in stones
and earth, samples of which they took away in bags. This turned out
to be an expedition sent from Belém by CPRM (Companhia de Pesqui-
sas e Recursos Minerais) to explore for minerals. It was a brief
encounter.

In the dry season of 1969 a number of Nipukú people who had been
visiting the / Kamara̧ra-ko / (the French Wayãpí, see below) on the
Igarapé Pirawiri arrived back on the Nipukú with a Brazilian named
Cuelho Brito (called 'Prono' by the Indians) and his companions

'Antonico' and 'Espio'. They were *garimpeiros*, gold prospectors, who had been working in the Cuc area. Apparently they had heard of the visit of the *companhia* and hoped to make contact with them to buy lead shot. Capitão Waiwai (as he likes to be known nowadays), a headman of the Nipukú group, still holds the document I transcribe below. This scrap of paper was important to me because it was dated – real documentary evidence. But it is also an intriguing fragment that gives a glimpse into the life of those *garimpeiros* and frontiersmen who leave their homes to spend months on end in remote stretches of the forest. It is a page torn from a notebook, carefully folded, with 'amigos amazonas' (amazon friends) written on the outside. Inside it runs:

Maloca dos oiapi
15 – 7 – 69
amigos de exploração eu esteve nesta maloca afin de falar com os Senhores que estou aqui neste mato tambem explorando eu temdo informaçao que os Senhores estavão aqui eu vim aqui ter uma comonicação que eu estou na mesma luta entre cuqui [i.e. Rio Cuc] e Nipucu Varei nesta agua no Locar Denominado araramira e continuo esplorando sempre no mesmo trecho eu vim afin de comprar um chombo que eu tenho ja pouco eu para Dezembro torno vir aqui o talvez antes pelu Mes outobru
                                                        Cuelho Brito
Something of the tone does come across in translation:
Maloca of the Oiapí. 15 July 69. Friends in the exploration business. I came here to this maloca to speak to you since I am here in this jungle also exploring (for minerals). Having information that you were here I came here to let you know that I am in the same struggle between the Cuc and the Nipukú. I came through on to this river at the place called Araramirã and I am going on exploring in the same area. I came to buy some lead shot since I have very little left and I'll come back here about December or perhaps earlier in October.
Waiwai's instructions were to give it to the next 'Amazon' to arrive, but Brito never returned to the Nipukú nor was the letter ever passed on.

On the use of the word 'Amazonas', a member of a subsequent CPRM expedition explained to me that this was the Wayãpí word for Brazilians. It is not. The Wayãpí word is /karai̯-ko/ which has been recorded in similar forms in numerous Tupian languages since the 16th century. The Indians explained that 'Amazonas' was one of the places where the Brazilians on the *companhia* expeditions said they came from. To them it was on a par with 'Belém' or 'São Paulo', one of a list of settlement names that Brazilians gave as their homes. Both Indians and Brazilians used the word but neither party was precisely aware of what it signified to the other. According to Pierre Grenand

(1972: 103) the French Wayãpí say that a long time ago they came from 'Mazone', or 'Amazone' as it would be put in French.

During 1971 CPRM were again working on the Nipukú. Waiwai has another priceless slip of paper, this time a company receipt which runs: '7 December 1971. Capitan Mota [another of Waiwai's names]. Hammock, machete, knife, torch, mosquito net. Services rendered'. Amongst the services rendered was the preparation of a clearing to allow helicopters to land. Also during this year there was another contact which had graver consequences.

In April 1971, three men – Alberto Rodrigues, 'Diko', and 'Algimiro' – from the Macapá / Porto Grande area in Amapá, were doing some sort of work on the Jarí along with the *patrão* or boss who had hired them. For some reason that was not explained, there was a disagreement and their boss abandoned them. They decided to make their way eastwards on foot in the hope of finding the Rio Amaparí and Serra do Navio, the ICOMI manganese mine and town. They were making their way up the Igarapé Aroá, quite lost and 'without salt' – a dangerous predicament according to Sr. Rodrigues who told me the story – when they came upon a Wayãpí settlement. They stayed on the Aroá for two months and while there discovered traces of gold in a small stream called Karwowo or Karamumu. The Indians later guided them over the watershed into Amaparí waters and they made their way down to Serra do Navio. The discovery of gold led to the inevitable invasion. It is estimated that about seventy *garimpeiros* arrived that year, coming in from the Amaparí side, to set up their *garimpo* or panning operation at Karwowo, about eight kilometres from the Wayãpí settlement on the Aroá. During the time the *garimpo* was working there thirteen Wayãpí that I know of were taken down by *garimpeiros* to visit Porto Grande, Macapá, and Santana. There must have been others. Two youngsters were 'given' to Brazilian families, remaining there until 1973/74 when FUNAI heard of their presence and brought them back to the Wayãpí settlements. With the arrival of the *garimpo* the Indians on the Aroá suffered outbreaks of influenza and diarrhoea; more seriously, during 1972 there was an outbreak of measles. FUNAI later established that at least eighteen Indians died in the epidemic.

During 1972, ICOMI, the manganese mining company, began to survey for minerals on the Nipukú (again by coming up the Jarí) and were also active in the headquarters of the Amaparí and Felício. While these explorations were going on, an ICOMI public relations officer, Sr. J. L. A. Freire, had the good sense and foresight to alert FUNAI to the presence of isolated Indians in the area. It was considered important to contact these Indians since a major new highway was planned which would cut directly into their lands. At the end of 1972 a FUNAI expedition was organized in Belém which was to enter the Wayãpí area by way of Serra do Navio and the Amaparí and Felício rivers.

From this point on there was to be no further contact with the Wayãpí by way of the Rio Jarí. The area was to be opened up from the east through the Amaparí. With the help of ICOMI, the FUNAI team reached the area in February 1973 and began setting up a Pôsto Indígena, meeting the groups living on the Igarapé Onça and the Igarapé Aroá. That month the team reported back to Belém. The Wayãpí had been officially discovered.

From the earliest days of the European invasions of Amazônia the great rivers were highways that allowed settlers to move into the area. Indian groups rapidly disappeared from the banks of the major rivers. Those who survived the epidemics and the slaving raids were either already in the more inaccessible interfluvial and headwater areas or else moved off into them. I have to be careful to say 'those who survived'. Hurault (1963:101) points out that: ' ... la plupart des auteurs ont admis avec une grande légèreté que les Indiens "s'étaient retirés dans l'intérieure des forêts" ... ', the point being that the casual notion of Indians retreating into the interior rather than dying where they were is responsible for beliefs that there are still dozens of 'uncontacted tribes' lurking in remote parts of the Amazon forest. Surviving groups of isolated Indians are very few and their populations are tiny. This particular group of Wayãpí was not a discovery. These people had been forgotten. And as for them being uncontacted, I will explain how much they suffered from our illnesses *before* any major intrusion into their lands took place.

Under Western eyes the history of the Wayãpí is reasonably well known. Peter Rivière (1963:184–194) and Pierre Grenand (1972, 1978, 1980) give summaries of the literature that mentions the Wayãpí. It is generally agreed that they moved north from the middle Xingú, crossed the Amazon, and moved into the Guyana area by way of the Rio Jarí. The *Handbook of South American Indians* cites the following evidence:

> On the upper Jarí (Iratapuru) River, Nimuendajú found open sites near a stream which yielded pottery of considerable excellence ... Nimuendajú attributes these vessels to the *Oyampí*, who, he believes, left them on their journey northwards into the Guianas in the early 18th century. The sherds are similar to material from old *Guaiapy* sites on the middle Xingú river, and *Waiapy (Guaipay)* is the *Aparai* name for the *Oyampí*. The *Guaiapy* disappeared from the Xingú River about the same time that the *Oyampí* appeared in Guiana; and the trip from the Xingú River to the Jarí River would be easy because the mouths of these two rivers are opposite each other on the Amazon River.
>
> (Gillen 1948:824–825)

An official French document entitled 'Mémoire des irruptions des

Portugais du Pará sur les terres de la Guiane de la France' mentions attacks made by the Wayãpí across the Serra do Tumucumaque and into the Oyapoque in 1736, 1742, and 1744 (Rivière 1963:185). Although they were certainly established in the Jarí by that time, they may not have finally established settlements in the Oyapoque until the early 1800's (Rivière 1963:163). These details are widely accepted and are summarized in Métraux's general history of the various Tupi-Guaraní migrations (1927:30–34), but Rivière's review of the literature adds an interesting suggestion. A book by Father Labat published in Paris in 1730 entitled *Le Voyage du Chevalier des Marchais en Guinée, Isles Voisines et à Cayenne* gives credit for much of its information on Cayenne to an earlier work by Milhau: *Historie de l'Isle de Cayenne et province de Guyane* published in Paris in 1702. Rivière was unable to trace a copy of Milhau's book (and I have also been unsuccessful) but Labat's contains:

> ... a map drawn by the famous cartographer D'Anville who based it on information supplied by Milhau. The significant features of the map are a tribe called Oyanpiques to the east of the Oyapock, and another called Merillons [i.e., Emerillon, the only neighbouring Tupian speaking group] near the source of the Mana. In the text there is mention of the Ouiampies who live in the Coripy, on the east side of the Oyapock mouth.
>
> (Rivière 1963:185)

D'Anville's map is included in the illustrations of this book.

This evidence does not accord with the standard account that the Wayãpí (and Emerillons) came north, up the Jarí, over the Tumucumaque, and down the Oyapoque. 1736 is the date of the first recorded attack by the Wayãpí into the headwaters of the Oyapoque yet here is evidence of them already at the mouth of the Oyapoque well before that date. Rivière therefore suggests that there was an early migration of a Tupi-Guaraní group northwards *along the Atlantic coast* from the mouth of the Amazon (not up the Jarí); that this must have occurred before 1650; that the spearhead of the migration was Emerillon who, reaching a district populated by Caribs, turned inland. Metraux's account of a Wayãpí migration across the Amazon and up the Jarí would then follow, with the major invasion of the upper Oyapoque valley taking place in the early 1800's (Rivière 1963:194).

Population estimates for Indians in the Amazon forest are to this day notoriously unreliable. But the figures for Wayãpí population published during the 19th century do show a shocking decline. Bodin (1825:57) states that 6,000 Wayãpí were living along the Oyapoque in 1824. Towards the end of the century Crevaux (1883:217) says he must have seen only about 200 Wayãpí in both Cayenne and Brazil. Coudreau (1893:572) guesses a total Wayãpí population of 300. However wayward these estimates may have been, the Wayãpí seem to have suffered terrible losses during the 1800s. The major cause seems to have been smallpox, although judging from better-known contacts between Indians and Europeans there were probably many other contributory illnesses. It appears that during these epidemics the areas of Wayãpí population contracted around the Oyapoque and the Cuc on the one hand, and around the Nipukú and Amaparí areas on the other. In this second area, the 'Coussaris' referred to by Adam de Bauve (1833:273; 1834:166–7) and by Leprieur (1834:224) were no doubt Wayãpí. So were Coudreau's 'Caicouchianes' (1893:369, 529) and Farabee's 'Paikipiranga' (1917:126ff) found well to the south on the Igarapé Maracá.

In these two areas, Cuc and Oyapoque on the one hand, Nipukú and Amaparí on the other, lived those whom for convenience I call the French Wayãpí and the Brazilian Wayãpí respectively. The Brazilian Wayãpí probably lost touch with the larger group of French Wayãpí around the end of the last century and probably made contact with them again in the 1950s. It was this group that the Brazilian authorities knew nothing of until 1972, and it is this group that I know. In February 1974 there were 152 of them.

It is curious that both Brazilian surveys mentioned above (Galvão 1960 and Ribeiro 1977) done in the late 1950s both state that the Wayãpí were extinct in Brazil. Clearly there was no reason for either Galvão or Ribeiro to suspect the existence of the group I call the Brazilian Wayãpí. No one had reported on their area. But reports of those French Wayãpí living on the Rio Cuc in Brazil were appearing regularly. The 'Brazilian Commission for the Demarcation of Frontiers' mentions them there (Diaz de Aguiar 1942:341ff). Rüe (1950) had visited in 1948–49, Sausse (1951) in 1948, and Hurault (1963) in 1958. These reports were overlooked in the Brazilian surveys.

The French Wayãpí now live entirely on the Oyapoque River in French Guiana. The Cuc was abandoned after a series of epidemics in the 1960s and the survivors crossed over into French Guiana to settle with their relatives there, making a total population nowadays of about 350. There has been regular contact between the French inhabitants of the territory and the Indians on the Oyapoque since last century. For a number of years now, Françoise and Pierre Grenand of ORSTOM (Office de la Recherche Scientifique et Technique Outre-Mer) have been living with these Indians.

When the Rio Cuc people moved off into French Guiana, a small group of about twenty individuals led by a man called Sarapó went instead to a spot called Morokopoti near the source of the Jarí in Brazil. I have no clear idea of the composition of this group. Relatives of the Brazilian Wayãpí were certainly there; but, say the Brazilian Wayãpí, Sarapó was not himself Wayãpí. He was an Aparai who came from downstream on the Jarí when he was young and settled on the Cuc. Sarapó appears in my account as an *éminence grise*. I never met him. Since my departure, FUNAI made the colossal error of moving the Morokopoti people to the Brazilian Wayãpí villages. Sarapó was promptly killed by them.

My distinction between French and Brazilian Wayãpí is reflected in their own usage. According to Summer Institute of Linguistics missionaries, and also according to reports from the Grenands, the French Wayãpí called the Brazilian Wayãpí / wayãpí-poko /, perhaps 'long Wayãpí'. I knew this term before I met the Wayãpí and when I first asked about it some people at the Nipukú said that this was *their* name for the *French* Wayãpí. But there was obvious disagreement on the matter. I think the answer is that they know they are referred to in this way and do not care for it. My friend Kasiripinar's rather petulant conclusion to the discussion was that 'we here' together with all the Cuc and Oyapoque people were 'all the same'. 'We are ALL Wayãpí.' The term the Brazilian Wayãpí use for the French Wayãpí is / kamar-ara–ko /. This covers all those who formerly lived on the Cuc and those who live on the Oyapoque. I suspect the word is derived from the French *camarade*, just as the Wayãpí word for the Wayana is / panari̵–ko / from a word usually transcribed *banare*, loosely translated as 'friend', which is widespread in the indigenous languages of the Guyanas. (Peter Rivière tells me that the root *pana* – is not adequately translated 'friend' since it refers to a contractual relationship. He suggests something like 'bargaining partner'.)

The French and Brazilian Wayãpí share a common history which can be pieced together from the reports of travellers and missionaries and from official documents of various kinds. The general outline of this story is well known, and as far as the French Wayãpí are concerned the record runs quite clearly through to the present day. But the Brazilian Wayãpí lost touch with the others towards the end of last century and there is a gap with regard to them which the records cannot fill.

Names are odd things. When they appear in great numbers they are obscure, ominous entities to some; irresistible hypostases to others. When I do my naming of parts, the place names and people's names which are so familiar and so resonant to me (and to the Wayãpí) easily bewilder readers, as I know from reading other ethnographies. As with the cumbersome names of characters presented early on in a Russian novel, one looks at them apprehensively, aware that they have to be remembered or else one gets lost. I assume that when I say 'the Amazon' I catch the imagination of every reader. 'Rio Jarí' means much less, although the name carries important connotations for most people in Northern Brazil and may creat the odd echo here and there because of Daniel K. Ludwig. But 'Nipukú', the name of the river and the settlement where I spent most of my time, was known only as a coarse pun ('*limpo cu*') in the talk of the advancing roadworkers.

On the other hand, those professionally absorbed in the Amazon forest can approach names as an intriguing collection of things to classify. The *Handbook of South American Indians* scrupulously catalogues every mention of an Indian 'tribe', but when confronting these enormous lists of names it is not at all clear what lies behind them. A name overtly suggests reference to a discrete, identifiable group, and given that we are all bound to construct impressions of the past, it is convenient and orderly to think of the large indigenous population, which was certainly there in previous centuries, as being clearly divided into many hundreds of named categories. A name suggests a tribe and a tribe suggests a discrete culture, perhaps even with its own language or dialect. But identifying discrete groups and recognizable boundaries between groups would never have been a straightforward matter at all.

A traveller on a brief visit to the Nipukú might easily go away with the impression that here was a group called the Wayãpí, that to the south of them was a group called the / I-singu-wanako /, as the Nipukú people might casually refer to their relatives living on the Aroá, and to the north was another tribe called the / kamarara-ko / as they refer to the Wayãpí living in French Guiana. But these names do not catalogue groups. Each name in this example refers to a different mode of reference identifying a different kind of relationship. The names have different intensities. But our commentators – travellers, government officials, and anthropologists – either did not or cannot now check this in the tribal lists; hence, the names are there to be appropriated as things, enticing commentators to slip into both fallacies of misplaced concreteness and the unnecessary proliferation of entities, so abusing the best known lessons of A. N. Whitehead and William of Ockham. The things in the world that are being classified in this way are only the names themselves: names that name names.

There is a further curiosity in the way representations of the past are created. Two points are indisputable: (a) that published sources since the European intrusion mention countless tribal names across the tropical forest and (b) that when compared with that evidence from the past there is a relatively small number of isolable, named groups today. Given these points, reconstructions of the history of Amazonian groups seem always to follow the same formal pattern, beginning with an initial simplicity, moving through the complexity of historical sources, and returning again to the simplicity that is found today. Thus a 'proto-Tupi' or 'proto-Arawak' migration might explain the complicated composition of a certain area over the past few centuries, and the remnants of these peoples explain the simpler composition of existing groups today either as sole survivors of a particular group or as amalgamations of two or more groups. The odd outline of this historical design – simplicity — complexity — simplicity – is the result of the numbers of names that are available.

Asking the Wayãpí about old names also produces mystifying answers. There is in the area a long-standing question about the existence of a group referred to as the 'mysterious Amikouanes or Longues Oreilles' or Namikwan (cf. Nambikwara, 'ears with holes') and mentioned by Coudreau, Grenand, and a 1972 FUNAI report on the Wayãpí. When I asked at the Nipukú, Waiwai responded with alacrity:

> Tamoko [grandfathers] talked about them. They were called the Wariken. They had huge long ears made by big holes. Also they had long dangling scrotums. Also they had no / kamisa / [loin-cloths] only / koroa / [a small piece of basketry]. They lived down-stream on the Arawari [the Amaparí].

Attached to this account as if it obviously followed was the obser-vation that 'there are certain kinds of Brazilians who have huge mouths in their chests. They eat people'. What sort of world is this? Some editors suggest that Othello's lines: 'The Anthropophagi, and men whose heads / Do grow beneath their shoulders' (*Othello* I, iii, 144–5) are a direct reference to Sir Walter Ralegh's book on the discovery of Guiana. The Indians he met told him of the Ewaipanoma: '. . . they are reported to haue their eyes in their shoulders, and their mouths in the middle of their breasts, and that a long train of haire groweth backward betwen their shoulders' (Ralegh 1928: 56). Other editors prefer *Mandeville's Travels*, written in French about 1357 and first translated into English about 1375, more than a century before the Europeans found the New World:

> And in another isle toward the south dwell folk of foul stature and cursed kind, that have no heads. And their eyes be in their shoulders, and their mouth is crooked as an horseshoe, and that is in the midst of their breast.
>
> And in another isle also be folk that have no heads, and their eyes and their mouth be behind in their shoulders.
>
> (Seymour 1968: 156)

So what, then, were the Wariken? Is the name a fragment of mythy fantasy and was Waiwai talking in Jungian archetypes, or might the word have referred to an actual group to which the mythy features were attached? Take either choice and doubts will remain.

When I reconstruct their history as they remember it, I put together two sets of names: the names of places (most of which I have not seen and of which there are no maps) and the names of people (there being no precise way of finding out when they lived and died). Responding to a question that begins 'how many years ago . . . ?' is difficult for people who have no words for numbers beyond four. Sometimes they'd point to a child or an adolescent and answer that it happened around the time that person was born. Once, in answer to a 'how long ago' question, Kasiripinar began to count back on his fingers the gardens he had made – here this year, there the previous year, no garden that year – and so on until he held out a clutch of fingers for me to count saying 'and that's when it happened'. Cuelho Brito's letter and the CPRM receipt were the only dated documents I found.

Although precise chronologies cannot be presented, once in possession of the names of people and places I can easily produce schemes and charts that give the *appearance* of precision, that appearance being created by the very lack of detail. The fewer the details the clearer the picture, but what kind of clarity is that?

Place names reveal the impermanence of settlements. I arrived in the Wayãpí area at a time when they were arranged in three settlements. I counted and named the inhabitants of each of these, and the arrangements I recorded remained largely unaltered during the first year or so of my stay. Hence I still think of settlement arrangements in terms of the Nipukú group, the Aroá group, and the Capoeira group. They certainly did not. I had come across a brief temporary grouping. The area between and beyond these three settlements was an immense empty tract of forest to me and to the invading Brazilians, but all adult Wayãpí could detail that emptiness in their own way with the names of the *igarapés* and the tiny streams (which are used to indicate where previous settlements were), with memories of their own previous movements, and with memories of those who gave their names to the triangles and circles on my genealogical chart.

> Place names refer to permanent features. Occasionally a name might refer to a hill (/ uruwu-ra'ɨ̈rë / for example, 'urubu's child', 'vulture's child', which has a just-so story to explain the ascription), or to a striking feature such as /takoro-sɨ/, 'white stone'. But I have few examples like that. Nearly always it is water that is named, everything from large rivers to tiny trickles. Hence a particular settlement will be referred to by the name of the nearby water. It is the water that is permanent, not the settlement.

The names of people allow me to construct a genealogical chart covering the entire group. It shows at a glance a kind of obscurity impossible to penetrate. One section of the chart has eighty people, fifty seven of them alive during my stay, set out on the same genealogical level. Counting from that level, the +1 has twenty-eight people (two of whom were alive) and the +2 level has eight: nine men who were named and two women whose names had been forgotten. The further back one goes into those times when the Wayãpí were more numerous, the more the names dwindle away. One person (Sirò) could do a genealogy back to +4, but by that time the reference points for the whole population had been reduced to the names of two brothers.

Names used as indicators in this way, like the grammatical problem that there are no morphologically indicated plurals, involves obscurities about numbers. For example, I am first given three names to indicate the very first Wayãpí who made contact with the Kamarara-ko, the French Wayãpí, by travelling through to the Igarapé Pirawiri on the Cuc. Later, when I am visiting another settlement, I am given different names. When I ask about the discrepancy I am told that X from my first list and Y from the second are brothers. The first idea I had formed of three intrepid Wayãpí setting off north had already grown a little. It turned out, of course, that a large group had made the journey. A typical fragment of history runs: 'Then Sarapó arrived here and said: "Come to Koroapi – lots of red cloth – lots of shotguns". ALL of us went. Then Sarapó took Tsako on a long trip to see the Wayana on the Parú.' What has to be read into this is that Sarapó would have arrived with a group of people; that it was not a total evacuation to Koroapi since many, especially older people, stayed behind; that the trip to the Parú would again have involved a large group, Tsako being the most significant person from the speaker's point of view. It's rather like having to remember that when we're told that in April 1917 'Lenin' was allowed to cross Germany in a sealed train, there were twenty-nine other Bolshevik exiles on board too.

The difficulty cannot be resolved simply by formulating more precise and searching questions. Even when I could ask a question in the form: 'Was it they and they only who went?', the answer would be 'yes'. Something that ran: 'No, there were a number of other people who went with them but I cannot remember their names', is a form of answer I learned not to expect. Specificity or nothing is the formula for this sort of statement, and names supply that specificity. My genealogical chart may *look* precise, but so many of the secrets of population and movements and of events are lying in the large blank spaces of what the chart does not represent.

Although I complain that this scaffolding of names (or catafalque, to be more blunt) is too flimsy to carry the weight of history, there is a sense in which these lists that I have in my notes are an embarrassment of detail. There is far more there than ever became immediately significant to me and the lists of people now dead and settlement places now abandoned became a resource from which to make connections between their geography, their memories, and my knowledge of the area. At the most unexpected moments I would be allowed to make the connection between a name, a place, and a time. It would happen, for instance, when journeying along a familiar path, many days out from the village. I would have passed along there a number of times before, only now I would be led off the path and taken to a spot with the tell-tale signs of secondary growth, almost now obliterated and the primary forest almost restored, and I would be told that 'this is Kani-Kani where Sirò's people lived' or 'this is where Sawa died' or 'this is where Yanuari was born'. Sometimes a laconic comment was added to these revelations – I remembered it as /aŋgè'è rèkoa/, 'now you know'. The lists of names were an important preparation, but only seeing it counted as knowing it. And it is in the nature of names that most of them are never seen.

Many times names would be corrected or confirmed or added to, but the outlines of their past remained blurred. The additional fragments were only further warning of the insubstantial nature of the account that I put together. There cannot be a completed picture. People genuinely forget names and relationships. Had the population remained stable perhaps it might have been possible to learn more, but the death of so many Wayãpí has obliterated many of the significant links that could name people in the past.

There is not much point in looking for a pattern of settlement and movement. Since contacting the Kamarara-ko the Wayãpí have suffered heavy losses during the epidemics. More recently the FUNAI contact is having a profound influence on their lives. It would therefore be a scholastic fantasy were I to present a pattern of settlement and movement explained perhaps in terms of ecological constraints and influences, or perhaps in terms of internal social determinants such as rivalries and disputes, loyalties and obligations. Living with the Nipukú people over a relatively untroubled spell of two years, I saw not a pattern but a casual impermanence where a village formed by a few families would be joined by a single family from elsewhere, or where a single family or two closely co-operating families might split off from the larger group and go to live elsewhere. Indeed there are hints that, left to themselves and with a thriving population, the Wayãpí show something of the 'anarchy and dispersion' that Marshall Sahlins says the 'domestic mode of production' tends towards (1974:95–99).

Five heads of families living at the Nipukú said they came from different settlements scattered around the headwaters of the Felício. The places mentioned are only two or three hours' walk from each other. Remembering the problem of number, it is possible that these five men were survivors of five different villages; but when pressed they would say that there were 'only us' there, 'only one house', 'only father's people'. Asking if the men would ever take on the women's work of preparing manioc, I was told that Sirò's father used to do it after his wife died. He did indeed live on his own. At Yarɨta, a short way downstream from the settlement on the Nipukú, there is a large solitary /òka-wɨrɨ/ (see appendix) where Paseta and Arama, two brothers, lived with their families for a few years.

After FUNAI set up their post on the Igarapé Onça in 1973, the large settlement on the Aroá was virtually abandoned. Everyone moved across the watershed to be nearer the FUNAI operation. It

seemed that the new arrangement was to be a string of five or six
settlements along the Onça.

I divided the genealogy into a North group and a South group, that
is, those principally resident at the Nipukú, and those resident along
the Aroá and the Igarapé Onça. There is some evidence that this
reflects arrangements in the past. A number of Wayãpí refer to the
two oldest settlements as Kumakakoa and Kumakarɨg. The first is on
the Aroá. The second is the Wayãpí name for a stream to the north of
the Felício which the Brazilians call Agua Preta. I think it would be
wrong to take this as evidence of two original villages which then
scattered throughout the territory. I think these names, like the
names of the two brothers in the genealogies, are remembered as
important settlements that indicate the two main areas where they
lived: the North group around the headwaters of the Felício and the
South group along the Aroá.

If there was a stable residence pattern in the past it was disturbed
after contact with the Kamarara-ko. The enticement of material goods
to be had on the Cuc caused the journeys that were to bring back the
diseases. Time and again the reason given for moving a settlement is
that 'everybody died'. There is now the new enticement of the FUNAI
'attraction front' as it is officially called. It remains to be seen what its
final effect will be. But it would be fictional to give an account of their
traditional way of life that ignored the collision with Western civilization, even if one was guessing about their time of isolation when
they lost contact with the Kamarara-ko to the north. That very isolation, which lasted for more than half a century, was a consequence
of the disastrous effects of contact. For 150 years, isolated or not,
theirs has been a way of life that results from, and tries to adapt to, the
ravages of Western disease.

They described the first time they re-established contact with the
Kamarara-ko as follows:

> It was the people from Kumakarɨg who knew the Kamarara-ko
> first. They always knew that there were other Wayãpí to the
> north of them. Their grandfathers told them there used to be a
> path. They spent a long time finding a way through to the Cuc.
> They knew which direction to go because they were shamanistic.
> They found the Kamarara-ko at Pirawiri. They were very afraid
> when they first arrived. They took back to Kumakarɨg red cloth,
> knives, machetes, matches, mirrors. There were no Brazilians on
> the Cuc at that time. The Pirawiri people got hold of these things
> on the Oyapoque. They also took flu back with them and a lot of
> people at Kumakarɨg died. Then Apeyawar and Ɨta went. Apeya-
> war went with a large number of bows and / ini / [a closely woven
> hammock as opposed to a net hammock; bow wood and / ini /
> were their major trade items].

The chronicle goes on like this, mentioning those who were the first to see the Wayana, the first to go to the Oyapoque, to the Litany River on the Surinam border, and to the Parú. Sèrèmètè who remembered names particularly well said that he was born about the time of the initial burst of coming and going. I thought him to be about twenty to twenty-five years old, and hence they probably first made contact with the French Wayápí in the early 1950s. Two fatal illnesses mentioned again and again as a result of this contact are influenza (/ aɨ̈gma'è̩ / 'fever') and dysentery (/ tèp̩òsiwɨ̈g̈ / though they often adopt the Brazilian frontier word *caganeira* for this). Finally in 1967 there was a particularly serious epidemic on the Cuc. As a consequence of this the Cuc Wayápí moved off into the Oyapoque and the Brazilian Wayápí who were staying in the area returned home.

At the time of the epidemics, before the exodus from the Cuc, there was an event remembered by everyone: the Big Fire nearly came. There was a lot of mist (smoke), the waters were a trickle, and, most significantly, / ar<u>ai</u> /, red sky arrived. The *arai* continued for many days and they thought the end of the world was coming:

/ ö-pa okɨ̈rɨ̈ngwèrë-rèmè   owa̯i ta̯ta /
when the children are finished   the fire comes

This is also referred to in a myth where it is put that Yaneyar ('our master') looks down and sees that there are still children about and therefore says: 'That's good. I won't send the fire yet'.

It was certainly a crisis. Everyone who told me of the *arai* asked if I too had seen it wherever I was at the time. Were the atmospheric conditions particularly strange then? Or were the red skies of a particularly dry summer seen as portents of doom following the epidemics?

When the Cuc Wayápí moved north to French Guiana and most of the Brazilian Wayápí returned home, a number of Brazilian Wayápí stayed on in a settlement on the Igarapé Pirawiri with Sarapó. In 1968 the first Brazilians arrived on the Nipukú and then in 1969 Cuelho Brito came through from the Cuc, shown the way by Sarapó and the remaining Brazilian Wayápí. Sarapó urged everyone to move to the Cuc area to work on a landing strip for the Brazilian Air Force. Many of them went through. This seems to have been a particularly sorry affair for the Wayápí. They said there was 'only one' Brazilian there; that there were 'only ourselves' since the Cuc Wayápí had all moved out; that they had been promised guns, machetes, and red cloth, but got nothing; and that once again there was illness. They stayed on the Cuc during 1970 then finally abandoned that area and returned home during the rains of 1970–71.

During 1971 the *garimpeiros* arrived on the Aroá and the *companhia* came to the Nipukú again. In early 1972 news came to the Nipukú of the epidemic of measles amongst the South group. In late 1972 four Brazilian hunters arrived at the Nipukú. After they left, five Wayápí died of diarrhoea and fever. In early 1973 FUNAI began its operation and in October of that year an ICOMI helicopter arrived at the Nipukú carrying a FUNAI official: / 'ẹ̀kwa Tatairɨg̈ nèrẹ̀na rẹ̀sa' è'i / 'Go to the Igarapé Onça and have a look at your [future] home' he said. With quiet compliance, half a dozen young men went through to the newly established FUNAI Post, stayed three nights, and returned to the Nipukú with flu. There were about sixty living at the Nipukú then. Six of them died. Since FUNAI had not made an accurate count of people living there is it nowhere documented that their first contact with that settlement resulted in its decimation, in an exact, antique sense of the word.

My arrival was part of this state of affairs. The conditions of my encounter with the Wayãpí, both from my point of view and from theirs, were furnished by the processes of this contact.

INFERNO VERDE:
making contact

I am for the woods against the world
But are the woods for me?
Edmund Blunden, 'The Kiss'

1. CONTACT

When there is word of 'contact' between previously isolated Amazonian Indians and representatives of the various nation states that now claim the forest, this is a euphemism for confrontation over possession of land and use of resources. Where there is no confrontation, all sorts of casual encounters between Indians and outsiders go unheeded and remain forgotten. And all along, the Indians themselves have their private histories of relations with other Indian groups.

The 1970s saw the construction of a grid plan of roads across Amazônia, the best known being the Transamazônica project. A sophisticated aerial radar survey of the entire area was completed. Mineral exploration was stepped up to an unprecedented degree. Powerful financial concerns in the Brazilian cities became increasingly interested in land speculation. And as a direct consequence of the road programme, there was a vast influx of poor settlers, also on the look-out for land, into various Indian areas.

Wayãpí territory was not seriously violated until 1975. The geological surveys carried out by CPRM and ICOMI in the early 1970s apparently found nothing of any interest to them. The *garimpo* that invaded the Aroá in 1971 was a serious blow; but had access to the area remained difficult, that kind of incursion would have been relatively easy to prevent. The main force that destroyed the integrity of Wayãpí land was the construction of the eastern stretch of the Perimetral Norte road, the BR.210, which was to run from Amapá up to the Surinam border and connect with another stretch being built from the west, the plan being to have a road running from the Atlantic seaboard along the northern frontiers to Colombia and Peru. I visited the FUNAI Indian post, on the eastern extremity of Wayãpí lands, during 1975 when from miles away in the still night we could *hear* the road coming towards us. The gigantic machines which flattened ridges and filled up valleys worked twenty-four hours a day. The planned route of the road ran directly through the Wayãpí area and would later cut off the Nipukú people in the north from the Capoeira and Aroá people in the south.

The building of these roads is an astonishing affair. It moves forward like lines of those leaf-cutting ants. What we were hearing, and what we would eventually see many months later, was a total force of some 1,000 men stretched out in a thin straight line through scores of miles of forest. First came the surveying team, a tiny group with a few surveyors and their labourers. They would mark the *linha base*, the base line, and would cut a path little wider than an Indian path but which ran dead straight between marker posts, and any turn was a clean angle. These men worked many miles ahead of the main force for months at a time, supplied by helicopter drops. Behind them, following their path, came the *desmatamento* teams, groups of between thirty and sixty men with axes and chain saws. Their job was to cut a wide swathe on the path of the *linha base*. The teams were formed on the *empreiteiro* system of contract labour, where the main company paid a *patrão* to get the job done and it was the *patrão*'s responsibility to get his team together and pay them. It was a rough life, and I heard they were paid very low wages. Some miles behind the *desmatamento* teams, a narrow winding undulating track was cut by a solitary bulldozer. Sometimes this ran along the swathe cleared by the *desmatamento* teams. Sometimes because of boggy ground or some other impediment (which would later disappear) it would find its own way round the obstacle. This allowed access for the petrol tanker trucks that supplied the machinery.

Back along the service road was the main activity – bulldozers finally clearing up the swathe so that the road was free from the danger of falling trees, and right down the centre the massive roadgraders digging out the main track of the road into a straight red scar. These were the huge machines we heard which never stopped. In hilly country they would move over the top of a hill gathering the red earth into their insides, then run down and deposit the stuff on the floor of the next valley on top of a previously constructed culvert, then turn and repeat the process the other way, time and time again, day and night. The completed road then undulated through huge cuttings and over huge embankments. It was in constant use – petrol tankers, trucks, and jeeps driven at violent speeds. (There were numerous accidents and deaths on that road even though it was not a public highway at the time.) Back down the road was the centre of operations – a group of prefabricated buildings serving as offices, canteens, and dormitories. It was also a helicopter base. The camp was temporary, the idea being that it should be moved forward when the lines of communication became too stretched. As it turned out, that was the only operational camp constructed on the BR.210. Right down at the start of the road, near Serra do Navio, was the base camp with the road company hospital, an air strip, and the main offices and residences of those who were running the operation.

In the dry season of 1975 the road entered Wayãpí lands on the south bank of the Felício, crossed to the north bank, and got as far as a small river called the Igarapé Jacaré. Work then stopped for the rains. The service road ran on for some distance beyond; the *desmatamento* team had got even further; and the surveyors' *linha base* had got as far as Ɨto Wasú, a large waterfall on the Nipukú, well downstream from the settlement. But by 1975 the Brazilian economy was in trouble and could no longer afford the grandiose scheː e of the Perimetral Norte. Work was not resumed in 1976 and to date the road still stops at the Jacaré.

It is such an unfortunate intrusion. Had the economic recession hit the Brazilian road programme just one year earlier the integrity of Wayãpí territory could have been maintained for many more years. As it is, the road now allows easy access right into the centre of their land and that facility is being used. Furthermore since the road is there, the lands on either side of it come under government scrutiny and have to be 'demarcated'. What will happen is that traditional Wayãpí land will be drastically reduced to a few patches of 'reservation'. The eastern section of the Perimetral Norte has been a failure in terms of the government's plans and it has been abandoned. But it has come just far enough to let loose its deleterious consequences on the Wayãpí and to put them through all the disturbances and disruptions that they are now having to face.

I entered the Wayãpí area in June 1974 and I am glad that I got to know it before the road arrived. I first saw the road in October 1975 when travelling through from the Nipukú to the FUNAI post with my friend Kasiripinar. I was breathtaken, but more to the point, it was Kasiripinar's first encounter with it — only a few miles from the spot where he had been born. He had once seen a helicopter, but never a road or a truck. We were on the fourth day of our walk and had already crossed a new picada which I recognized as the *linha base*. Suddenly we saw daylight appearing through the trees and knew we were approaching a clearing where previously there had been none. In a few minutes we were out in the sunlight gazing at the huge swathe cut by the *desmatamento* teams and found we were at a point where the service road had already been pushed through. It was rolling country and we had emerged into the clearing at the bottom of a shallow dip. In both directions the service road disappeared over a huge gap in the skyline cut by the swathe of the clearing. There was an uncanny silence. The big machinery was many miles away. We sat by the side of the track for a long time, taking all this in, until we heard the sound of a vehicle approaching. I think we were both pretty agitated. A large Mercedes truck appeared over the rise and came down towards us. As it approached, Kasiripinar fled across the clearing to the edge of the woods. In my concern to arrange a lift with the driver I did not pay much attention to Kasiripinar's movements, but after the truck stopped he came running back to join me. He paid no attention to the driver but began to stroke the side of the truck feeling what it was made of. His face was very close to it and I think he may have been smelling it. We got our lift and arrived at the post two days earlier than we had expected. Since the arrival of the road, the post had been moved a few kilometres to its present site at the edge of the road. On our arrival at the new post Kasiripinar gave it its name by which it is still known: Aramirã – 'Red Earth'. He had earlier been astonished by the red earth which the road had exposed and here the bulldozers had done FUNAI a favour by making a clearing for them. The new post sat in the middle of a large rectangle of the astonishing red earth.

Goodland and Irwin's study (1975) of the fragile ecosystem of the Amazon tropical forest and of the damage done by the roads and the profligate development schemes is called *Amazon Jungle: Green Hell to Red Desert*. I hope that 'red desert' is not an accurate prophecy. It looks like a colourful exaggeration, but the threat is indeed colossal. 'Green hell' on the other hand refers to a fanciful tradition in Brazil which describes the forest in novels and travel books as the *'inferno verde'*. I found it nothing of the sort, although I am sure that a large part of the reason why I found the forest so benign was that I was looked after so well by the Wayãpí.

2. THE FOREST

In an essay called 'Wordsworth in the Tropics', Aldous Huxley suggested that Wordsworth (and Meredith and Cowper) and anyone else smitten by daft Nature-worship should go and see Nature nourished by the equatorial rains. There, 'to travel is to hack one's way laboriously through a tangled, prickly, and venomous darkness':

> The sparse inhabitants of the equatorial forest are all believers in devils. When one has visited, in even the most superficial manner, the places where they live, it is difficult not to share their faith. The jungle is marvellous, fantastic, beautiful; but it is also terrifying, it is also profoundly sinister. There is something in . . . the character of great forests . . . which is foreign, appalling, fundamentally and utterly inimical to intruding man.
>
> (1929:116 and 114)

Well, it's a splendid essay on Wordsworth: elegant, perceptive, and witty. But I never came across that terrifying, foreign, appalling, inimical something. Nor did I do much laborious hacking. Let's just say that removing the word 'sparse', and reading 'London' or 'New York' or 'Rio' for 'the forest' and 'the jungle', then the matter would be put quite well. Turning to something like Bates's *The Naturalist on the River Amazons* (1930) or following the journeys of Wallace (1853) and Spruce (1908), one finds in work like that a wholehearted and sensible extraversion to all the creatures, plants, and processes of the forest.

The worst I can say of the forest is that sometimes on a grey day it can look messy, ragged, and depressing, and that after many months of seeing the sky from village clearings and gardens I longed for a view. Only once, towards the end, when I got a lift in the roadmen's helicopter (taking half an hour or so to cover a distance that took us five to eight days to walk) did I see from above the awesome extent of the forest canopy. Flying towards the Nipukú settlement, the clearings and gardens were not visible until we were almost on top of them when they looked like accidental tears in the endless undulations of tree tops. Within the forest, it was difficult to get a sense of the height of the various trees. The edges of clearings were the only places where I could see the habit of larger trees and there are many I only know by their trunks.

The fauna does not come teeming round the traveller. One can be out for hours and see next to nothing. But the noises are always there. To me, the extreme contrasts of bird song were between the *paipaia*, a small nondescript bird with an interminable whoop like a very loud wolf-whistle, and the *uirapurú*, a tiny plain bird with a repertoire of delicate songs that sounded like a person playing a bone flute. (Some Wayãpí are good at whistling the various tunes.) The *paipaia*'s brash cry one hears everywhere, all day long. Hearing the *uirapuru* is a rare, exquisite event. (Restaurants in Amazonian towns called 'Uirapuru' show a brightly coloured tanager on their illuminated signs, not the proper bird.)

Night sounds came through the blanket of whistling and croaking made by the insects and frogs. There were strange bird cries at night: a long growl from the / anyɨreatɨ /, the *passaro mau*; a bubbling noise like a turkey from the / ya-po / (*japu*); and the plaintive falling cry like our curlew from the / soi / (*sovi*). The / òrǫwa / (perhaps the *tovaquinha*) has a similar sad hoot which the Wayãpí say is 'singing of sadness'. Occasionally we would hear a long muffled crash in the distance. / 'ɨwɨra omano'/ (tree dies) was the offhand comment. From time to time these huge old trees simply keeled over, not blown down, since anything stronger than a light breeze is unusual in the forest. A few people indicated in the genealogies were said to have been killed by falling trees.

The most arresting sound is that of howler monkeys crying in full voice. I thought it sounded like the kind of effects that can be made up on a synthesizer and I think the weird effect is due to a complex

collection of overtones. The male howler monkey has a boney spherical cavity in its throat which produces the resonance of its cry. It can
come in the night, or in the twilight of morning or evening, the deep
cry rising and falling, seeming to come nearer and then recede. When
heard from nearby, the cry loses much of its resonance and one is
more aware of it as a series of barking grunts.

Accidents from snake bite are rare, three in the area during my stay,
none fatal, but it is a hazard. In my short genealogies there are a
number of deaths mostly from the *jararaca* (a small pit viper sometimes called the 'fer-de-lance' by Europeans), and one from the *suru-
cucú* (a snake of fearful size, rare in that area, called the 'bushmaster'
in English). I had difficulty seeing snakes on the path and frequently
walked over or past *jararacas*. Scorpions are a nuisance. They get into
the thatch of houses and shelters and fall onto people in their hammocks below. They also get into one's belongings. The sting is painful
and needs a day's rest with the comfort of analgesics to get over.
Spiders, including the large tarantula, are not a significant hazard.
Mosquitos were present but sparse, being much worse on the lower
stretches of the Nipukú. We were spared the misery of *piuns*, the
vicious black flies that people who know other parts of Amazônia
describe as a particularly horrible pest. Mites get on one's skin when
travelling and chiggers were common especially in the dusty floors of
abandoned houses. (Chiggers, /tõ/, are fleas carried by dogs. They
lay their eggs in the skin of one's foot or under the toenail. The cluster
of eggs swells into the size of a small wart.) But mites and chiggers are
easily removed. The settlements suffered a permanent plague of
various varieties of cockroaches. It is a repellent sight at first, but one
soon gets used to these things being everywhere.

Travelling at the height of the dry season along dried-out paths is
easy, pleasant going. But the rains of the wet season make any
journey a misery, slopping through mud and water, unable to see
where your feet are going, slipping and tripping on submerged roots
and branches, wading long stretches with water up to your knees,
occasionally even chest high. Travelling with one or two men was
always strenuous since we aimed to get the journey over as quickly as
possible. But travelling with a family was a leisurely affair. If game
was shot or fruit found, that was the end of walking for the day and
shelters would be built at the nearest convenient stream. When a
group was approaching the end of a journey, either near a settlement
or near the FUNAI post, everyone stopped and rested at the last
stream and gathered the stragglers together. They would wash the
mud off their legs and titivate themselves as best they could, putting
on red urucu dye if they had any, before going on to announce their
arrival.

Although we were only one and a half degrees north of the Equator
it was never uncomfortably hot. At night I used two blankets in a close

woven hammock. The Indians like to get hold of thick Brazilian hammocks and blankets, and some have mosquito nets which protect against the cold. Those who do not have such luxuries make small fires of glowing embers under their hammocks at night. These need tending (and it is usually the woman of the household who gets up and sees to it). I got the impression that the Indians did not need the long sleep of our standard eight hours. A night's sleep was more a matter of cat-napping and resting.

The notion of the *inferno verde* is a nonsensical exaggeration of the discomforts and dangers of the forest. Apart from recurrent attacks of malaria, which certainly were troublesome, and apart from periods of lassitude, which may have been due to intestinal parasites, my life was very comfortable. I hunted and fished with the men, but I was supported by the hospitality of my hosts. I did very little work in the gardens and did no cooking except when travelling alone. While they guaranteed my welfare I was able to treat their illnesses with the medicines at my disposal, but the risks they faced to their lives were infinitely greater than those facing mine. If there is anything infernal about the Amazon forest, it does not come either from the natural surroundings or from the way of life of the Indians who live there. Misery and suffering in Amazônia are a result of the penetration of our civilization in its various modes. It is Aldous Huxley's 'intruder' who is utterly inimical to the place.

3. ACCULTURATION AND MORAL JUDGEMENTS

I arrived in the Wayãpí area as part of that intrusion, with various expectations about isolated people which, however vague, gave some sort of initial direction towards what was later to interest me. Circumstances changed my mind with respect to a number of assumptions: about the relationship between Indians and outsiders; about government Indian policy; and about anthropological interest in Indians. It was not so much a matter of Neurath's desperate image of 'rebuilding one's ship at sea'. Rather, reflecting and writing afterwards about what happened is like the dry-dock of Wordsworth's 'emotion recollected in tranquillity'.

I arrived at the FUNAI post on the Rio Felício at midnight after a sixteen-hour journey by motorized canoe from the manganese mine, Serra do Navio. There were four Indian families visiting the post at the time, and as we came in they were standing in a line, side by side, on the high bank above us, silhouetted in the moonlight. 'And round about the keel with faces pale . . .' It was to be some weeks before I had any clear idea of what I had come to. The first few days saw a series of nasty jolts to my expectations, making me suspect during the initial days I spent on the post that I had come upon a tragedy. I had arrived suspicious of FUNAI's policy of 'attraction', which was simply to encourage the Indians to move their settlements from remote sites either on to the post itself or else to new sites near the post, concentrating the population, making it easier for FUNAI to exercise its role of protection and control. The policy seemed to me then to be dangerous and immoral and I have not changed my view since. But I had not realized how seductive the presence of a single post, staffed by four to six Brazilians, would be to the Indians. Since it was an 'attraction front', extra funds were available, and the Indians were liberally supplied with shotguns and ammunition, machetes, aluminium pots, knives, electric torches, hammocks, salt, and so on. The largesse was short term, of course, and would stop when the 'attraction' was completed, leaving habits and dependences but removing the means to satisfy them. There was also a pharmacy on the post which seemed to the Indians a guarantee against illness and death, but careless access to the post and careless health standards on it made it more a dispensary of illness. All the epidemics of coughs, flus, and skin complaints in the villages were brought in by Indians returning from a visit to the post.

I was dismayed both by the apparent compliance of the Indians and by the speed with which they had apparently been affected by this contact. A number of young Wayápí men were dressed in shorts and T-shirts and wore plastic construction helmets (as did the FUNAI employees). Also, many of them seemed to speak Portuguese. I saw every sign of Brazilian influence as implying immediate cultural decay, and in those early days I thought I had found myself in just the sort of field circumstances I most wanted to avoid.

'Capitão Waiwai' and the Nipukú villagers were due to arrive – all of them. These were the people from the most distant settlement where I had decided to go and stay. They had been summoned to receive immunization injections and to be encouraged to prepare a clearing for their future home near the post. After a week with no sign of them I arranged for three Wayápí boys to guide me through to the Nipukú and to help carry my belongings. At the start of the journey, even the signs of Brazilian penetration into the woods added more to my dismay: a large clearing made by the manganese company for helicopters to land; the remains of a helicopter which had crashed some years previously; jaguar traps made by Brazilian hunters; a pit dug close to the path where a gold-prospector had worked; initials carved on a tree trunk. Furthermore I was tired, sore, bad tempered, carrying far too much, and finding the walking extremely difficult.

On the third day of our walk we met the Nipukú villagers travelling towards us. It was early in the day, but a camp was immediately made. It was a moving encounter for me since, apart from the three youngsters, it was the first time I had been with Wayápí when there were no Brazilians about.

Many months later Waiwai's account of our meeting went something like this: 'We asked the boys who you were. They didn't know. We asked if you were . . . (the Brazilian in charge of the post). They said no. We asked if you were / karai-ko / (Brazilian). They said no. We asked why you had come. They said they didn't know. We were all afraid of you.' I saw nothing of their fear, only an ebullience of smiles, numerous offerings of food from giggling women, and a circle of men round me making enthusiastic, if broken conversation.

Round the fire at night they asked me to sing. I sang a few songs and played the harmonica for some time. Then I asked them to sing. 'Wayãpí don't know any songs' was the tenor of the reply. But after some pressing one man offered to sing a song he had learned from the Wayana. He began to sing and a number of others joined in. I did not understand the Wayana words but the tune was 'Jesus loves me, this I know' (660 in the Presbyterian *Church Hymnary*). Warming to my feigned appreciation he said he knew another. This time it was 'When he cometh, when he cometh to make up his jewels' (158 in the *Hymnary*). They were delighted that I knew the tunes and asked me to teach them more songs about *papai do ceu*, a Brazilian phrase meaning 'daddy in the sky', just as the / amerikana-ko / had taught the Wayana. I assumed the Americans were from one of the missionary organizations. Perhaps for the sake of balance I should have taught them 'The Red Flag' and the 'Internationale'.

Finding children's hymns as an introduction to Wayãpí culture is the best epiphany of my dismay. But as events grew more intense I was not allowed to sulk for long in damaged expectations. The three youngsters and I turned back and accompanied the others on their slow journey towards the post. We all finally camped about an eight to twelve hour walk from the post at a spot called the Sabão, the Brazilians' name for a beautiful series of rapids on the Felício which marks the highest point on the river of easy access by motorized canoe. Some young men went on to alert FUNAI. A few days later the FUNAI people arrived at the camp by motor canoe to give the injections, bringing back with them the young Indians who had gone on to the post.

The injection encounter at the Sabão was a lethal fiasco. The FUNAI men left after a couple of hours. Within a few days every single person in the camp with the exception of myself fell ill with influenza symptoms. My medicines ran out and with one man who had recovered I went to the post to get more. It turned out that the illness had been taken in by three workers from the road survey team, still many miles away, who had come upstream to visit the post. They were still there. From their point of view it was simply a neighbourly call. They were quietly lounging around watching, expressionless, the movements of the bare-breasted Indian women.

Back at the Sabão camp, people were recovering and families began to drift back to the Nipukú. No one was entirely well during the

48INFERNO VERDE: making contact

journey. The coughing lingered on and a number suffered relapses into high temperatures. The group I went with took seven nights to get through to the village. Morale was low during the following weeks. Night after night Waiwai would begin a loud monologue from his hammock, heard across the village. I understood very little but the main point was that 'we were told to go to the post for medicine – we were told we would get manioc flour – we got hunger and influenza'. Two infant children died. Their coughs had been getting worse and worse. By this time the crises had dispelled my expectations and taken me into these people's lives.

The presence of FUNAI was essential. Certainly carelessness and ignorance in the way the staff fulfilled their roles led to unnecessary suffering and death. But there would have been wholesale confusion had the Indians confronted on their own the arrival of the road and the influx of prospectors and settlers. FUNAI did play a protective role or sorts, but more than that, standing as they did between the Wayãpí and the Brazilians, these half dozen or so FUNAI staff were the major influence that changed the Indians' lives.

The notion of acculturation is difficult to use. An obvious indicator of it would seem to be speaking Portuguese but that is unevenly acquired. As a rule the men pick up far more than the women. Contact between Brazilians and Indians is man's talk. It is Brazilian men who go into the forests and it is Indian men who are taken on as labour or who go hunting and prospecting with the Brazilians. But not all Wayãpí men have made these contacts. Those who have picked up a bit of Portuguese go on improving it rapidly while those who have not get left behind.

Of the Nipukú people, four men and one woman had been taken down to the frontier town of Porto Grande by *garimpeiros* and had picked up enough Portuguese to enable them to get on fairly easily with the FUNAI people on the post. The best Portuguese speaker was a boy of 12 who had been 'given' to a Brazilian family for about a year. But for the most part the rest could do little beyond the basics such as 'it is very good', 'it is very bad', 'do this', 'do that', and the indispensable *da para mim* (give to me). On the other side of the area there were better Portuguese speakers because of the 1971 *garimpo* and because of regular contact with FUNAI

Acculturation can be seen in terms of the breakdown of material self-sufficiency and an increasing dependence on outside goods. But this indicator does not measure very much either unless it is obvious that in becoming dependent on those material goods the Indians are handing over the last of their political self-sufficiency too. Some of the outside goods gave greater strength to the material conditions of their lives and it would be hard to grudge them the gifts. Machetes, axes, and files immediately made their lives immensely more secure, although I still doubt the wisdom of introducing shotguns, since once that dependence is established a constant and expensive supply of shot and powder is required. (By the time I left no one at the Nipukú was using bows and arrows.) Since Indians were most persuasive when they described the advantages of shotguns over bows and arrows, I suppose theirs should be the last word. As for Western clothes, T-shirts and flip-flop sandals are useful in the forest while hats were as much a novelty for them as wearing a loin-cloth was for me. (There is a view that shirts produce skin diseases since Indians are not supposed to know how to keep clothes clean, but that is humbug.)

Their aesthetic of appearance was not undermined, at least not in the villages. The youngsters who had helped carry my belongings had been given shorts to wear while they worked on the post, but they put on loin-cloths as soon as they were out of sight of the FUNAI workers. Most of the men at the Nipukú plucked their eyebrows and eyelashes in spite of the teasing they got for doing so when they visited the post. (Both men and women plucked their pubic hair.) The business of facial hair was explained to me as follows:

> In the old days we never plucked our facial hair. The old men had beards just like you. Then we met the Wayana and they said 'Ho ho ho, you all look like howler monkeys' so we learned to pluck the hair on our faces. Now we meet the Brazilians and they say 'Ho ho ho, you all look like spider monkeys' [which have black fur but pale, bald faces].

Some of them have now stopped removing their eyebrows and eyelashes.

The story about their facial hair, doing what others say they should, illustrates a more general pliancy. Though culture and acculturation are not sturdy enough terms to be put to very much work, one can say that there is something about Wayãpí culture that makes it prone to deculturation. One of the first FUNAI reports on the newly dis-covered Wayãpí stated that 'their ceramic is weak and crude'. I suppose it is when compared with similar artefacts from other parts of Brazil, and perhaps their pottery can be seen as a token of their culture as a whole. A note struck again and again in their own descriptions was that 'the Wayãpí don't know anything', 'the Wayãpí don't have anything'. This often went along with descriptions stating that 'we did not know this in the old days but the Wayana taught us how to do it'. [See Appendix.] It seems they managed to give the same impres-sion 100 years ago. 'Pauvres Oyampis,' says Coudreau, 'les voici bien décadents.' And in his judgement, 'les Roucouyennes [i.e. the Wayana] sont de beaucoup plus intéressants que les Oyampis. Plus nombreux, plus laborieux, plus artistes' (1893:548 and 371). In the 1930s a German traveller on the Jarí who buried an expedition casualty under a swastika, and who takes time off in his account to extol the brilliant record of Germany's explorers, comes to a similar conclusion. He finds that the Wayana and Aparai who are travelling with him 'evidently want to keep me away from the Oyampi, who are inferior to the Oayana and more or less ruled by them'. He goes on:

[The Oyampi are] . . . people of an entirely different breed from the Aparai and the Oayana, far more primitive. Many of them have their eyes close together, like monkeys . . . More and more Oyampi come in, regular wild men of the jungle. They are plainly under the influence of the masterful Oayana.

(Schulz-Kampfhenkel 1940:237,239,240)

I sometimes heard FUNAI staff discuss their postings, where they had worked and where they would like to work. They frequently mentioned their admiration for some of the Gê groups they knew in Southern Pará and Mato Grosso – the Gorotire, the Txukahamãe, and so on. Points which were usually mentioned were the sturdy build of the men, their wrestling matches, their physical bravery, and their fierce pride. 'Look at these people', they said of the Wayãpí. 'Compared with the Kayapó these people here are *uma banda de mulheres* [a pack of women]'. The point being discussed was invasions by *garimpeiros* and it was suggested that whereas the Gorotire had in the past attacked and killed Brazilians who invaded their lands, the Wayãpí were too docile to do so.

These moral judgements expressed through similes of monkeys and women and through images of weakness are outrageous no matter what lies behind them. When others say that the Wayãpí are timid or docile, I would rather note their kindly approach to outsiders. There is a long-standing distinction in frontier Brazil between *índios bravos* and *índios mansos*. *Manso* means 'tame' and fits well with the rest of the animal similes. Why some groups should resist contact violently while others put up no resistance at all is a question I cannot answer, although in case after case it is quite clear that the bellicosity of *índios bravos* is a result of their being terrified by the encroachment of outsiders. Darcy Ribeiro documents a number of cases where from the Brazilians' point of view they were 'pacifying' hostile Indians while from the Indians' point of view it was they who were 'pacifying' the Brazilians (Ribeiro 1977:184–186). There is a common response of fear underlying both violent and compliant reactions, and I suspect that the distinction between *bravo* and *manso* reflects episodes in a complicated history of misunderstanding rather than differences between temperamental types.

Wayãpí life is simple and unadorned, but that simplicity is intriguing. Looking behind both the embellishments of contact (the aluminium pots, the machetes, the fish-hooks, and so on) and its disasters (the terrible epidemics), there is still an astonishing self-sufficiency and contentment maintained with the minimum of cultural fuss. It would be better for them were this self-sufficiency to last, but the very simplicity of their way of life makes it vulnerable to influences from outside.

They are fully aware of the danger they are in. A phrase I learned early on in my stay, as the first epidemic was taking its course, was /wayãpi õ-pa/, 'the Wayãpí are finished'. They said that in the old days everybody had many children but that now all the children die and there are no old people. The losses they suffer through illness are their major anxiety, and when I visited them ill in their hammocks it was not through hypochondria that so many of them would say, partly as a question, partly as an announcement, /amanǫ-ti ki'i/, 'I am dying now'. They were ambivalent in the way they approached contact with Brazilians. On the one hand they were afraid: afraid of illness and afraid of violence. On the other hand the presence of the FUNAI post brought medicine to guard against illness and death, and it also brought the goods. I cannot say how clearly they made the connection between meeting Brazilians and picking up dangerous diseases. The analogy of us visiting a supermarket knowing every time that we ran the risk of catching bubonic plague is too flamboyant. I do not think it was cupidity that overcame their fear. Neither is it explained by any clear conception of the causality of death, where some of their rationalizations might appear to be that illness is not itself the cause of death – that illness makes us vulnerable to witchcraft and it is the latter that kills us. I will look at these ambiguities later. I think it was rather that they saw themselves permanently surrounded and threatened by disease whether Brazilians were there or not, and that whatever risks the Brazilians brought, there was a greater advantage in the protection given by injections and pills.

There is no *necessary* relationship between the changes in the material conditions of their lives and their compliance with Brazilian influence and power. Explaining their relation to the Brazilian frontier in terms of changing conditions of production and reproduction, to use the Marxian phrases, is not as useful as emphasizing that the principal determining conditions are those of extinction. They are easily deculturated because their culture is simple. They are *mansos* because they are afraid. They do what they are told because they can see no alternative. They see contact as giving a better chance of survival than isolation.

4. ILLUSIONS OF DIFFERENCE

Suppose I had been a solitary adventurer. Suppose I had arrived at the Nipukú as a wandering *déraciné* coming upon a lost tribe. What a melodrama; and what a sham. It is mysterious to reflect on what my arrival meant to them. There was no difference between me, with my university degrees and anthropological prurience, and someone who might represent the worst of the Brazilian frontier, brutalized by poverty and cruel conditions, and impelled by a different appetite. I came with beads and red cloth and medicines, but would my reception have been any different had I arrived with nothing? I suspect I would have been looked after in just as generous a way. Waiwai's comments show that they were puzzled by my arrival but the reason for my presence was never questioned throughout my stay. They were always anxious to please me and anxious to look after me. This is an extraordinary state of affairs. Having the medicines gave me an important role in their lives and they were pleased with the various goods I brought, but that is not enough to explain the respect I was given.

I had brought far too much. Some kind of token exchange at the beginning would have been quite enough. I thought I might have to pay my way with exchanges of goods for food, but such an arrangement is impossible over a long period in such a community. I gave away nearly everything when I first arrived, but made the mistake of holding back various things. I should have given everything away immediately since they all knew exactly what I had left, and it was all the more difficult to find a proper pretext later to get rid of the things I had nervously held back in case of unforeseen events.

My principal gifts were beads and red cloth. The Wayãpí wear a strip of red cloth /kamisa/ held by a cotton string /koaŋ/ around their waists. Women wear the cloth like a mini-skirt, wrapped round and tucked in. Men wear the length through their legs and hanging down over the string fore and aft. In the old days the cloth was woven from cotton and dyed with urucú. The colour fades fast, and for men the cloth can become uncomfortable when walking in the rain since it becomes heavy and inflames the inside of their thighs. The dye in Brazilian cloth is much faster, the colour is found more attractive, and the garment is lighter.

The beads I brought produced a tremendous reaction. When I first produced them the village burst into a chorus of glottal gasps. People ran from all sides and crowded round, and from then on I was constantly asked for gifts of /mò'ïrë/. They had hardly any when I came. There were a few necklaces of large, dull beads which they said they had got on the Cuc. Mine were small, bright, *rocaille* beads which they said were the best possible. I once heard that I had been criticized by a FUNAI official for 'infantilizing' the Indians by giving them gifts of beads. I was shocked when I heard of the allegation. It is after all an accusation I am quick to make against FUNAI and against missionaries. I can see no harm in imperishable articles which have no effect on their physical well-being one way or the other and which give them so much pleasure. I wore them too.

There is a popular notion that anthropologists cannot step into a primitive culture without altering it in some way. It is a trivial thing to say, since all these meetings alter the participants in some way or another. The friendships I made there were reciprocal. I learned a lot from them and I am sure they learned a lot from me. But more to the point, compared with what has happened to the Wayãpí since Cabral first landed on the Brazilian coast in 1500 (given for instance that dogs and bananas are now as much part of their lives as manioc is), and compared with the impact that the road was going to have, my arrival as an anthropologist is of no consequence. The notion of an un-contacted group is a fantasy of our culture. Anthropology is only possible within the conditions of contact.

Just as there is no such thing as an uncontacted group, so there is no such thing as an innocent arrival. My inquiry was *not* made possible because I came with goods and medicines and exchanged the things I had and the knowledge I had for their hospitality and their infor-mation about themselves. My work was made possible because the force of the Brazilian frontier was behind me. My presence was backed up. I suppose the proper perspective is that my presence was respected because the FUNAI enterprise was behind me; that FUNAI was powerful because it represented the most effective en-croachment of the Brazilian frontier; and that the frontier in its turn was the particular face in Amazônia of the expansion of western industrial civilization. Behind us all, like a distant *papai do ceu*, was the force of world commerce.

It would be misleading to ignore these conditions. Judith Okely shows how much is revealed in Malinowski's *Diary*, and how much is concealed in his ethnographies, regarding the effect of the colonial administration on the Trobriand Islanders. For Malinowski this was an irritating intrusion that would adversely affect the 'objective' and 'scientific' status of his account, hence he deliberately eradicated any concern with it, whereas what was 'objectively' the case was that: '. . . the ideal model of the isolated, simple society didn't exist, even at the outset of intensive anthropological fieldwork' (Okely 1975:181). What is the point of presenting an account of the 'political and social organization' of the Trobrianders or of anyone else if such pivotal facets of their lives are ignored?

It is not just an anthropological predicament. Conor Cruise O'Brien pointed out that in the United States there is a great deal of scholarly interest in the history, politics, and economics of Third World countries, especially those that are under the politi-cal and economic hegemony of the United States. Latin American countries are represented particularly strongly. A great deal of this work is presented with scrupulous scholarly care for facts and for sources. It is often massively detailed. But the account can be presented with no mention whatsoever of the role of the

United States. 'The result is not scholarship but mystification with scholarly apparatus' (O'Brien 1967:69).

In anthropology, the fantasy is very attractive and those who manage to resist it do so with regret. 'When', asks Lévi-Strauss 'was the best time to see India? At what period would the study of Brazilian savages have afforded the purest satisfaction and revealed them in their least adulterated state?' He goes on:

> And so I am caught within a circle from which there is no escape: the less human societies were able to communicate with each other and therefore to corrupt each other through contact, the less their respective emissaries were able to perceive the wealth and significance of their diversity. In short, I have only two possibilities: either I can be like some traveller of the olden days, who was faced with a stupendous spectacle, all, or almost all, of which eluded him, or worse still, filled him with scorn and disgust; or I can be a modern traveller, chasing after the vestiges of a vanished reality. I lose on both counts, and more seriously than may at first appear, for, while I complain of being able to glimpse no more than the shadow of the past, I may be insensitive to reality as it is taking shape at this very moment, since I have not reached the stage of development at which I would be capable of perceiving it. A few hundred years hence, in this same place, another traveller, as despairing as myself, will mourn the disappearance of what I might have seen, but failed to see. I am subject to a double infirmity: all that I perceive offends me, and I constantly reproach myself for not seeing as much as I should. (1974:43).

Anthropology takes a primary interest in alternative modes of thought and action. That implies that what is interesting is difference and contrast between us and them. To the extent that that difference is emulsified, so the interest will be diluted. The 'vestiges of a vanished reality' which Lévi-Strauss refers to are really vestiges of vanished differences. The best contrast appears when we find something that carries on its own life with no interference from the mode of life that is familiar to us.

In order to make an effective contrast with what we recognize as familiar, it is important that what we encounter as alien be seen as self-contained. If the boundaries of that self-containment are broken down, it will be all the more difficult to identify the singularity of what we have encountered. Hence the obvious tendency in ethnographic writing to emphasize the uniqueness of what is found. It is a well-intentioned respect for a people's *integrity* – a good word with which to bundle up an ontological notion and a moral one. Furthermore it reflects the way that most writers, including me, want to 'chase after the vestiges of a vanished reality' and satisfy initial expectations of what traditional cultures look like.

On the moral question of interference with Indian groups, there is a lot of work done within anthropology. There are excellent chronicles of what happened to the Indians, Ribeiro (1977) and Hemming (1978) for example. There is also a line of work dealing explicitly with the sociology of contact and the theme of inter-ethnic friction. Oliveira (1964) and Laraia and Da Matta (1967) are two such examples. And there is a great deal of responsible documentation of the more brutal aspects of contact – violent clashes, epidemics, land invasions – as well as accounts of the adaptations the Indians are making in response to government activity, missionary activity, and trading and work arrangements with Brazilians. The broad outline is clear: the remains of Indian cultures in Amazônia are being eradicated, and no one who knows the area can fail to be moved by the tragedy of what is taking place.

But the outline of the related academic questions is blurred. In looking for an alien mode of thought and action there is a danger of pursuing an illusion of difference and perceiving what is encountered through all sorts of exaggerations and elisions, composing an account of the culture in question that satisfies those initial expectations of self-containment and singularity.

Folk studies of rural Scotland, for example, vigorously pursue such distortions. In this case, the illusion of difference is sought with rhapsodic intemperance, and folk cultures are made to appear out of meagre bric-à-brac. I recognize the appetite that is being satisfied by this way of looking at things. Anthropologists in Amazônia are stimulated by it too, although it might be said in favour of the folk cultures that they produce some lively entertainment, in music and song, whereas there is little to raise the spirits in the bleaker technicalities of the ethnographies.

Many examples show that even when Indians have lived for decades on the edges of Brazilian society, certain aspects of their lives such as language and a relationship terminology, some practical skills, and a certain ragged lore of cosmological notions, can show a surprising resilience to the effects of contact. But there are Indian groups in Brazil who can tell the time and who have watches, who use money, and who can catch a bus into a nearby town. I would expect that their understanding of the world is closer to mine than those who have never seen a road or a motor car or a brick building, and some kind of appreciation of the shared familiarity, or lack of it, has to be attempted before I am to understand what it is about those cultures that is self-contained, homogeneous, contrasting, and therefore alien.

Written accounts can control the picture they want to give. But when photographs or films or even spoken comments back up an ethnographic report, all sorts of odd ectopic details break through the integument of self-containment. In the beautiful run of photographs in the original edition of *Tristes Tropiques* (Lévi-Strauss 1955), plate 27 shows curare being prepared in tin cans. Ethnographic films are a rich source of similar clues. Besides revealing through these unintentional hints that material self-containment is a fiction, these films and photographs also show how much a degree of contact and acculturation is a necessary precondition for any kind of anthropological report to take place. We cannot stalk these people like some jungle paparazzi, trying to catch our victims in unguarded private moments which we can record unknown to them. Just as these odd things, the tin cans and the T-shirts, reveal a relationship between them and others, so all the things that we take back – photographs, museum artefacts, and reports – show that we have taken part in that wider relationship in which they were already involved.

If the material conditions of self-containment are so flimsy, what of those conditions by which we recognize an alien mode of *thought*? A temporary distinction between material self-sufficiency and something like 'epistemological self-sufficiency' sets up the question for the moment, although the distinction cannot be maintained for long. It illustrates only that if an illusion of material self-containment is so easy to produce (by hiding the tin cans and asking the people to take off their T-shirts for the camera, or by writing in the cheerful convention of the ethnographic present), then the illusion of epistemological self-containment makes its appearance with even less effort. When I read an account of a collection of beliefs and cosmological notions, a few curiosities about space and time, perhaps, or an odd taxonomy, am I to take this as an alien mode of thought? What exactly do these details illustrate of a difference between us and them? Surely if there were such a thing as an isolated, singular, self-contained, alien mode of thought, there would be no conditions for us to know anything about it. There would be no way in. Hence the presence of the tin cans may seem a trivial material intrusion, but their clanking reminds me that I share a common world with the people I am visiting. Contact does much more than set up the practical and material conditions that make an inquiry possible. It reveals conditions of mutual comprehension between me and the people I am with.

At this point the provisional distinction between things and thought, between material conditions and epistemological conditions, can be put aside. Both are aspects of the same predicament. It is misleading to think of a mode of thought and action as something comprehensively or coherently alien (along the lines of all those 'different forms of life' arguments). An abstraction such as 'Wayãpí culture' is a useful expository device, not much more than a syntactic convenience, since in a strict sense it can only refer to a demographic division, in this case defined by many miles of empty forest, and by marriage and residence arrangements that keep these people interrelated amongst themselves and separated from others. Consider the rest:

A language: shared by another group on the Oyapoque showing only dialectal variations, and related to a string of cognate tongues going back as far as the first records of the European invaders.

A cosmology: fragments of myths and stories, and a number of notions about the world which are found throughout the Amazon forest.

A material culture: with not a single feature that could not be found somewhere else.

A relationship terminology: 'simplicity itself' (see Chapter 7).

A present crisis of contact with the Brazilian frontier: a sorry scene which has been repeated countless times before.

A growing familiarity with the encroaching frontier.

There is nothing alien in any of this. Other Amazonian ethnographers would find themselves professionally at home here, while all other people who are not individually wedded to their own collective identity of race or caste or place or pedigree would find themselves equally at ease living with the Wayãpí.

The quick answer to the question 'what does "Wayãpí" mean to the Wayãpí?' is that it means 'not Brazilian', 'not Wayana', 'not Aparai', and so on, and 'not quite / kamarara-ko /'. This is a matter of their self-identity and the inter-ethnic friction theme I mentioned earlier, and the question of how the boundaries of ethnic groups are maintained. I have nothing helpful to say on this matter. The boundary between them and the half dozen or so FUNAI staff they had to deal with was absolutely unambiguous.

The most convincing way to put the question is to ask whether I can produce an account of a significant difference between them and us. Can I produce an intelligible account of the differences between my knowledge of the world and theirs, between my interpretations of what goes on around me and theirs, between my experience of life and theirs? 'Experience of life' is not a particularly crisp phrase, but it is easy to see that much of the difference between me and them and much of what is interesting about that difference consists of differing practical acquaintance, differing knowledge, differing courses of events that we have undergone.

I cannot chart those differences as if the matter could be expressed like co-ordinates on a map or a reading from a barograph. It is not a question of measurement or experiment, nor is it a systematic inquiry. I have to be alert to whatever indications of these conditions may appear fortuitously in what they do and what they say. The anthropological intuition that it is better to get as far away from the tin cans as possible does have an advantage. Finding Indians who speak Portuguese and who can tell the time makes for comfortable conversations, but to the extent that the initial contrast is blurred by shared experience and shared knowledge so the questions become that much

more obscure. What *is* the difference between us? will be a much more
elusive question. Some kind of contrast that I can take for granted also
helps guard against my creating an illusion of difference where I take
along my baggage of expectations, anthropological and otherwise, as
to what is primitive or archaic, and make sure I satisfy these by
emphasizing what conforms to these and ignoring what does not.

There was a reasonable clarity about that initial contrast, although
even in a small group like the Wayãpí acculturation does not appear
as a homogeneous characteristic of the group. Some of them had been
taken down to the frontier towns and had become familiar with that
way of life. Many others had never been outside the forest. My
expectation that it would be more interesting to find people with
minimal experience of the Brazilian frontier was borne out in that
there was a difference between my conversations with those who
were familiar with the towns and those who were not. For example,
with the first, people talked of their impressions, what they had seen,
what had happened to them, what was 'good' and what was 'bad'
about life down there. But that went along with an absence of curiosity and speculation, as if they had no more questions to ask. I am
not suggesting that firsthand familiarity with the Brazilian towns
changes people's way of seeing the world so as to make them significantly different from other Wayãpí. Perhaps it did, but I cannot judge
that. What I found was that there was a greater reserve and self-
consciousness amongst these people when it came to talking about
themselves. They could share a familiarity with me by telling me their
stories of what happened to them there, but they were not so willing
to comment on what was going on round about us. So often it was the
lack of a shared familiarity, shown through their questions and speculations about the outside, which gave me glimpses of a different
imagination.

The following anecdotes are examples of hints I start from. The
point is not that they reflect naïvety, or ignorance, but that they
indicate significant contrasts between my knowledge and theirs:

Returning to the Nipukú after a trip to the post, I heard that in my
absence a young man called Tora had died in mysterious circumstances. He had gone hunting alone and had not returned. After
two days of searching for him they found his body, but no one
could suggest how he had died. The day after my return it was
announced that a number of people were going to visit the place
where he had been found and buried. It was made clear that it
was very important that I come too, and Waiwai twice checked
up before we left that I was taking my notebook and pen. We
arrived at the spot where the grave had been made, with a small
shelter above it. Some tobacco and food had been hung from the
roof, while some of his other belongings had been buried with
him. From the grave we went down a steep slope to where the

body had been discovered.

I began questioning and taking notes. He had been found naked, with his loin-cloth tied loosely round his neck and his cotton string belt tied round his wrist. He lay on his back with a hole in the crook of one arm, a hole in the back of his leg, and a hole in his stomach. His bow and arrow were propped against a tree and his knife was stuck into the ground near his body. There were no signs of Brazilians in the area, no signs of snakebite, and no signs of jaguars or any other large animal. I can find no explanation for his death.

My companions often conversed in a curious way. A man some way away from me would ask questions of someone standing just beside me who would relate the question to me, even though I had heard the initial question perfectly well. I would reply to the man at my side, and my answer would be passed on to the questioner. Waiwai began questioning in this way: 'Has he written it all?' 'Have you written it all?' 'Yes' . . . and so on. 'Has he finished writing?' 'Have you finished writing?' 'Yes.' 'So now he knows.' 'So now you know.' Immediately I realized I was going to let them down. I could not provide an explanation of Tora's death and I had to say so. During the following few days, Waiwai repeatedly queried if my writing had not allowed me to solve the mystery.

Writing, / èkòsiwarë /, is seen to create knowledge as well as to record it. The act of writing is diagnostic as well as mnemonic. The word / èkòsiwarë / also describes any design such as urucú and genipapo designs on the body, designs etched into pottery, and the designs on the anaconda and the jaguar. And according to the myths it was the anaconda who taught the Wayãpí / èkòsiwarë / as well as all sorts of other things. Designs and patterns are not just embellishments, but are part of what constitutes knowledge.

Early on in my stay, Waiwai asked what kind of houses Brazilians lived in. I tried to explain as best I could what brick houses were, using the words 'earth' and 'mud' to get the idea across. 'Yes, yes, I know', he said. 'Long ago in the time of the grandfather-people the Wayãpí knew about mud houses. Ask Sirò. He knows.' I wondered at that time if Waiwai might not be referring to some kind of missionary contact where, perhaps, the Wayãpí might have been regimented into neat rows of adobe huts. But that was quite wrong. Many months later I found out what Sirò knew. It was the familiar myth about the great fire and the great flood which involved a mud house.

This mild euhemerism, on both my part and theirs, hints at how short their historical memories are. When I try to reflect on what the notion of 'grandfather-people time' must look like, I have to remember that whereas my sense of historical time is organized fairly precisely back to Homer and in a vaguer way back through geological ages, my notion of last century is mythy time to them. The great fire and the great flood are not so very far away.

A compendium of differences like these would be interesting enough. Each example prompts further reflection on *our* notions of writing and knowledge, or of the scales of history and time. But these contrasts are genial surprises. They are not areas of profound perplexity. The next example, though, is:

> Towards the end of my stay, relaxed into all kinds of familiarities with them, I was sitting at the post using a typewriter. Looking on was a youngster called Kumari who had been living on the post for some time as an employee. I had always considered him one of the most genial people I had met. He was confident, cheeky, and witty. He was familiar with the ways of the Brazilians on the post and could handle the outboard motor, the generator, and so on. I had no sense at all with him that I was in the presence of a representative of an alien culture. He had not seen a typewriter before, and was fascinated when I set to work. Speaking Portuguese he asked: 'What makes it work? *Tem gente ahi dentro*? [Are there people inside it?].' That left me speechless, seized by a stupid confusion where I felt that my impressions of him had been completely mistaken.

Time and again it was causal statements that brought the sense of being among the alien corn.

At the Sabão, 1974 (the child pointing died a month later, see page 48)

Resting in the afternoon

Kuyuri and Ato

Matam and Piko'i

Karimo and Sirò

Werena at the Sabão, 1974

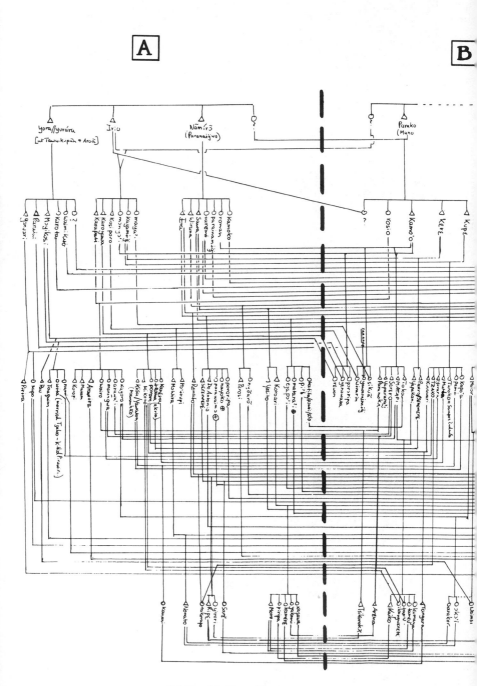

Relationship Term Chart

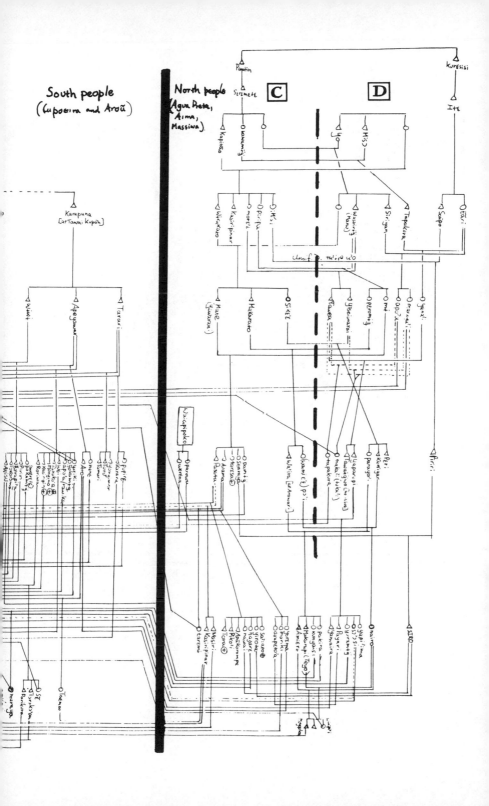

D'Anville's Map

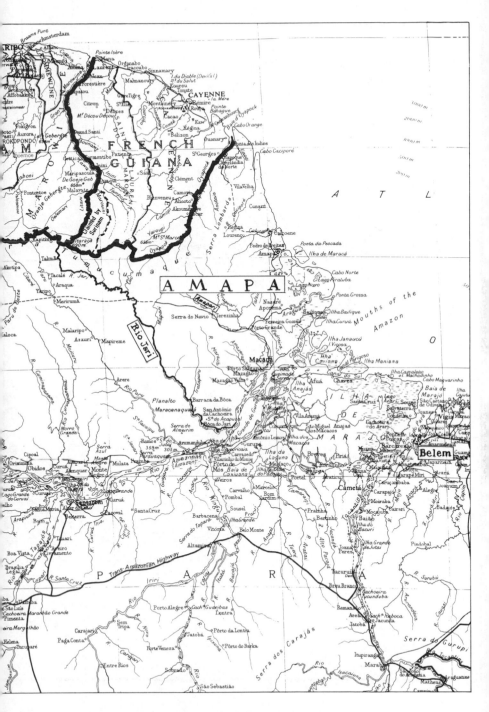

The Lower Amazon: Belém and Amapá

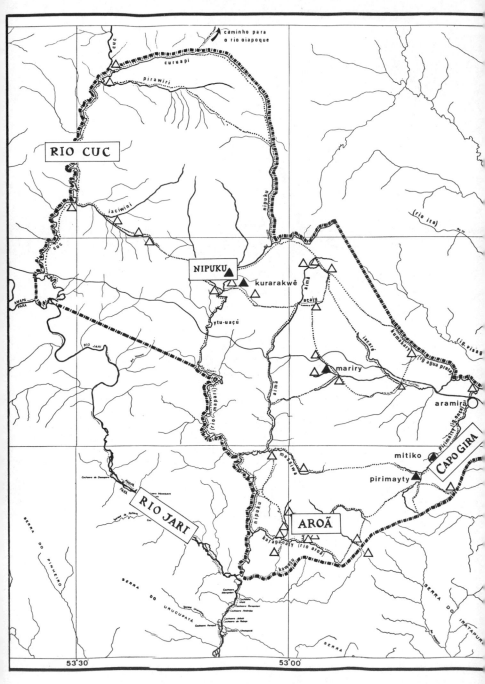

The Wayãpí Reserve *(courtesy Dominique Gallois)*

CAUSE:
animating nature

Spirits are simply personified causes.
E. B. Tylor 1903:108

I

Causal statements reveal the most vivid confrontations between different ways of thinking. Time and again they are a touchstone where one's charity and openness towards other people's views are tested and challenged. Looking back on those occasions when Wayãpí people managed to jolt me out of a sense of familiarity with them and confront me with their strangeness, I find that these were always related in some way or another to causal observations, that is, to statements in 'the homespun language of "making something happen"' (Black 1958:20).

My stay with the Wayãpí leaves me convinced that there is no profound difference between us and them; in knowledge and practical acquaintance, yes, but not in moral responses and emotional responses. Yet there is a peevish residue of assertions, descriptions, explanations, and performances that disturbs this placid conclusion. These make up the loose bundle I have called causal statements and which are illustrated below. While they obviously reveal a discrepancy between my way of seeing the world and that of the Wayãpí, does the difference have any significance, or it is inconsequential when compared with the essential characteristics all human beings share? The discrepancy turns out to be considerably more puzzling than, for example, locating and explaining differences between moral evaluations: what counts as good and bad, what counts as worthwhile and reprehensible. But before presenting the examples I want first to look at the notion of cause.

II

I want to contrast my approach with two others which I shall illustrate by turning them into commonplace questions. The first might appear as the exasperating query: 'Do the Wayãpí have a word for "cause"?' The question is squint, rather like the more familiar one that non-specialists ask anthropologists: 'Do your people have a religion?' To dispose of it properly, consider the following parallel example.

Edmund Leach begins an essay on 'time' by pointing out that it is 'oddly difficult to translate' this word even into French:

> Outside of Europe this sort of ambiguity is even more marked. For example, the language of the Kachin people of North Burma seems to contain no single word which corresponds at all closely to English *time*; instead there are numerous partial equivalents.
>
> (1966:124)

Eight examples follow, 'and that certainly does not exhaust the list'. It is an awkward approach. The word 'time' is presented as something whole or complete, of which Kachin words are 'partial equivalents', but the English word not only refers to obscure philosophical questions, it also appears in a large number of different contextual uses. Hence there is nothing either ambiguous or odd in finding only 'partial equivalents' in other languages. Indeed it would be astonishing if we did find simple equivalents of the English word, and it does not seem particularly useful to go looking for them. Nor is 'time' oddly difficult to translate. Leach gives examples of numerous possibilities in French and Kachin. The only oddity, as Leach later considers, is how such a collection of ambiguities has become bundled up in the one English word. The introductory query is taken no further and the article goes on to other things. But the 'do they have a word for it?' question has a widespread appeal and it is instructive to note its appearance in this prominent essay.

At the back of that approach is a presupposition essential to that view of language and culture called 'Whorfianism', where mental life, world views, or culture are seen to be in some way determined by or dependent on language. (One of B. L. Whorf's most intriguing essays, 1956:57, opens by noting the lack of a word for 'time' in Hopi.) Hence finding lexical variations or a lack of lexical fit between languages is enough to encourage the conclusion that a different conception of the world has been discovered. Max Black's aside on the question is caution enough at this stage: 'The temptation, which I also feel, to jump to picturesque conclusions about "different forms of life" should be resisted' (1969:32–3).

The lesson is simple. When I am asked, 'Do the Wayãpí have a word for "time"?', I have to convince the questioner that the query does not make sense as it stands. It looks like a request for a translation from English to Wayãpí, but it really isn't, since it does not make clear what I am being asked to translate: 'What, then, is time? I know well enough what it is, provided that nobody asks me; but if I am asked what it is and try to explain, I am baffled' (St Augustine 1961:Book XI, 14). A proper request for a translation would be something like: 'How do you say "a long time", "the present time", "it's time to go" in Wayãpí?' Searching for lexical equivalents with questions of the form 'Do they have a word for X?' are really disguised questions about what X means in the questioner's language. Hence when I approach the question of cause, looking for a native equivalent of the term is an unnecessary diversion. I need only recognize that 'there are surely . . . various means of expressing a causal inference or connexion' (Needham 1976:87 note 11), and having recognized that, the question to ask is how adequate are our translations between that language and our own when we are dealing with such expressions.

The second approach is a more sophisticated version of the first. It asks a more interesting question but is open to the same kind of objection. The question could be put: 'Do the Wayãpí have a different conception of causality from ours?' Again I follow a particular example. In Rodney Needham's essay 'Skulls and Causality', he suggests that the institution of headhunting in Borneo had been misinterpreted by the older ethnographers because they were led astray by a notion of cause embedded in the scientific idiom of their day. He locates the misunderstanding as follows: 'But the reality of the issue is that underneath the mutual bafflement there is a confrontation between two quite different conceptions of causality' (1976:84). The Kenyah headhunters of Borneo have one conception of causality and we have another. Their way of thinking has been misrepresented because categories in their thought and in ours are assumed to be equivalent when there is no evidence that they do in fact fit.

That restates the argument in the simplest possible way, but reflecting on the approach it is difficult to see the question being asked in the first place. The essay can be read in three different ways:

(a) The concept of cause (to us) is not problematic. We know what causal explanations entail. Corresponding Kenyah accounts which we want to carry over in translation as 'causal explanations' do not fit with our notions of what causal explanations should be.

Hence: the Kenyah have a different conception of causality. 'Our categories' and 'their categories' do not fit.

(b) The concept of cause (to us) is not problematic. We know what causal explanations entail. Remembering the epigraph from Kant which introduces Needham's essay ('The concept of cause . . . signifies something different from "that which happens", and is not therefore contained in this latter representation'), we find, in Kenyah, not causal explanations, but statements of the 'that which happens' variety.

Hence: Kenyah accounts of headhunting are not causal explanations at all. 'Our categories' and 'their categories' do fit, but our previous identifications were mistaken.

(c) The concept of cause (as we use it) is problematic. In examining the question of Kenyah headhunting we are really writing footnotes to a debate in western philosophy that puzzles about the notion of cause (whether ours or anyone else's).

Hence: the result of a confrontation between their categories and ours is that ours are undermined and require revision or reformulation.

This is a paradigm of the hidden ambiguities in all anthropological inquiries that set out to compare 'alien categories of thought' with our own. The initial question is ambiguous enough to include all three possible answers, but each indicates quite different results. The first leaves us at a loss: we have failed to understand them. The second indicates a successful attempt at understanding where their categories have been adequately translated into ours. The third shifts the matter to another level where the question is not so much to understand them, but to use pecularities of their way of thinking as a means to throw light on our own. And it is frequently the third answer, the self-reflective impulse, which anthropologists appeal to when they are asked to justify their inquiry. Needham, in a different essay, puts the point as follows:

> The chief effect, namely, is to turn the attention of the comparativist back from the comprehension of alien categories and to direct it into a more critical scrutiny of his own. It is not possible to study, for example, the concept of cause . . . in another culture, without at the same time holding in full view the range of connotations that the word has acquired in western philosophical discourse.   (1972:184)

Notice that it is still suggested here that 'another culture' will have its 'notion of cause', its 'alien category', which will be distinct from that of 'western philosophical discourse'.

If we accept the third way and take the question not as 'Do the Wayãpí have a different conception of cause from ours?' but instead as 'What is the conception of cause in the first place?', there might be a temptation to side-step any further inquiry by saying 'And at this point the philosopher takes over from the anthropologist', as Evans-Pritchard handed over further queries about Neur religion to the theologian (1956:322). But there are two good reasons for not doing so. The first is that if it were the case that western philosophical discourse could tell us what causal statements are, we would find ourselves on a carousel of questions where, having arrived at question three (What is the notion of cause to us?) and having resolved that, we would find ourselves back at question one (Do they have a different conception of cause?). The second is that western philosophical discourse is not very adept at explaining our notion of cause. An entry under 'causation' in a modern dictionary of philosophy considers the shortcomings of contributions by Hume, J. S. Mill, and Russell, and concludes: 'Modern analyses regard it as explicable through the subjunctive conditional "If e_1 had not occurred, e_2 would not have occurred", but little is clear about what makes such a remark true' (Flew et al. 1979:54). This is not very helpful.

As with the search for lexical equivalents, here too there is something wrong with the initial question. Comparing alien categories
with our own seems a sensible sort of inquiry only because we think
of a number of vague and sometimes baffling abstract notions of ours
as having some kind of substantial definition. Even if we cannot at
any particular point give a wholly adequate definition, we nevertheless feel that there is one somewhere. Hence we describe these
notions of ours as categories, concepts, or classes, which will allow
comparison with alien categories, concepts, and classes. But all this
depends on a difficult step described by Willard Quine as 'the hypostasis of abstract entities'. He is discussing a traditional distinction
between general terms, such as 'square', and abstract singular terms,
such as 'squareness', and he comments:

> Use of the general term does not of itself commit us to the
> admission of a corresponding abstract entity into our ontology;
> on the other hand the use of an abstract singular term . . . flatly
> commits us to an abstract entity named by the term. There is
> every reason to rejoice that the general terms are with us, what-
> ever the cause. Clearly language would be impossible without
> them and thought would come to very little. On the admission of
> abstract entities, however, as named by abstract singular terms,
> there is room for divergent value judgments.
> (Quine 1963: 76 and 77)

Seeing 'our notion of cause' like one of Quine's 'abstract singular
terms' makes the difficulty with the initial question more obvious. By
putting the question in that way we give the notion of cause some
kind of ontological specificity. It exists, like an article in our conceptual lumber-room which we can dust off and compare with the exotic
souvenir we have returned with from across the seas.

Pointing this out does not necessarily repudiate the abstract term,
but it makes us more aware of what we are doing when we use it.
Quine's conclusion in the article referred to is not quite the point
I want to make but it suggests a way of getting there. His query is
that since these abstract entities are unendingly created by our
language, and since they are therefore part of our conceptual scheme,
it becomes difficult to see how we can check that conceptual scheme
of ours against reality, given that we cannot talk about the world
without imposing our conceptual scheme on it. This is a
well-known theme in anthropology, but Quine's conclusion is particularly well put. Given this state of affairs, he says, we need not
jump to the gloomy conclusion that we are stuck with the conceptual
scheme that we grew up in. Like the mariner rebuilding his ship at
sea:

> We can improve our conceptual scheme, our philosophy, bit by
> bit while continuing to depend on it for support; but we cannot
> detach ourselves from it and compare it objectively with an

unconceptualized reality. Hence it is meaningless, I suggest, to inquire into the absolute correctness of a conceptual scheme as a mirror of reality.   (1963:79)
This can be turned into a lesson for ethnographic comparisons. Just as we cannot detach ourselves from our conceptual scheme and check it out objectively against unconceptualized reality, so it is equally unhelpful to suggest that we can objectively check out our conceptual scheme *against another*, comparing similarities and differences and pointing out where adjustments would have to be made in order that they be brought into agreement. I am sure that in many contexts it is a useful and convenient linguistic device to describe our conceptual scheme as a collection of categories and concepts, such that individual categories and concepts can be abstracted, examined, and discussed. But it does not make much sense when this image is hypostatized into a set of conceptual items which can be abstracted and compared with a similar set of items taken from another society. We can talk about a notion of causality because the conventions of our language allow us to do so. But it does not make much sense to ask if the Wayãpí have a different notion of causality since there are no conditions by which we could recognize another, foreign, abstract entity as a *bona fide* instance of 'the notion of causality' and still hold that it was a *different* one from our own.

Just as the question 'Do they have a word for cause?' looks like a request for a specific translation but is not, so the question 'Do they have a different conception of causality?' seems to ask about understanding a different way of life, but does not. Here too the priority of the question is not to understand the Wayãpí but to use any evidence that can be found to help further the questioner's interest in the concept of causality. In this matter the Wayãpí are a fortuitous and replaceable presence, like a lover to Lothario or like a comedian's stooge. Do those who ask these questions really want to get down to learning the language and to participating in these people's lives? If not, what *is* the point of their questions?

I have loosely identified that area of difficulty in understanding the Wayãpí as a collection of causal statements or statements about how things are made to happen. And the proper question is not 'Do the Wayãpí have a different conception of causality from our own?' but simply 'What is it about these statements that makes them seem odd to us?' Why is my sense of familiarity with them so unnerved when Kumari asks if it is little people inside the typewriter which make it work?

III

The following examples begin with the most prosaic and move towards the most difficult, namely, Wayãpí explanations of death. While looking for an outline of distinguishable kinds of statement I have tried to keep the distinctions simple, and I would also suggest that they be used as landmarks, not as boundaries.

The first example is the same as that pleasant trick with beaker and straw which philosophy teachers sometimes use to make a point about illusion and reality:

(1). Shooting fish with a bow and arrow requires considerable skill since you must learn how to aim lower to hit the fish you are looking at. When possible you get as close as you can to the fish without disturbing it and carefully place the arrow point in the water to get the correct line; it is easier to aim and shoot with the arrow partially submerged. Kasiripinar explains why an arrow or stick seems to bend (or rather *does* bend) when it is stuck into water: 'Bamboo and wood are not hard – they float on water. When you put a stick or an arrow into water, the water pushes it up.'

This is a quaint, ingenious explanation but it indicates nothing significant about different perceptions, different capacities, different ways of seeing the world, or different assumptions about how the world works. Most people educated in our schools would agree that the arrow only *seems* to bend. Some would be able to take the explanation further and say something about refraction. I believe the phenomenon occurs because of the different refractive indices of the two media, air and water, but I cannot be much more precise because I'm not sure what a refractive index is.

How far these details can be taken is not important. What has to be resolved is the disagreement as to whether the arrow bends or whether it does not. I have access to both explanations, and I hold that the explanation that says that the arrow does not bend is the better. Kasiripinar has access to only one, yet I am fairly sure that with the help of the beaker and the straw I could convince him that my explanation was better, just as I was convinced in the school laboratory. The disagreement reveals a disparity between his knowledge and my knowledge, one that I can remove by *showing* him the better explanation. It is also worth noting that even if we did not agree on whether the arrow bends or only seems to bend, the decision would not affect our skill in catching fish. Armed with the better explanation I always missed. Kasiripinar was an expert shot.

Changes in the weather are often a source of causal speculation:

(2). The sky becomes suddenly overcast. A number of explanations are offered in an offhand way. 'Perhaps *coatas* [spider monkeys] are copulating over there', 'a jaguar has perhaps killed a *caititu* [collared peccary] and is eating it', and so on.

The most common source of speculation of this kind was thunderclaps. 'If there is thunder and lightning in a certain direction there are /tayau/ [*queixadas*, white-lipped peccaries] there. Grandfather-people said ''go that way tomorrow and you'll find *tayau''*. They would go that way and they would find them.' A peal of thunder may also mean that someone absent from the village is returning. Towards the end of my stay, when the road construction teams had entered the Wayãpí area, the Brazilians were then held responsible for every thunderclap and every shower of rain. It so happens that most storms and changes in the weather come in from the east, the same direction the road was coming from.

Like the first example, these appear to be statements about natural philosophy, only this time instead of explaining regularities they speculate about the cause of irregularities. Speculation is an important feature in these statements; they are frequently qualified by the word / maịǧwò/ (perhaps). Why does a storm suddenly arrive or thunder suddenly break out? Well, *perhaps* because something else a little unusual has taken place: animals copulating, killing, or being on the move. It is not terribly difficult to see, more or less, what an appropriate explanation would look like: something people have seen, and which is unusual and dramatic, and especially something *noisy*.

Queixadas, those peccaries or 'wild pigs', are appropriate, for instance, because their herds are large; while feeding they move through the forest in a most agitated way; they can be heard and often smelled from a distance; they are the most important source of meat; they are dangerous if disturbed, and you don't come across a herd of them without your pulse quickening. Regarding this example I also suspect that 'what grandfather-people said' is a fragment of a myth. It did not appear in any of the myths I collected, but so many other similar statements did.

These statements are not particularly puzzling, but the type of explanation offered is one I cannot accept: a disturbance in the weather is the result of a disturbance among living things. I will compare statements (1) and (2) later.

The next three examples form a separate group.

(3). House-building is a man's job. When the last of the thatching has been done and the house finished, the women come along with bowls of mud and spatter the inside of the thatch, the roof-beams, and the house-posts. 'Why are they doing that?' 'Because it's good.' 'Why is it good?' 'Because it keeps the scorpions away.' 'But there are scorpions in all the other houses.' 'Yes.' 'So won't they come anyway?' 'Yes, but only LATER.'

The mud throwing is done in high spirits. I doubt that the apotropaic effect of the mud is very much on anyone's mind since the comfort of a new, vermin-free house is so short lived. Throwing the mud is not important as a technique; it is important as 'the appropriate thing to do', just as people here might throw confetti at a wedding or break a bottle of champagne against the hull of a new ship. The example is best seen not in causal terms: 'throwing mud on a new house prevents scorpions and vermin arriving', but in normative terms: 'throwing mud to keep scorpions away is the proper thing to do when a new house has been completed'. It is a benediction.

(4). In making a canoe, the lengthiest part of the work is felling the tree, cutting the log to size, and hollowing it out. This may take weeks to finish. But the most unpredictable part comes right at the end when the hull is placed over a fire and the sides forced out from a sharp U-shape to a more gentle concave shape. During this operation, the log is liable to split and weeks of work can be lost in a few minutes. Before firing they smear alternate stripes of white tapioca and brown mud along the length of the hull. This is to stop it cracking when it goes on the fire.

(5). Men whose wives are pregnant should not go near the spot where the canoe is being hollowed out since this will cause it to crack on firing. An expectant father who wants to go into the forest in that direction will make a detour, keeping well away from the place where the work is being carried out.

The last example (5) is unacceptable to me. The interesting feature of example (4) is that I'm not sure whether the stripes of mud and tapioca have any effect on the wood. Perhaps they may indeed do something to minimize the risk of cracking. According to a Brazilian employed in the post who was, as the Indians recognized, an excellent canoe maker, this was 'no more than a belief of theirs'. Whether it helped or not he was unwilling to say with conviction, but he was doubtful that it did. But even if someone were able to say with authority that these bands of mud and tapioca had no effect whatsoever on the wood, we still would not find the practice strange. We might say that it was a bad, inefficient, unnecessary, or ill-informed technique but we would not say that it was an odd belief as we say of example (5).

Two further preparatory examples:

(6). When preparing a new garden an area of forest is first felled and left several weeks to dry. A few of us go out one day to set fire to the tangled clearing. Having started a number of fires around the edge we gather to watch it take, and while standing there, my companions break into a chorus of long drawn-out undulating whistles. It is an eerie sound since the pitches criss-cross slowly and produce overtones. The purpose of this is to make the wind come so that the fires will be fanned and the burning will go well. (The fiercer the fire the less clearing that has to be done afterwards.) I willingly join in whistling up the wind.

(7). We set off on a fishing expedition and require bait. We make our way to a shallow stagnant creek where we are likely to find / warapą / (a fish about six inches long, like a miniature *trahirão*). (The old Wayãpí word for this fish was / yoyo /. From this and

from von Ihering's description, 1968, I would guess that it is the
Brazilian *jeju*.) We approach the creek stealthily but find nothing
there. My companions break into the same kind of whistling we
used to whistle for the wind. Again I cheerfully join in. To my
astonishment a small shoal of half a dozen *warapá* come whizzing
round the corner making straight for us, obviously attracted by
the sound. We quickly got the bait we needed.

Although previously sceptical, I now know that it is possible to
whistle up fish. But with all possible anthropological charity on my
part, the Wayãpí will never convince me that they can whistle up the
wind. A point to note is that in coming across a disagreement like this,
I am not at all inclined to try to convince them of my scepticism or to
test their credulity. It is a charming and pleasant procedure standing
there whistling and watching the gusts of breeze bring the flames on.
But more to the point, it would be awkward to try to *show* them
reasons for my scepticism. Felled jungle never burns out completely.
Even if the first burning has gone well, the area always has to be
cleared up and burnt a second time leaving as far as possible only the
large trunks. Whatever happened one could always complain that the
first burning might have gone better. Trying to convince the Wayãpí
of their error by a little practical science would get one nowhere.

IV

I am going to group these examples together following the distinctions set out by R. G. Collingwood in his essay 'On the so-called
idea of causation' (1938). I have been unable to find any commentary
on this essay which seriously qualifies its conclusions, nor have
I found any alternative approach as illuminating as this one.
(For example, it seems to me that Stephen Toulmin, 1953, and Max
Black, 1958, take the same line as Collingwood.) I also draw a number
of supplementary observations from Hart and Honoré (1985: chapter
2).

Collingwood's essay clarifies a confused area of our usages by
looking at a range of causal propositions and distinguishing them into
three kinds. If we follow Collingwood's scrupulous distinctions, and
if we are made aware of the ambiguities in our own expressions, we
are better able to see the discrepancies between our statements and
Wayãpí statements. We are using distinctions, however ambigu-
ously, that they are not using. But Collingwood's argument cannot
solve the problem. It can only present it more clearly. It cannot say if
or how the discrepancy between our ways and their ways can be
negotiated.

According to Collingwood, causal propositions compound three
meanings of the word 'cause'. In the first and oldest sense of the
word:

  ... that which is caused is the free and deliberate act of a

conscious and responsible agent, and 'causing' him to do it
means affording him a motive for doing it. For 'causing', we may
substitute 'making', 'inducing', 'persuading', 'urging', 'forcing',
'compelling' according to differences in the kind of motive in
question.   (86)

In other words this sense, sense I, refers to interaction between
human beings.

The second sense is this:

In sense II, no less than in sense I, the word cause expresses an
idea relative to human action; but the action in this case is an
action intended to control, not other human beings, but things in
'nature', or 'physical' things. In this sense, the 'cause' of an event
in nature is the handle, so to speak, by which we can manipulate
it. If we want to produce or to prevent such a thing, and cannot
produce or prevent it immediately . . . we set about looking for its
'cause'.   (89)

The search for causes in sense II is 'natural science' in that sense
of the phrase in which natural science is what Aristotle calls a
'practical science', valued not for its truth pure and simple but for
its utility, for the 'power over nature' which it gives us . . .(90)

The argument then goes on to show that the cause-effect terminology
in sense II really indicates a means-end relation. And why is a means-
end relation expressed in a cause-effect terminology?

The answer, I think, is not doubtful. The cause-effect terminology conveys an idea not only of one thing's leading to another,
but of one thing's forcing another to happen or exist; an idea of
power or compulsion or constraint.   (95)

And that is carried over from our social life, from our relations with
other people, and applied to 'physical things'. We 'cause' inorganic
nature to act just as we 'cause' other human beings to act, hence the
word implies:

(1) That there are certain ways in which natural things behave if
left to themselves;

(2) That man, being more powerful than they, is able to thwart
their inclination to behave in these ways, and by the exercise of
his superior magic to make them behave, not as they like, but as
he likes.

And if anybody is so truthful as to admit that, in our exper-
imental science, we do constantly use language which taken
literally implies all this, but argues that it is 'mere metaphor' and
never meant to be taken literally, I reply: then express yourself
literally; and you will find that all this language about causation
disappears, and that you are left with a vocabulary in which all
that is said is that we find certain means useful to certain ends.
(96)

Sense II, means-ends vocabulary, is the vocabulary of 'practical science', and again the notion of cause has to be conceived in relation to human activities.

Sense III is concerned with the descriptions in what he calls 'theoretical science' as opposed to practical science. Briefly, causal propositions in sense III are 'descriptions of natural events in anthropomorphic terms' (103) and following Bertrand Russell's 1912 paper on the subject, Collingwood agrees that propositions about causes have to be replaced by propositions about laws. Max Black puts the same point as follows:

> A cause is something that we can or might be able to control. But we invoke causes also when we are interested in explaining something rather than controlling it. And as our accepted patterns of explanation become more complex, our notion of a cause becomes correspondingly more elusive, until it threatens to vanish altogether into the abstract conception of a law, a parameter, a boundary condition, or some combination of all of these. As scientific modes of investigation develop, the language of cause tends to its own supersession.   (Black 1958:29)

Cause sense I, then, is interaction between human beings;

> inducing, compelling.

Cause sense II is practical science, human beings interfering with the world;

> means which achieve ends.

Cause sense III is theoretical science, explanations about the nature of the world;

> laws and conditions.

Cause III: regularities. To begin with sense III, Collingwood and Russell suggest that when we are explaining regularities in the world, 'cause' disappears and is substituted by 'law'. Toulmin also notes that in engineering and medical journals, i.e., where sciences are applied to practical purposes, we do find the word 'cause', but the term hardly ever appears in work on the physical sciences (1953:119). In his helpful image, theoretical science constructs maps while practical science constructs itineraries (121, 123). Similarly Waissman puts it that if we ask questions about the motions of the stars we cannot say that one configuration 'causes' the next. In this kind of explanation the vocabulary of cause disappears and is substituted by concepts of *functional dependence*. After Bacon first applied the Latin *lex* to material phenomena, 'laws of nature' were conceived of as commands of God which were 'obeyed', and only gradually did notions of 'principles', 'ratios', and 'proportions' emancipate the inquiry into an impersonal determinism (Waissman 1968:209 and 220).

The point is that these statements may look like causal explanations or be phrased in causal language, but they are more precisely general descriptions of how things happen. I suggest that when we compare unfamiliar statements of this kind, descriptions of natural events which can be rephrased in terms of conditions, as accounts of 'the way things usually occur', we will not find there any insurmountable obstacle between our statements and the alien ones. Their propositions (and ours for that matter) may be wrong, ill-informed, incomplete, or in some way inadequate when compared with alternatives. But the competing explanations are *compatible*, taking that word with its older connotations of sympathy and sharing. We understand how that view can be held even if it counters our own. We know what it is like to see the world in that way. So to return to example (1), the arrow in the water, we have no difficulty understanding the explanation about the arrow bending when it is stuck into the river.

Why is the river water warmer (or why does the river water appear to be warmer) in the early morning than at other times of the day? Because at night the sun goes back under the earth and warms the water there. It comes out warmer.

The causal aspect of this statement can be easily translated into a description of natural events, of conditions, of the normal state of affairs, and as such, these statements can take their place alongside those other descriptions of the world which are not causal at all, but which simply state what is the case.

The sky is blue because it is stone – in the same way that blue hills when seen from a distance turn out to be stone. [I expect this refers to those granite outcrops in the Serra do Tumucumaque]. There is stone away beneath us, and stone away above us.

Do you know why you don't see butterflies during the rainy season? Because butterflies and some species of flies spend the wet season in the sky and only come down during the dry season.

And so on. The images in this natural philosophy may be refreshingly quaint, but there is nothing remarkably odd about them. There are dozens of similar notions round us in our everyday lives here (see, e.g., Keith Thomas's history of changing attitudes to the natural world, 1984).

Sometimes, to grasp their explanations, we have to appreciate their distinctions:

Everyone who stayed in the forest for any length of time found themselves with tiny black spots all over their hair. When I first discovered them I thought I had been infested with lice eggs, but they seem to be some kind of fungus. The Wayãpí word is / èapɨtą 'ɨğ /. The black spots, I think, are the result of having one's hair constantly wet. They say: 'If you get your hair wet in the rain and don't wash your hair in the river you'll get them.' But, I protest, people have them throughout the dry season too, and the reason for that is that everyone bathes so often in the river, keeping their hair constantly wet. No, I'm told firmly, it's rain / amạn / and not [river] water / ɨg̃ / which brings the black spots. It's a distinction I have to learn.

A clean pan which I had left on a tree trunk had filled with rainwater, some of which I took to use while giving out medicine. Immediately people protested. Rain was no good. It was quickly thrown out and someone ran to the river for 'water'.

A man covered a pot of prepared *açaí* (a forest fruit), already mixed with water, to protect it from drips of rain that were coming through his leaky roof: 'If you drink rain you get a pain in your belly.'

Obviously, then, getting one's hair wet in the rain and getting it wet while bathing in the river are two quite different matters. Finally, none of these collisions with cosmological speculations were as disconcerting as one that took place not in the forest but at the moment when I stepped out of it:

Serra do Navio, the manganese mine, is where you suddenly step from the forest into the outposts of urbanization. At the end of my first spell in the woods I found the transition disconcerting. I was taken down to the Serra by the FUNAI *motorista*. We turned the last bend in the river and saw houses, a single moving car, and various other commonplace sights which at that moment I found unusually agitating. We moored at the landing stage and walked up to greet the solitary guard, waiting for us in immaculately ironed khaki, shining black boots, leggings, peaked cap, dark glasses, and revolver – an intimidating spectacle since police in Brazil sometimes flex their authority in unpredictable ways. Nevertheless, although cautious in front of this apparition, I felt I had returned to familiar comforts. It was particularly relaxing to be able to use language easily and to understand everything that was said. Portuguese was like my native tongue after my struggles with Wayãpí. While waiting, the FUNAI *motorista* and the guard talked together. I paid no attention until I heard: 'Ask him. He'll know.' The conversation went on:

Motorista: 'Doctor,' [anyone vaguely connected with the professions may be addressed as Doctor in rural Brazil] 'have you, in all your studies, ever found mention of where the world finishes?'

Guard: 'Is it true that it doesn't finish, that it's round like a ball?'

Me: 'Yes, if you went that way for long enough you'd come back this way.'

The guard grinned and nodded and looked up to the sky where there was a daytime moon shining: 'Yes, it's difficult to understand, isn't it. And when these Americans go to the moon they land on it like this [the underside] don't they? And they don't fall off.'

What kind of somersaulting was being played in front of me? The intimidating dark glasses had come off to reveal a kindly, warm-

hearted *ingénu*, while at the same time the familiarity of shared
knowledge and experience had evaporated.
If I want to gather funny notions about Aristotle's ten predicaments
(his 'categories': time, space, substance, quantity, and so on), why do
I have to go to the tropical forest when I can find them at my own back
door? We all share the appearances of what we refer to as our civilization, making it easily discriminable from the world of the Wayãpí;
but the cosmological notions we carry around privately can, when
told, destroy that sense of homogeneity. No doubt my description of
the solar system would sound oddly ignorant to someone who had
studied astronomy. So many people have next to no sense of orien-
tation or direction, being unable to point to where the sun rises. I
conclude from these examples that other people's descriptions, propositions, explanations, and laws of this kind are interesting, but not
perplexing. We are familiar with disagreements of this kind and they
do not baffle us.

Cause III: irregularities. But this is not the end of cause in sense III. The
writers mentioned give a convincing account of scientific inquiry into
regularities and successfully identify the nature of these statements.
But the notion of cause creeps back when considering *irregularities*.
We understand the mechanics of the stars and their nightly swing
above us, but when a distant star explodes we ask 'what was the cause
of that?' This leads Hart and Honoré to make a distinction between
causes and *conditions*, 'between what is abnormal and what is normal
in relation to any given thing or subject-matter' (1985:33). Mere conditions are always present. Causes are interesting because they 'make
a difference'. Stars do not usually explode. Why did that one explode
just now? It might be possible to get round Hart and Honoré's
example by suggesting that causes can be reduced to conditions; for
example, that star exploded just now because there were certain
conditions under which all such stars explode. This successfully gets
rid of the notion of cause. But it is quite proper to say that lightning
was the cause of a fire, and it seems difficult to get round that
example. (It was introduced by Hart and Honoré as a corrective to
Collingwood's view that the 'cause' was always that condition among
many others which we could produce or prevent.) Having pointed
that out, there is no need to go further into the controversy. Max Black
explains that:

> Anybody with a logician's desire for clear-cut distinctions may
> well be exasperated by the lack of systematic principle in these
> patterns of analogical and metaphorical extensions of causal
> language . . . Abstract and simplified formulas fail to do justice to
> the actual uses of 'cause' and its cognates.   (1958:28)

And to show how 'peculiar, unsystematic, and erratic' a notion it is
(ibid.:30), consider how the example of the arrow bending in water

can be regarded either as a regularity, an example of conditions (arrows bend when they are put into water), or as an irregularity requiring causal explanation (arrows in the ordinary course of events do not bend like that – what is making the difference?). As soon as the distinctions are made they can be emulsified again. Hence distinctions suggested by these writers are useful only as guide-posts that we will eventually be able to do without.

Accepting Hart and Honoré's distinction, the point of example (2) – the sky becoming overcast, a peal of thunder, an unexpected shower of rain – is that they are sudden events. Something irregular or unusual has happened and a cause is sought. The agency held responsible for these happenings is human or animal. The elements respond to a disturbance among living things.

If you shout and play while you are bathing in the river, rain will come. It's all right to shout and play in the river at the village because you're at home, but when you're travelling and heavy rain can be a danger (making rivers impassable and flooding the path) it is important not to make a noise. In camps, children were frequently scolded for splashing noisily in the water. On one trip we were held up for a few days with rivers in front of us and behind us too full to cross. We were caught like that 'because Brazilian roadworkers were moving up and down the Rio Felício. Everybody knows that when Brazilians push a canoe up rapids they make a lot of noise shouting at each other'.

Thunder might signal the return of someone who has been away for some time, or that visitors are approaching.

Waiwai had been away for some weeks. Sirò said, 'Perhaps Waiwai will return today.' 'Why?' 'Because I heard *macaco prego* monkeys crying yesterday evening.' We had had no visitors for months, but early that afternoon a family from another settlement arrived.

Perhaps the last example was coincidence, or perhaps it shows Sirò's alertness. When monkeys are disturbed they create quite a commotion and this could have signalled the arrival of the family. We don't accept the other causal connections because we don't reason that inanimate forces are going to respond to animal or human behaviour. 'Spirits', said Tylor, 'are simply personified causes' (1903:108). Another way of putting it is that something about which we require an explanation in terms of cause III is given in terms of cause I. It is expressed as an interaction between living things.

To sum up cause III: Disagreements about conditions, about regularities, are not usually puzzling. We do not feel that they proceed from profoundly alien assumptions. When cause III *irregularities* are explained through an animistic idiom in terms of a relation among living things, we do suspect profoundly incompatible assumptions.

Cause II. In sense II, the cause of an event in nature is 'the handle, so to speak, by which we can manipulate it'. There may be many conditions that contribute to an event taking place, but the cause of the event, in this sense, is again that particular one of its conditions that 'makes a difference' (lightning caused the fire, *coatas* copulating caused the thunder), only here, in cause II, that condition is one that a given person is able to produce or prevent. (Notice again how the question wanders. This aspect is contained in the last example where the noise we made caused the rain to come.) We should expect to be able to reformulate causal statements of this kind in a means-end vocabulary 'in which all that is said is that we find certain means useful to certain ends'. Example (4), painting the stripes of tapioca and mud on to the canoe before firing, is straightforward because that is one of the means at the maker's disposal to prevent cracking. Whenever we can carry out a translation of this kind we will have no difficulty with the statement.

Like so many other groups in the tropical forest, Wayāpí people know how to use *timbó* / mèko /, a vine that produces fish poison. When the men come back to the village after a day preparing *timbó* for a poisoning expedition to be carried out the following day, they do not bathe in the river, but use calabashes to throw water over themselves in the manner of those bathing prohibitions that menstruating women and parents of newborn children observe. Asking about this, Kuyuri, who was not taking part, answered: 'It's no good if they bathe in the river – they wouldn't kill any fish tomorrow.' Waiwai, who had also stayed at home, said: 'It's no good if they bathe in the river because the tiny fish and the shrimps will go and tell all the big fish "Don't eat – get out of here – it's dangerous – let's go", and tomorrow there won't be any fish.' Kasiripinar, who had been working the stuff that day, said: 'We all have *timbó* on us and if the smell gets into the water the fish will all go away and there won't be any around tomorrow when we are ready to put the rest of the *timbó* in.'

These are straightforward means-ends explanations. Waiwai's colourful pictures of the process do not change the matter or make it any more opaque. The explanation is about what happens if they inadvertently let *timbó* get into the water. I don't know whether such small amounts as are on the men's hands and bodies would have any premature effect on the catch, but the substance has spectacular effects when it is introduced into the river and I can understand why it is treated with care.

There is a series of prohibitions which it is said men should observe before a *timbó* expedition. The emphasis is on continence, although the list does show a mixture of what would be acceptable and unacceptable to us. A man should not (1) have sex for several days beforehand, (2) get drunk, (3) fart while prepar-

ing the stuff, (4) sniff while preparing it, (5) bathe in the river
having prepared it, (6) kill any game during the previous few
days. If these are not observed the *timbó* will not work. But I am
not sure how firm the prohibitions are, given the casual way the
outing is organized.

Causal statements that can be translated into mean-ends statements, into descriptions of technique, into descriptions of those
conditions that we are instrumental in producing or preventing are
usually straightforward. The worst we tend to say of them is that they
are ill-informed, inadequate, or inefficient. If we come across means-
ends statements that baffle us, we then usually start talking about
'magic'. In other words, while those cause III puzzles led us back to
Tylor and his animism, these cause II puzzles lead us back to Frazer. Is
this the answer to the difficulty about example (5) where a man whose
wife is pregnant can, if he sees the canoe, cause it to crack on firing? A
man in such a condition can provoke failure by being near, or by
looking at the unfinished canoe. Clearly this does not correspond to
psychokinesis where the person involved is said to will inanimate
things to act in a certain way. It is just that the person's state has a
baleful influence on the technical process. And, since the canoe is an
artefact and apparently not an animate object, it seems that this
example cannot be translated, as in cause III, into that of interaction
between living things. Is this just 'magic'?

I will return to this example in section V of this chapter to show how
this particular configuration which appears as 'magic' can indeed be
translated into one that can be seen as 'animism', or rather, as interaction between living things. Although the subject of magic is only
referred to briefly in the examples below, I suggest that it occupies an
ambiguous position between straightforward means-ends statements and cause I statements (inducing, persuading, compelling).

Cause I. Finally, cause in sense I is the 'first and oldest sense of the
word'. In place of 'causing' we can substitute 'making', 'inducing',
'persuading', and so on: 'I did it because *he* said it was a good thing to
do.' In a previous chapter I explained how the Waỹapí appeared to me
to be particularly open to influences of all kinds, as if their will were
peculiarly pliant. So much was done this way or that way, or thought
to be good or bad, 'because the Wayana said so' or 'because Sarapó
said so'. Similarly I found that often when I asked a particular individual directly why he or she did something, I would often get the
answer that someone else had supplied the motive. In asking for a
reason I am given a cause.

Teyo decides one day to take his family on a trip to the post. He
makes it clear that he might be away for many weeks. Why has he
decided to go? Because *his sister*, who lives near the post with her
husband, said 'It's good that you visit'. He has not seen his sister

for over a year, and no one has recently arrived who could have brought instructions.

Of course it may be inappropriate for a person to make intimate motives and inclinations clear. Teyo would be unlikely to say that he felt like seeing what he could cadge off his sister's husband for a while, or that he had his eye on a certain woman over there. But explanations like this appeared again and again, as if attributing the reason for someone's action to the motivating agency of someone else offered the line of at least resistance.

Why did you go off to Pirawiri that time many years ago when you knew there were epidemics there? Because *Sarapó* came and said 'Come on. I'm taking you all to Pirawiri'.

Why did you start making gardens at the Sabão last year if you didn't want to leave the Nipukú? Because . . . (a FUNAI official) came and said 'Off you go and make a garden over there'.

Yanuari explains that it is dangerous for a man to hunt game when he is under 'couvade' or birth precautions because his newly born child might die. For instance, he himself once killed a howler monkey when his own son was still very small, and his son nearly died. But since he knew about the precautions, why did he go out and kill the monkey? Because *his wife* said 'I'm hungry. I want meat'.

I'm sure that Wayãpí people make decisions, pursue their goals and desires, change their minds, make mistakes, rationalize and justify what they do in much the same way as the rest of us. There are usually obvious and acceptable reasons for travelling, visiting, moving home, or making a new garden. But when I challenge them to explain their actions and decisions they deflect reasons and explanations on to other people, as if the explanation sounds better if it can be said that 'she said it should be done' rather than 'I felt like doing it'. Passing the buck is an essential aspect of causal explanations:

All philosophic terms have necessarily begun . . . from a simpler, concrete usage with a human reference point. For a example the concept of a 'cause' *aition*, is clearly a development from the idea of 'the guilty one, he who is to blame', *aitios*.
                                              (Kahn 1974:116)

In the previous chapter I suggested that their passivity or malleability is related to fear of extinction. That accounts for a lot of what they *do*. Here, in accounting for what they *say* I'd suggest that deflecting reasons on to others is the easiest way to find a reason or justification for one's actions. If I found it strange that so many of my questions about motives were answered by blaming someone else, it was also clear that they found it unusual to be asked such questions in the first place. Like the awkwardness and effort I put them to with frequent questions about 'how many?' and 'how long?' (awkward because they have no words for number beyond four), so my persistent

questions about why this or that course of action was taken made
unusual demands on their readiness to explain things. The idiom of
self-justification was not a very practised one, and these deflected
explanations were a convenient way round the difficulty I presented
them with, since it shifted the burden of explanation on to someone
else. But the main point is that however much I was struck by their
tendency to explain their decisions and their actions in terms of their
being motivated, predisposed, incited, or induced by others, there is
nothing mysterious or opaque about this form of reasoning.

To go back to the example of whistling for fish (example 7), is this
cause in sense I or cause in sense II? When a dog is trained to respond
to our commands or when Wayãpí lure spider monkeys and *jacamins*
(trumpeters) towards them by imitating their cry, are we all just
'manipulating nature' (cause II) or are we affording a motive to a
conscious agent so that the agent performs a free and deliberate act?
What is the difference between inadvertently scaring an animal away
by startling it, and luring it into a trap by making sounds that attract
it? These questions do seem pretty forced, but the difficulty is that
Collingwood reserves sense I for action intended to influence other
human beings while cause II is intended to control 'things in
"nature", or "physical" things'. I'd rather take these questions as yet
other examples that blur the distinctions and suggest that it does
make sense to say that we can make, induce, force, or compel an
animal into a deliberate act. Hence, whistling for fish and luring
spider monkeys by imitating their cry are causal in sense I. Nevertheless, these are also means-ends procedures and therefore are also
causal in sense II.

Whistling for the wind is presented in exactly the same terms but
we cannot accept it as a reasonable explanation. There is no causal
connection for us because we do not consider the wind as a living
thing. Again, then, the difference between them and us is not something to do with a different conception of causality, a different logic,
or a different rationality. It is a disagreement about a distinction. We
make a certain distinction between what is living and what is not.
They don't.

v

In trying to get round the area of cause, I have followed the itineraries
suggested by the various writers to whom I have referred. And before
leaving them it is worth mentioning one point. In making their
distinctions these writers imply that our causal language is confused:
that it was originally animistic but that somehow over the years we
have changed our ideas about the world without changing our
language to keep up with our ideas. Our careless, unreflective use of
this idiom makes our thought untidy. If that is so, the conclusion is
inescapable that those Wayãpí statements we object to show a com-

mendable clarity. The idiom of causality reveals, with vivid accuracy, just what they want to say.

The statements we find unacceptable (the sky turning overcast, a thunderclap, a sudden shower of rain, *and* whistling for the wind) would be straightforward were we to agree that the relation referred to is one between living things. Whether or not we have the imaginative ability or the intellectual freedom to understand this vivification, we should appreciate how extensive it is.

Kasiripinar had lost both his infant daughters during one of the epidemics and had been depressed for a long time. We were sitting on a rock in the middle of the river, lazing about, when he said:

Why do we die?
Stone doesn't die.
Earth doesn't die.
Trees do die but only after a long long time.
Why do we die?

Our parlour categories of animal, vegetable, and mineral are supported by the formal divisions of the three kingdoms; hence we are provided with our neat distinctions between animate and inanimate, and between what is a living organism and what is not. Controversy about Protista, a proposed biological kingdom intermediate between Animalia and Plantae, including protozoans, bacteria, algae, and slime moulds, is a mere curiosity to most of us, although Jaques Monod (1977) produces some genuine surprises (starting with crystals) which question our presuppositions about what living matter is. But our disagreement with Wayãpí statements is not a matter of *different* distinctions. Leaving aside artefacts, it seems that there is no distinction at all between 'being' and 'living'. Existence and life are the same thing. (Ontology would be all biological.) Stone and earth, wind and water 'don't die'.

There is a further complication. Water, stone, and every animal and plant has / yạrë /, master, the word one would use for the owner of a pet animal. A man who is observing birth precautions will not go near any of the big trees, the *sumauma* or the *angelim*, because of the baleful influence of / yạrë / which is in them. *Yaneyar* is literally 'our master'. (/ yạnè / is 'we inclusive' as opposed to / òrè / 'we exclusive', a use indicating that the word has become more a proper name than an indication of a relationship. They would not say / òrèyạrë / when talking to an outsider.) Yaneyar appears as the authority figure and demiurge in many of the myths; but with the caution that there are no singular and plural forms to guide us, it is best to keep in mind that depending on the context there can be many Yaneyars. Yaneyar will eventually send the fire that will destroy the world, but apart from that, he/they are not an everyday cause of concern. The most active / yạrë / is / mòyo /, the anaconda, who is / iğ-yarë /, master of water.

The rainbow is / i'ŭ /, the 'soul' of *moyo*. If you point at a rainbow your arm will hurt. It might even break. If you want to indicate a rainbow you have to point with your lips.

The colours in birds are *moyo*'s excrement. *Moyo* appears in a myth about the origin of the Wayana as the person who taught the Wayãpí how to make body designs with genipapo dye. When Montaigne met Brazilian Indians (who must have been Tupian) in Rouen in 1562 he collected a love song, worthy of Anacreon, he said. The refrain went: 'Couleuvre, arreste toy; arreste toy, couleuvre, afin que ma soeur tire sur le patron de ta peinture la façon et l'ouvrage d'un riche cordon que je puisse donner à m'amie; ainsi soit en tout temps ta beauté et ta disposition preferée à tous les autres serpens' (Montaigne 1962:244). I wonder if *couleuvre* was *moyo*, the *sucurijú* or anaconda. No English translator to the present has broken away from Florio's original rendering of it in 1603 as 'adder'. No doubt *serpent* and *couleuvre* were used loosely in Montaigne's time as 'adder' was in Elizabethan England, but to maintain what is now a precise English term for the vague French one is silly, especially since there are no Viperidae in the New World.

/ mòyo i-paye / – 'anaconda is shamanistic'. I once shot one. I am immensely ashamed remembering that – a senseless and unnecessary slaughter. I was the first to see it, in the sand of a shallow creek a few feet below us down a small bank. I had fired a shot just as I was being told not to. It was such a magnificent creature. At one point in its agonized writhing its head came slowly up the bank towards us, its mouth wide open as if in a horrible silent scream. There were six of us in the line going out that day and it was clear that what I had done upset everyone. I tried later to get people to talk about the implications of what I had done, but no one was willing to do so. Nine days later I fainted while bathing alone in the river. They say they found me caught in the branches of a submerged tree. I nearly drowned. Although no one said so, this is just the sort of incident that would be put down to *moyo*, master of water.

Amongst all the chirping and whistling of insects at night, there was one kind of whistle that was said to be *moyo*. When Kasiripinar and I visited Belém we stayed in apartments in the Museu Goeldi which stands in a small, beautiful botanical and zoological park. There were anacondas and boa constrictors in a deep pit at the far end of the zoo. Looking at them did not alarm Kasiripinar at all. What did alarm him was when, on leaving by the side gate in the dark one evening, and stepping out on to a quiet street, we heard the whistling. I thought it came from the mango trees, so common on the pavements of Belém. 'Hear that,' he said, 'that's *moyo*.' What *moyo*? The ones in the pit? 'No, not

THAT *moyo*. OTHER *moyo*. *Moyo* we taught you to hear at nights at Nipukú.' But there's no water here. 'Yes there is.' I had previously explained what gutter holes were for. 'Water goes off down there, doesn't it? Well, that's where the water is and that's where *moyo* is.'

There is a mystery here about identity and difference which is difficult to follow. Shamanistic *moyo* both is and is not the actual creature we see, in the same way that when we are in a shamanistic trance and meet tapirs and jaguars they are 'as ourselves' not 'as animals'. It is as if the personifications made in our children's stories or in Orwell's *Animal Farm* existed out there in the world both as part of the animals that are represented and as separate and different from them. *Moyo* is *both* the creature we see *and* the personified shamanistic presence but these are not 'the same'.

/ ta̱koro-yarë /, master of stone, is described as a frightening being. Other *yarr* are just described vaguely as 'like us', although there are differences in their powers. Every plant and every tree has *yarr*, but the reason why a man observing birth precautions will avoid *sumau-mas* and *angelins* is because these *yarr* are / moa'a̱rowa i-pa̱ye /, vastly shamanistic. (I would expect large boulders and cliffs to be avoided where there are any. There are none in that area, except rocks in the river, and that is dangerous because of *moyo*.) The clue to hold on to when considering causal statements is that *yarr* are thought of as people, with wills, temperaments, and with power to influence events.

Siriyan's wife Sikuá gave birth on 2 October 1975 in a small shelter near the village. On 6 October Siriyan went to see the child. (The umbilical cord had almost dropped off.) That was the first time he had left his house. Also that day he crossed the Nipukú river to go to his garden. Before going he covered himself from head to foot with urucú (red dye). First he tells me that with urucú on, *moyo* won't *see* him as he crosses the river. Later he says that *moyo* doesn't like the *smell*. (This is a common synaesthesia.) *Moyo* dislikes the smell of our bodies and without urucú, *moyo* would come and kill us. (And in other contexts it would be said that it was the infant child which was in danger.) At the fall of the evening there was a high wind and heavy rain. No one in the village is fond of Siriyan. A number of men say that the reason for the disturbance in the weather was that Siriyan crossed the water. *Moyo* saw him and is angry. *Moyo* being / pa̱ye / (shaman-istic) 'sees' or 'knows' that Siriyan has a child and says 'I'm going to kill it'. Siriyan heard that I'd been given these explanations. He denied them vigorously. He visited me twice the following day to explain himself, loudly so that the village could hear. First he said that the rain and wind were brought by the thunder and there was thunder because his brother Taweya was on the path return-ing home after a long absence. The second visit was to explain that a lot of people were playing noisily in the water yesterday, therefore *moyo* got angry and brought rain. On 8 October Siriyan again crossed to his garden. Late that afternoon there was a very gusty shower which blew everything around wildly. One of the men came, quietly this time, to explain smugly, 'You see, I told you so. I was correct.'

Causal explanations are eminently satisfactory when there is someone to blame. The example here, putting on urucú to cross the river, may first appear to be Collingwood's cause II, a means-ends matter where human beings interfere with the world, finding out what they can produce or prevent. But the personification of *yarr* is the crucial intervention, turning the matter into an interpersonal relationship. We make *yarr* angry and then something goes wrong. I'd risk the guess that this is the answer to the example left unresolved: the harmful influence a man, whose wife was about to have a baby, could have on the successful burning of the canoe. Although I did not follow it up, it is the sort of example which, if pursued, results in attributing the harmful agency to *yarr*. The 'magical' appearance is due to the preliminary means-ends character of the explanation. It has not reached its causal terminus by blaming a personified agency.

There are numerous examples of procedures that are simply 'magical' in the sense of means-ends procedures that do not go through such an agency.

The FUNAI *sertanista* (senior post official) visited the Nipukú. While he was there, there was a spree and he joined in the dancing. He was a well-built man and the exertion made him sweat profusely. While he was resting at one point, various women approached him, rubbed their hands on his body, then rubbed the babies they were carrying or the children that were near them 'so that the children would be strong'. Piripa, a young, unmarried woman, in good spirits because of the beer, rubbed her breasts vigorously against him saying that she would thereafter be able to carry a heavy load of manioc without falling and without getting tired.

Yanuari came to my house one day with a herb which he rubbed on my shotgun chanting the names of all the animals which were urged 'not to fear the gun' (hence I would kill a lot of game).

An even more useful contrast is the following example where I expected *yarr* to be blamed eventually, but such an explanation did not appear. It is the matter of / pane /. The word is known throughout Brazil as *panema*, usually translated as 'bad luck'. Charles Wagley shows how vividly this notion appears amongst Brazilians in a small Amazonian town (1976:78ff). I understand that Ipanema (the name of an expensive district in Rio de Janeiro, now known worldwide since Frank Sinatra popularized a samba tune called 'The girl from Ipanema') comes from Tupi *y*, water, and *panema*. / pane / is specifically bad luck at hunting.

Having skinned and gutted game, the refuse must never be thrown in the river. This will certainly result in / pane /. In the village, once you have eaten meat you don't discard the bones in case dogs eat them. You return the bones to the woman who gave you the food, and she later removes them. The forest around the village is full of small bundles of bones wrapped in palm leaf baskets and stuck into the forks of trees. It seems that were I to be careless with the bones both I and the hunter who originally killed the game would be liable to be afflicted by / pane /. There is no fuss about fish bones. You get rid of them in the river.

If you kill game and leave it in the forest, you will get / pane /. 'But Kurapi'a killed a tapir at Łyɨ-piyon and he left it.' 'Ah, but that was all right. A jaguar had torn its hindquarters, so it was all right to leave it.'

Not long after his daughters died, Kasiripinar said he was off to find some / tapia'ɨ /, a stinging ant, smaller and less venomous than the tocandeira, to let them sting his arms and so remove the / pane / which had been inflicting him for about two months or so. 'Why do you think I don't go hunting? I don't kill anything any more. I have a lot of / pane /.' Yanuari says that the Wayana apply the true tocandeira and also / ka /, hornets, and even scorpions, as remedies for the affliction.

The space is there for the affliction of / pane / to be attributed to one of the *yarr*, as if a clever theologian could push the reasoning that far. But it is not done. This is in contrast to the following:

I return from hunting with the blood of the game I killed on my hands and legs. I cannot bathe in the river or *moyo* will either kill me or give me fever. Water is brought in a calabash to remove the blood before I can bathe.

/ pane / is a matter of 'magical' connections. My washing off blood in the river is a matter of 'animistic' connections. Both aspects are conflated in the procedures that must be followed on a girl's first menstruation.

/ ònyimòndɨ'a / refers to a girl's first *two* menstruations. After that, a period is just referred to as / wɨ̈g /, blood. At each / ònyi-mòndɨ'a / she has her head shaved and is confined to a hammock. Strips of palm leaf are woven into the shape of a small belt. / tapia'ɨ / ants are collected and held in the belt, the head and thorax on one side and the abdomen sticking out the other. These ants have a painful sting in their abdomens. In the case I saw it was the two brothers of the girl's mother who prepared the strip of ants, and the brother of her father (her father was dead) who applied it – arms, legs, chest, back, and brow. She was held firmly by her mother as it was applied. When the father's brother had finished one of the mother's brothers applied it twice more in an offhand way. They say that the tocandeira ant is never used because it would kill her. If the ants were not applied she would be lazy, do no work, make no hammocks, spin no cotton thread, make no *caxirí* (beer).

There are two different causal strands going on here. The first is the straightforward rite of passage, what people do to the girl's body 'so that she won't be lazy': cutting her hair off and applying the stinging ants. But the seclusion, whatever we may say about liminality, is to protect her, and follows the pattern that is now familiar:

> Do you know why Okòsi's elder sister died? She bathed in the river during her first menstruation. *Moyo* killed her. She got dizzy and then died of fever.

The point about keeping the girl in her hammock has a similar rationale:

> During first menstruation it's bad for women to walk on the ground. /ewò'i/, earth worm, will rape her. It's all right if she walks on wood, for example on a raised floor or along tree trunks.

After the second menstruation the tight seclusion is relaxed although bathing in the river is always dangerous for a menstruating woman:

> /sa̱'i-ko/, grandmother-people, bathed in the river while they were menstruating. They were carried off by *moyo* and raped. Also /sò'ò/, deer, came and did the same thing. (Statements like these suggest fragments of myth.)

When women are menstruating they are /o-si/. I understand this term as 'shy', 'self-conscious', 'reserved'. It implies that one is un-willing to leave the house. (When visitors arrive they are /o-si/, and stick to their houses. They don't walk about much. Kasiripinar said he was /o-si/ when he first went to Belém because everyone stared at him in the streets.) Menstruating women are expected to remain in their hammocks and spin cotton. But what they must not do is bathe in the river 'because *moyo* will make them dizzy or give them fever or perhaps kill them'.

The mortification of the girl's body and her seclusion, the two main aspects of this rite of passage, reflect two distinguishable kinds of causal connection. The first is a means-ends technique, cause II; if the belief in the efficacy of the mortification is strong and explicit we would call the connection magical; if weak we would fall back on seeing the procedures as a mark of transition between statuses. The second depends on the ascription of power to a personified agency, cause I. The second kind of reasoning is the more difficult for us to understand. Magic is not as difficult to understand as animism.

VI

Do *yarr* exist, then? 'Obviously there are no witches' said Evans-Pritchard, thereby upsetting Peter Winch (Winch 1970: 79). It is point-

less to say 'obviously there are no *yarr*' or 'we don't believe in *yarr*'
without first having a clear picture of what 'believing in *yarr*' is, and
that may be very difficult to achieve. I suggest the following three
questions. Is the guiding image that there really are these creatures
and little people running around (which are only seen in shamanistic
trances)? Or is the notion of *yarr* much vaguer: is it a conceptual
device, like a deeply embedded technique of prosopopeia which
allows a way of thinking of all one's surroundings as living things,
thus dissolving the distinction between animate and inanimate? Or,
in the blandest terms, is all this talk of *yarr* no more than a conventional response of not much significance; a response that takes the
place of our causal statements by turning round Tylor's phrase from
us looking at them: 'spirits are simply personified causes', to them
looking at us: 'causes are simply unpersonified spirits'? In that case,
as a conventional response, it reflects nothing more than differences
between shaking hands and rubbing noses.

Having abstracted these three aspects it would be wrong to say that
we now have to look for one amongst them as the correct answer to
the puzzle. They are better taken as referring to different intensities of
the notion as it appears in different contexts, where each context
presents its own kind of difficulty. Taking conventional responses
first, these may be shrugged off as insignificant by those who are
familiar with them. For example, when Kasiripinar asks 'Why do we
die? Stone doesn't die . . . ' and so on, I understand his mood utterly.
'*Timor mortis conturbat me*' expresses a universal foreboding. What is
interesting is that Kasɨrɨpɨnar's perplexity, which I share, has for him
a mythy answer:
Stone wailed.
A lot of Wayãpí gathered together.
'Come here', said Yaneyar 'that you may answer back, that you
may not die.'
They listened.
There was wood.
The warosi tree (it has light wood, it floats, it is not hard); the
warosi tree wailed.
They listened. There was a long wailing sound. They began to
answer.
'No', said Yaneyar. 'That's not the stone that's wailing. It's just
the wood, the warosi.'
It wailed in front of them.
Again.
'No, it's not the thing that you answer', said Yaneyar. 'That's not
the stone that's wailing. That's just a tree.'
Then wailing again.
(It's / ɨwɨra-yaɾë /, master of tree, that's wailing).
[This is a gloss in response to my questioning].

'That's not the sound', said Yaneyar. 'Not stone.'
So they all slept then.
Stone wailed . . . èèèèèèèèèèèèèèèèèèèèèèèèèèè . . .
'Listen. Answer', said Yaneyar. 'Answer quickly. Come on, come on, come on.'
Wailing went on and on.
Then just as they nearly answered it, it stopped.
. . . èèèèèèèèè . . . WÒ! / 'a /! Stopped now.
Only the French answered.
French are tall people.
Therefore French are very very old. They don't die young.
They get to be old.
They answered the stone long ago. Wayãpí didn't answer.
If they had answered "/ 'a /" Wayãpí would be the same.
Old.
They wouldn't die then.
'Why doesn't stone die?' they asked.
Stone doesn't die.
'That you answer back. That you may not die', he just said.
Then Yaneyar was angry.
'You'll finish like that. Old you will therefore be', said Yaneyar to his children, 'and after that you'll die' he said.
They very nearly answered the stone, you know.
Had they answered the stone they would not get old or lose their teeth.   (Waiwai)
Malinowski wrote that myth is:
. . . told in satisfaction of deep religious wants, moral cravings, social submissions, assertions, even practical requirements. Myth fulfills in primitive culture an indispensable function: it expresses, enhances, and codifies belief; it safeguards and enforces morality; it vouches for the efficiency of ritual and contains practical rules for the guidance of man.
                                                      (Malinowski 1948:79)
I recognize a faint reflection of this in myths Wayãpí tell, although there is no place for the strong language: deep wants, cravings, indispensable, codifies, enforces, rules. There is certainly a charter aspect to the myths they tell. They all know 'How the world was created by Yaneyar', 'Why Jacamin [trumpeter bird] has grey feathers on its back' (it danced with Winame's wife during a spree, and Winame, another bird, pushed him into the ashes of the fire), 'That the moon is a man who had sex with his sister', and so on through innumerable stories. But suppose you as a Wayãpí were not particularly interested in the way the myths answer questions. You would know them, but in terms of what they explain you might say 'and so what?'. Myths may not resolve perplexities at all. So often a person's moral response to the world, which I can share and understand,

overwhelms these conventional responses, as if the charter aspect of the myth were no more than a playful or fanciful embellishment.

I am treating Yanuari who is miserably ill. He says many times that he thinks he is dying. A little later, caught up in the enthusiasm of telling me a myth, he breaks off the narrative to explain something about Yaneyar's place in the sky where we go to when we die. One of the details of this delightful place is that we get washed in soap until we're wonderfully white. Yanuari is, of course, like good believers here, untroubled by the contradiction between his beatific vision of the hereafter and his fear of death.

Conventional responses may simply carry no weight. They may not connect with the matter at hand. And how can we judge the extent to which a connection is made?

There is enough evidence in the following chapters to show that there is a great deal more to say about these *yarr* explanations than that they are just an unreflective convention or a pleasant fancy, and it is those other two aspects of the puzzle, *yarr* as little people and *yarr* as a conceptual device, that present more difficult interpretative problems. Taking these in turn, does all this talk of *yarr* really refer to creatures running around everywhere? If this is the way to approach the problem it turns out to be a straightforward disagreement about ontologies. They think *yarr* exist. We don't.

There are three points to be made about ontological disagreements. First, they are very common indeed and are one of the usual ways by which people describe differences between themselves and others. But, secondly, although we can so often identify ontological disagreements with confidence (spirits, fairies, ghosts, gods, heavens and hells), these have a habit of slipping away into interpretative disagreements (witches, reds, subversives). In other words, the boundary of what counts as an ontological disagreement is blurred. Thirdly, if we think we have identified one, how do we respond? Is it negotiable or not?

If the disagreement is straightforward we should expect to negotiate it with confidence:

There are unusual communities in this country where people talk to plants to encourage them to grow. One of the best known is the Findhorn Community in the north of Scotland who, in their various publications, populate the world with devas, elementals, angels, and other beings. Roc, an elderly gentleman who is a member of the community, has published an account of his meetings with a faun called Kurmos in the Botanic Gardens in Edinburgh and of meeting Pan, with hoofed feet, horns, and smelling of pine, outside the National Gallery in Princes Street (Findhorn Community 1976:100–25). 'And why a faun?' he asks. 'That puzzled me. I had read no Greek mythology for years . . . As a child I had passionately believed in fairies and loved both

the Greek myths and their Norse equivalents, whose gods were
very real to me'   (107 and 111).
I know what to do with what is being said here because I share the
notions being manipulated. All of us know what Pan is, and we know
where we got the notion. It is part of my understanding of this notion
that I am not going to meet him on Princes Street. Hence the description offered flatly contradicts my presumptions as to what counts as
existing and what does not. My response to this is to say 'havers' and
that's that.

If I could identify the notion of *yarr* as a straight ontological disagreement, a disagreement as to what exists or not in the world, I
would have no hesitation in making a similar response. And there is
an aspect of the disagreement that does come down to their popu-
lating the world with extra creatures. The myth just presented, when
stone and warosi tree wail, first looks like simple personification of
stone and tree. But in response to my queries 'the tree is wailing?
Does a tree wail?', it was explained that it's not THE TREE that wails
but tree *YARR*. From my point of view, looking at it like that, obviously there are no *yarr*.

We could leave the matter there, as an ontological disagreement,
but that would be a crude rendering of the discrepancy. Our notions
of little creatures, like wee folk and hobgoblins, and of spirits, ghosts,
and witches, and so on, are a matter of extra entities, and the primary
question to be negotiated is whether they exist or not. But if there is
more to the matter of *yarr* than simply one more set of exotic entities,
then it would be misleading to attribute to Wayãpí statements simple
parallels or simple equivalents of our entities (spirits or fairies) and
say that the matter ends there. The earlier examples (whistling for the
wind, 'earth doesn't die', and so on) show that it is worth considering
yarr as part of a much broader linguistic and conceptual context and
to see them not simply as entities in the form of animals or people
but as conceptual devices for making intelligible the living nature of
everything that surrounds us. What deserves emphasis is not just
that the creatures are said to be there, but that these images are
metaphors through which the living world is expressed. They are not
just extra entities. And they are certainly more than our casual figure
of personification. They are the vehicle by which the living tenor is
conceived.

Tylor's hundred-year-old notion of 'animism' is undoubtedly an
illuminating image, but it has to be used with care. Animism in either
of its forms, whether the ascription of life (in general) to inanimate
objects, or the ascription of spirits (in particular) to natural phenomena, is a notion that depends on our fundamental distinction ani-
mate/inanimate. Given this distinction we then abstract one of the
terms (animate) and use it as an integument in which to wrap up their
thought. What we are doing is assuming that a notion of ours (what

counts as 'alive') is being extended by them to cover all these other
aspects of the world, that is, that one side of our distinction has
disappeared, having been blended into the other. This is a dangerous
assumption: we find a state of affairs where a distinction of ours is not
being made and we describe it by one of the terms of our distinction.

I. A. Richards describes a similar predicament in his attempts to
translate the notion of *Hsing* from classical Chinese thought. There
being no distinction between 'psychology' and 'physics' in that context, the notion refers both to Human Nature and Nature in general.
Translating the notion in any particular case we may find ourselves
having to make a choice and render the translation in terms of one
side of our distinction or the other:

> In attempting to choose one reading rather than another a very
> important consideration is soon forced upon us. As we shall see,
> Chinese thinking often gives no attention to distinctions which
> for Western minds are so traditional and so firmly established in
> thought and language, that we neither question them nor even
> become aware of them *as distinctions* [italics original]. We receive
> and use them as though they belonged unconditionally to the
> constitution of things (or of thought). We forget that these dis-
> tinctions have been made and maintained as part of one tradition
> of thinking; and that another tradition of thinking might neither
> find use for them nor (being committed to other courses) be able
> to admit them. And an analysis into separate alternative read-
> ings, such as the above, is likely (in a measure which we have no
> means at present of estimating) to misrepresent the original
> meaning, which may not correspond to any one of them but be
> nearer to a blend of several. But this blending metaphor will
> mislead, if we are dealing here with a meaning which includes, or
> treats as one, ingredients which for us may be distinct and
> separate, but were never analysed and then put together by the
> Chinese. And we should be rash to suppose that any blend we
> can achieve by abstraction and synthesis will really reproduce a
> thought which was not arrived at by these processes.
>
> (Richards 1932:3–4)

Similarly, Tylor's notion, which apparently works so well and which
apparently can be applied so generally, can lead us astray. Given our
distinction there is little alternative but to translate what we understand of their way of looking at things in terms of that distinction and
we bundle the whole matter into one side of it: 'animism'. Is there
anything we can do to ameliorate this regimenting of their thought by
our bullying logic? I suggest two strategies.

The first is to realize that describing their thought as animistic is no
more than a hesitant attempt at a translation. Hence our descriptions
in terms of 'a living world' or 'a living tenor' are always going to be an

'as if' matter: it is 'as if' they animated the world; it is 'as if' they used our terms in this way. Far from animism being a terminal definition we should see it as a landmark that suggests a way to go forward, a word that we can ignore as our familiarity with the area grows.

The second is to realize that animism is a matter of degree. As a terminal diagnostic description, animism suggests that we live in one reality with our comfortable distinction between animate and inanimate while they live in a separate reality teeming with an excess of life. This is nonsense. Animism is not a discriminable thing which they have and we don't. It is a matter of complexions and shades that change in front of us. If one is going to use the word at all it would be best to say that when looking at the similarities and differences between our experience of life and theirs, for much of the inquiry 'animism' will have no place whatsoever. And when it does become a term useful in alerting us to discrepancies, these will appear in varying degrees of intensity. What we call animism might appear as casual, offhand personifications which, like our own, are no more than embellishments or grace notes. At the other extreme it might appear with a profound intensity as the overwhelming rationale in their thought and action. Here we should properly ignore a recurrent theme in anthropology that discourages inquiry into imaginative constructs and inner states by repeating Durkheim's dogma about the distinction between social facts and psychological facts. It is more worthwhile to remember the point that the link between thought and action cannot be dissolved, as Stuart Hampshire explains:

> The actions of another may compel me to refer, in properly interpreting his intentions, to things and events that do not exist in fact, as I believe, and also to things that could not conceivably exist, according to the implicit or explicit philosophical principles that govern my recognition of the existence of things. I may learn to understand, and to recognise in his behaviour, what he is trying to do, even though I believe that what he is trying to do is something that could not conceivably be done, and that nothing whatever would count as actually doing it. There is a sense in which I could not possibly set out with the intention of doing what he is trying to do, because I think that the project, as it presents itself to him in his thinking, has no sense and cannot be formulated as a possibility ... [An example follows of a friend kneeling in prayer to ask for forgiveness of sins. This action can be imitated by someone who does not believe in the existence of God, but it cannot be the same act since the informing intention is absent] ...
>
> We cannot represent human conduct as detachable from the thought that directs it, as if actions were a universal system of natural signs, always intelligible on mere inspection.
>
> (Hampshire 1959:205–06)

As with all our encounters with others, access to the inner states and imaginative constructs of Wayãpí people is neither entirely blocked nor entirely free. The way in is through conversation, but because of the linguistic difficulties which limited the scope of our exchanges, I have only faint and fitful images to work with. Obviously, then, there is an advantage in dealing with these images when they appear at that more extreme intensity where what we call animism comes to our attention in exaggerated forms, and that is the area dealt with in the following chapters. The risk is equally obvious: it is so *easy* to make others look exaggeratedly strange by concentrating on the extremities and avoiding the subtleties of more prosaic examples.

Extremities appear in those causal statements where explanations are pushed to a terminus and those extra living agencies are blamed. To return to the beginning of this chapter, it should now be clear why those particular causal statements reveal so dramatic a discrepancy between us and them. Talking about *yarr*, as I suggested, leads to something much more comprehensive than a squabble about the existence of certain entities. *Yarr* can be seen as a particular aspect of what all statements that explain irregularities, misfortunes, untoward events look like. Just as there is no distinction between animate and inanimate so there is no distinction between living agency and non-living agency. Impersonal, natural, deterministic forces on the one hand, and personalized, intentional agencies on the other are the same thing. Hence the images we are looking at, while they are certainly the vehicle for the conception of a living nature, carry the even more crucial implication that they involve human beings in an intimate relationship with that world. Thus, in certain contexts, the relationship is going to make its extraordinary demands on their lives, and it is at those points that I am going to see the most vivid examples of their thought in action.

To sum up this section, I mentioned three aspects of the puzzle of these *yarr*: a conventional response, an ontological disagreement, and a conceptual device with far-reaching implications. All three should be accepted as different ways of approaching the problem in different contexts. To the extent that I am aware of *yarr* as a conventional response, shared familiarity with the world and shared responses to it will not be obscured. To the extent that a mere ontological disagreement is emphasized, I shall say 'havers' and leave it at that. To the extent that the notion becomes a generalized device that has implications for their ways of relating to the world, I shall look for those extreme situations where the hints of the intensity of the imaginative life that informs that relation will be the most obvious.

The following two chapters look at those situations *in extremis*: explanations of death associated with shamanism, illness, and those birth precautions ('the couvade') that try to protect the newborn from premature death.

PAJÉ:
causing death

It was Death that killed him and not the bullet
Iain Crichton Smith, 'At the Cemetery'

I

'Nature is perhaps the most complex word in the language' says
Raymond Williams (1976:184). Nevertheless there is a received turn of
phrase in anthropological writing which contrasts our views of death
with those of primitive peoples saying that whereas we have a notion
of 'death by natural causes' they do not. They attribute death to
'supernatural causes': spirits, sorcery, and so on. 'Natural' is the
fulcrum of the contrast and I want to find out how firm it is. Robert
Hertz's essay on death, a received anthropological classic published
in 1907, puts the point bluntly: '. . . primitive peoples do not see death
as a natural phenomenon: it is always due to the action of spiritual
powers . . .' (Hertz 1960:77). The formulation is exclusive and disjunctive. What's being said is (a) that we understand death as a
natural phenomenon and (b) that they do not. But is there such an
obvious contradiction between our thought and theirs? Is this description adequate? And what does it imply?

Numerous examples from ethnographies support Hertz's statement. The following are all from South America. The first begins with
an intriguing hint of doubt. This is J. M. Cooper talking about the
Araucanians, or the Mapuche, of Chile:

> *If we may take our sources literally,* death in all cases, even from
> accident or old age, was attributed to other than natural causes,
> viz., to sorcery or to evil spirits.
> (Cooper 1946:734, my emphasis)

John Murra writes of the Cayapa and Colorado of Colombia that:

> Death is not considered to be a natural phenomenon but is
> attributed to the presence of malevolent spirits in the body.
> (Murra 1948:283)

Paul Kirchhoff on the Caribbean Lowland Tribes:

> Death is thought to be due to sorcery or to the machinations of
> evil spirits.   (Kirchhoff 1948:226)

Peter Rivière, among the Trio, says:
> For the Trio sickness and death ... are not considered to be
> natural phenomena ... The Trio sicken or die as a result of being
> cursed.   (Rivière 1969:238)

Reichel-Dolmatoff says of the Tukano of Colombia:
> There is no 'natural' death in Tukano culture'; death and disease
> are always regarded as the consequence of evil magic exercised
> by an enemy.   (Reichel-Dolmatoff 1975:100)

And lastly, more than seventy years after Hertz's essay, Joanna
Kaplan describes the 'supernatural dangers' that beset the Piaroa,
who believe that all death is caused by sorcery. She emphasizes in a
footnote that:
> All of my informants insisted that the only cause of death is attack
> by *marimu* (sorcerers). Disease, accidents, only weaken a person
> making him more vulnerable than when in a normal state to
> *marimu* attack.   (Kaplan 1975:27)

Hertz went on to say:
> The ethnographers who report this widespread belief see in it a
> gross and persistent error; but we ought rather to consider it as
> the naïve expression of a permanent social need.   (1960:77)

And following Hertz, ethnographers have usually been careful not to
attribute gross and persistent errors to the people they have visited
but instead have presented numerous accounts of naïve expressions
of permanent social needs, that is, it is explained that death is a *social*
phenomenon and not simply a natural phenomenon. But the flat
sociologism simply obscures the question. If primitive peoples do not
see death as a natural phenomenon, then explaining that they see it as
a social phenomenon does not seem to do much to rescue them from
'gross and persistent error'. And if it is not an error, what is the nature
of the discrepancy between our ideas and theirs?
> During the first months of my stay I learned something of the
> unseemly aspects of FUNAI's attraction programmes. I had seen
> an incident early on when a few families were visiting the post
> and were struck down by influenza. A five-year-old girl died.
> That morning, while I was composing a letter to the FUNAI
> authorities pointing out that Indians should be positively dis-
> couraged from visiting Indian Protection posts until it could be
> guaranteed that these were properly managed and maintained
> free from fatal infection, the distraught mother of the dead child
> came to where I was writing and asked a number of times: 'Why
> did my child die?' I had very little of the language, but as she
> repeated her question I wondered if I should try to explain that
> the cause of her child's death lay with the incompetent personnel
> on the post who had allowed a roadworker with common cold
> symptoms to come up river on to the post, but attempting that
> was out of the question for all sorts of reasons, practical and

political. I said simply 'fever', referring to the symptom of high temperature which accompanies so many serious ailments in the forest. Through her sobs she responded with challenging firmness: '/paye òyuka/', which would usually be translated into Portuguese as *pajé matou* or into English as 'shaman killed'. Puzzled, I asked 'Who?' and she astounded me by naming another Indian who was also on the post at the time.

It was a disturbing encounter. There was certainly no quickening of the anthropological pulse that here was some grand primitive stuff for the notebooks. I was shocked that the Indian mentioned, one of the most amiable I had met, should be so bluntly accused of murder. I also felt dismayed and betrayed. What was the point of struggling with the authorities if the very person who had lost most through the tragic incompetence of this protection operation could not at this time forget such savage nonsense and see what had happened? Could she not find an appropriate target for her heart-broken accusations? 'Why can't they see?' became a familiar expression of my irritation in later months as the road teams moved into the area. But I should say that by the end of my time there with many of my initial ideas knocked out of shape I was saying to myself: 'Yes, they do see, but they feel it's worth the risk, and perhaps they accept the inevitability of contact with a more realistic and resigned grace than I do.'

Reflecting on the contradiction between the mother's account of her child's death and my explanation, there is one contrast which I must be careful *not* to make. Evans-Pritchard says of witchcraft: 'It is not a necessary link in a sequence of events but something external to them that participates in them and gives them a peculiar value' (1937:72). It would be easy to be misled by that statement and to describe *my* explanation of the child's death as a logically coherent account of the causal sequence of events that led up to the tragedy, an explanation that stands apart and immune from considerations of value, whereas *the mother's* explanation introduced a peculiar value that was external to the causal sequence. But there is nothing value-free about my account. It is a serious moral judgement and I can easily claim that the particular details of this sequence of cause and effect are the least important aspect of the matter. Furthermore I am ignorant of the necessary links in the sequence of events that often (though not always) turns what is easily diagnosed in our society as a cold or influenza into an ailment that afflicts Indians with temperatures of 104° to 105°F and that can produce severe pulmonary and respiratory disorders leading to death. Medical inquiry into pathology and immunology in isolated tropical forest groups still has many questions to answer regarding the precise mechanics of how this happens. But even if I knew the sequence down to the last antibody and pathogen it would make no difference to the tone of my explanation. I saw why it happened and I know that most five-year-old Indian girls do not 'naturally' die. I cannot describe the incident significantly without using words like 'carelessness', 'incompetence', 'lack of responsibility', and so on, nor without naming the people I thought responsible. My account is an accusation just as the mother's is, and to try to restate it expunging all moral judgement would empty it of all significance. If primitive peoples do not see death as a natural phenomenon, then in this case neither did I.

The difficulty is in the adjective 'natural'. The top layer of ambiguity is that the contrast Hertz and the ethnographers most obviously follow is that between 'natural causes' and 'supernatural causes' whereas in ordinary English usage the first term also carried a different distinction: that between 'natural causes' and 'unnatural causes' such as homicide, suicide, misadventure. Thinking of the second distinction, there is evidence that Hertz's generalisation is not satisfactory. Returning to Father Cooper's evidence, the first in the list given above which began with the healthy query regarding 'taking our sources literally', having stated that death is always attributed to 'other than natural causes' he goes on 'excepting only death from wounds'. He then adds with tantalizing brevity: 'Suicide occurred but was not common.' Leaving South America for a moment and stretching the 'among the so-and-so's' accumulations, Gregory Bateson says of the Iatmul of New Guinea:

> In this community where violent death is frequent, death by sickness (i.e. sorcery) is not very seriously regarded. There is very little of the almost paranoid fear of sorcery which is characteristic of many primitive cultures.   (Bateson 1958:55 note 1)

But the clarity of the distinction between un-natural and super-natural does not last for long:

> In general no deaths are regarded by [the Iatmul] as 'natural' but all are referred to sorcery. Even when a man is killed by the enemy, his relatives will suspect that some sorcerer in the village has sold the dead man's soul to the enemy before the raid.(64 note 1)

Wayãpí people make no reference to supernatural agencies when they describe homicide. Similarly, suicides are described in terms of 'the person didn't want to live' or 'the person was sad' with no reference to any further agency. (There have been a number of cases of people hanging themselves from the roof-beams of their houses, always, it would appear, during drunken episodes and sprees.) The usual examples of accidents are being struck by a snake and having your arrow come down on top of you (after you've aimed it straight up into the foliage – a tricky predicament). A common valediction runs: 'May you see on the path. May you not get hurt.' Danger of snakebite is the major anxiety when travelling:

Waiwai can do a splendid, spine-chilling talk-and-mime description of walking on the paths, bare-footed, where the little *jararaca*
lies coiled, unseen, just at the side, waiting to get you just below
the ankle. Some FUNAI people prefer the security of wellington
boots to the comfort of almost anything else.

In the recent genealogies there is one case where a woman was killed
by the branch of a tree falling on her, one where a man is said to have
bled to death after his arrow fell back on him, and one where a man
was killed by a jaguar. In none of these cases was 'supernatural' cause
invoked, as in those celebrated Azande cases of collapsing granaries
and charging buffaloes (Evans-Pritchard 1937).

Leaving aside the natural/supernatural distinction for the
moment, let us suppose that we are working only with that between
natural and unnatural. Hence, if these examples indicate that death
was not considered a 'natural' phenomenon, they might indicate the
idea that people were blessed with immortality and would only die by
some 'unnatural' intervention, in other words by 'being killed'. Surprisingly, this is more or less what I was told about animals and birds.
A conversation at the Nipukú produced the following information
which was discussed and agreed upon by others:

Animals and birds do not die. (The collective word is / miyarë /
which in other contexts I translate 'game'.) They are only killed.
Eagles kill howler monkeys. Snakes and jaguars kill pigs. Otters
kill fish. Eagles are killed by howler monkeys – the monkeys bite
them when they attack. Pigs and snakes kill jaguars. Hawks are
killed by hornets (which sting them in the eye). Hornets are killed
by smaller birds. Otters are killed by snakes and jaguars . . . (and
so on completing the circle). Yaneyar made this so.

The list was presented like that. Typically it does not try to be exhaus-
tive. Indeed it was my questions about eagles and so on that produced
the circularity. When it was over, Yanuari, who was telling me all this,
added morosely: 'Dogs die. So do we.'

The English word 'jaguar' is a loan word from the Tupi-Guaraní
languages. The Wayãpí word / yawarë / is a generic term for all
the forest cats as well as for the dogs around the village. When
necessary, dogs are distinguished by adding words which mean
'pet jaguars', 'village jaguars', 'our jaguars', or something of the
sort.

Yanuari had a pet macaco-prego monkey which died:

If animals don't die, why did it die? 'It didn't eat. It refused to eat.
Hunger killed it. In the forest macaco-prego monkeys don't die.
Eagles kill them.'

'Dogs die. So do we.' Taking the natural/supernatural distinction in
terms of dying and being killed we seem to agree with them when it
comes to human life, as Kasiripinar's questions 'Why do we die? . . .'

and the myth set out in the previous chapter show. Waiwai ended that myth (where Wayãpí failed to answer the call of stone) by saying:
'The French answered it, you know. If you go to the Oyapoque you'll see very very old French people.' Yes, but do they die? 'Well, yes, perhaps they die, but they're very very old. Wayãpí don't become *very very old.*'
Note the ambiguity where ageing and dying have been conflated. It is well reflected in our own myths, say Gulliver's Struldbrugs or the Tithonus theme, where the gift of immortality is given but no request for perpetual youth is made. The translators of Lévi-Strauss's *Le Cru et le cuit* find nothing odd in rendering a title that is originally given as 'la vie brève' as 'How men lost immortality' (Lévi-Strauss 1970: part 3). Waiwai stumbled over whether getting old was a good sign, longevity tending towards immortality, or whether it was decay tending towards death.

Is dying of old age what we mean by dying of natural causes? *Some* Azande *sometimes* say that old people die of old age: 'When a very old man dies unrelated people say that he has died of old age, but they do not say this in the presence of kinsmen, who declare that witchcraft is responsible for his death' (Evans-Pritchard 1937:77). Colin Turnbull (1966) writing of the Mbuti pygmies presents the old distinction: '. . . death itself is accepted by the Mbuti as being perfectly natural' (146); '. . . the Mbuti believe in natural causes rather than supernatural' (60); but when contrasting the Mbuti with the village cultivators who surround them and who do explain death in terms of witchcraft, he writes: '. . . if [the Mbuti] consider the death perfectly natural, they do not want to be bothered with a senseless preoccupation with causes' (75). This last statement is arresting. Considering death as 'natural' they are not concerned with causes *at all.* Man comes and tills the field and lies beneath and that's that. And if *that* is the clearest expression of an idea of death being a natural phenomenon, then we do not compare very favourably. We, like the Bantu village cultivators, are preoccupied with causes. In this country when anyone, including an elderly person, dies and is not under medical supervision, then an autopsy must be performed to diagnose the cause of death. Our specialists must have their say in divining the cause. 'He died of old age' won't do. Remembering the ground covered in the previous chapter we can see what a coroner's report is doing: the final verdict of 'natural causes' establishes (1) that no person is to blame and (2) that this was not an accident that could have been prevented. 'Natural causes' is therefore a residual category appealed to only when the question of human intervention, either producing or preventing, has been cleared out of the way. Hence the statement 'death by natural causes' is not really a causal statement at all. Like Collingwood's cause III statements or Hart and Honoré's 'conditions' it means 'conditions' it means simply, 'there is no specific cause; death in this case is part of the usual course of events'.

So far, then, our distinction between natural and unnatural causes does not reveal a discrepancy between their notions and ours. All of us share notions of death from old age and death by misadventure: being murdered, a tree falling, a snakebite, or starvation. As regards the connection between illness and death, can we imagine an ethnographic case stating that a certain people made no connection at all between illness and death; that they saw illness as something that comes and goes, and death as something that comes along once, there being no relation whatsoever between the two? Not surprisingly, Wayãpí are well aware that if one becomes ill one might die. They are also aware that disease can be transmitted. One of the first questions asked of a visitor is 'do you bring any illness?' Those who have been ill and who have recovered are often described, sometimes with a touch of exaggeration, as having 'very nearly died'. And when a visitor arrived with a cough, I saw a family pack up and get out of the village in about fifteen minutes and stay away for nearly a month.

There is no indication here of an alien mode of thought, of a discrepancy between our way of looking at things and theirs, or of the emergence of an error in their thinking about the causes of illness and death. Hence, so far there is no need for a disjunctive formula to describe what they think as opposed to what we think. The collision occurs when the shamanism accusations begin. It is a shock to encounter these for the first time, and it is initially difficult to avoid seeing them as examples of 'gross and persistent error'.

Just as some Azande sometimes say that people die of old age, or some Wayãpí sometimes say that people die of influenza or fever. But one man, who considers himself *paye* (shamanistic) and is recognized to be so, says:

> Measles, influenza, and fever do not kill. Only *anyang* sent by *paye*-people kill. If the Brazilians bring influenza then the enemy *paye*-people see / know and they say 'this is the time to kill them' and they send *anyang*. If no *anyang* are sent we get better. Other people who are not *paye* say that perhaps influenza and fever can kill. But this is because they don't know. When people die and there's no *paye*-people about, the others don't know if *anyang* were sent. Only *paye*-people can tell. Only *paye*-people can see *anyang*.

It may appear that Evans-Pritchard solved the puzzle about the relation between illness and death when he wrote:

> Zande belief in witchcraft in no way contradicts empirical knowledge of cause and effect . . . Belief in death from natural causes and belief in death from witchcraft are not mutually exclusive. On the contrary, they supplement one another, the one accounting for what the other does not account for.   (1937:73)

This is provisionally helpful. Witchcraft explanations are supplementary, supervenient explanations which add to and do not interfere with what we could be tempted to call the 'natural' explanation. But is this enough to justify the natural / supernatural distinction? A recent case in our newspapers explained that an elderly woman was found to have died of pulmonary oedema brought on by hypothermia and malnutrition, and her son and daughter-in-law were charged with manslaughter. Here too, the accusation does not interfere with, or contradict, the 'natural' explanation. Natural / supernatural, therefore, does not account for the difference between my view of the Indian child's death and her mother's view.

II

Consider the following six peculiarities of causal reasoning:

(1) Causal reasoning is typically *ex post facto*. It is retrospective, trying to explain events that have already happened.

(2) Causal reasoning allows for the supervention of explanations one on the other, the addition of supernumerary explanations in succession or perhaps better, in regression: 'he died – he died of a coronary – he died of a coronary because he worked too hard – he worked too hard because he was anxious to succeed – he was like that because his parents . . . – ' and so on.

(3) The result of extending the causal nexus in this way is that a plurality of causes is produced to which appeal can be made. (Evans-Pritchard makes this point clearly in *Azande Witchcraft*.)

(4) An adjudication goes on amongst these possible explanations which is not looking for the empirical, natural, logical sequence of cause and effect, but which is trying to decide which explanation has *significant priority*. If a government official explained that the Indian girl died of pulmonary oedema brought on by influenza, and if I allowed that as an explanation in the first place, I would add that the explanation is insignificant; that it misses the point.

(5) When a number of explanations competing for significance are discussed, we are impelled to support our priority by contradicting a competing one. We say 'not this but that'. When Collingwood discusses the relativity of causes, making the point about means / ends statements, he writes:

> The principle may be stated by saying that *for any given person, the cause of a given thing is that one of its conditions which he is able to produce or prevent* [original emphasis]. For example, a car skids while cornering at a certain point, turns turtle, and bursts into flame. From the car driver's point of view, the cause of the accident was cornering too fast, and the lesson is that one must drive more carefully. From the county surveyor's point of view, the cause was a defective road-surface, and the lesson is that one must make skid-proof roads. From the motor-manufacturer's

point of view, the cause was defective design, and the lesson is that one must place the centre of gravity lower.

(Collingwood 1938: 92–93)

Should we imagine a discussion between the driver, the county surveyor, and the motor-manufacturer, each justifying different and competing points of view, it would be full of negatives: 'No, that wasn't it . . . the *real* cause was . . .'; unless of course the circumstances you are in make you compliant enough to accept all competing explanations without demur:

And they hanged Private Simmons – hanged him high as Haman in hollow square of the regiment; and the Colonel said it was Drink, and the Chaplain was sure it was the Devil; and Simmons fancied it was both, but he didn't know . . .

(Kipling 'In the Manner of a Private' from *Soldiers Three*)

The rhetorical 'not this but that' appears in *Nuer Religion* where at an important point in the explanation of 'twins are birds' Evans-Pritchard writes: 'They say "a twin is not a person (*ran*), he is a bird (*dit*)", although, as we have just seen, they assert, in another sense, that twins are one person (*ran*)' (1956:129). The negatives are used to reinforce different points, the first to emphasize that twins are not TWO *ran* but ONE *ran*, the second that twins are not *ran* but *dit*. 'Not this but that' statements can be obscure since we may not be able to find out whether what is said is an absolute denial holding in all contexts, or a rhetorical denial, used to make a contrast, and specifically related to the speaker's interests at the time. In one of the examples above, Joanna Kaplan takes special care to write that *all* her informants *insisted* that the *only* cause of death is sorcery, and there is no reason to doubt that this is what was said: 'emphatically not this but that'. But do these statements hold at all times and in all possible contexts? In the Azande example referred to above, on the death of an old person unrelated people might say that it was old age that caused it, but they will not say this in the presence of related people who hold witchcraft responsible. Contexts force us into these disjunctive formulae where we say 'not this but that' instead of 'in some circumstances this, in others that'; 'yes this, but more importantly that'; or even poor Private Simmon's 'both this and that'. Evans-Pritchard suggests that what one is doing is 'fore-shortening the chain of events'. Another way of putting it is that one explanation is abstracted from a number of competing ones and emphasized in such a way that it obliterates the others by denying them.

(6) When we are adjudicating among priorities of significance, the reasoning is beyond the reach of scientific verification or intervention by philosophical 'counter-factuals'. Here the priority is judged, not proven. It could be argued that the accusations of manslaughter and incompetence in the examples given above could indeed be proven: 'If you had done this then that would not have happened, therefore

you are responsible'. But I don't think so. We could verify what happened and what did not happen down to the most minute detail, but we still have to *judge* matters of responsibility and guilt. We create responsibility and we create guilt. These are neither matters of apodeictic fact given in the natural order. (Nor are they whimsical personal opinions.) They are agreements between people.

Moral judgements and accusations appeal to a dimension of significance that is not given in the empirical sequence of cause and effect. They are assessed not as true or false, but as significant or insignificant, appropriate or inappropriate, by reference to grounding principles that are immune from verification and proof. What happened might never be in dispute. My accusation at the post (blaming someone for allowing the carrier of the disease access to the place) is grounded on assumptions of certain responsibilities and powers attached to certain roles. But those I accuse could easily refuse to accept that they had the authority or responsibility to do anything about the matter. We disagree not about what happened but about the grounding principles. They don't believe me. The manslaughter charge illustrated above is grounded on an ethical judgement regarding the proper way to care for relatives, and though our processes of law might convict in that case since the action of the relatives concerned is a moral affront to us, the Eskimos, 'if we may take our sources literally', might in the past have held that there was no charge to answer. And if these fantasy Eskimos refuse to accept our judgement there is nothing we can do to prove to them that it is *correct*. We disagree about the grounding principles. They don't believe us.

Returning to shamanism accusations, describing the discrepancy between our thought and theirs as a contrast between natural and supernatural will clearly not do. It suggests that our statements are grounded in the security of verifiable sequence of cause and effect: in 'empirical knowledge'. But both our accounts of these states of affairs and the Wayãpí's are much more complicated than that. Our 'death by natural causes' is a residual statement which means roughly 'nothing caused it'. Where possible, we too introduce properly causal statements which blame people, for instance in the way we blame lung cancer, cirrhosis of the liver, or heart disease on bad personal habits. To say that sickness is normal or natural is something we resist through the habits of our language, and the way we use medicine confirms this. Illness is pathological and medicine is there to combat the malevolent intrusion. 'Death is not considered to be a natural phenomenon but is attributed to the presence of malevolent spirits in the body.' How like our own view of the matter. What was said of the Cayapa could be said of our doctors describing the evils of alcohol.

These descriptions are grounded on all sorts of pre-conceptions regarding moral values, intentions, responsibilities, notions of proper and correct behaviour, notions of what exists and what does

not, notions of what is harmful and what is not, notions about health,
illness, and danger. These preoccupations and preconceptions are
not given in the events themselves. When we confront those descriptions that compete with our own it is not the sequences of events that
are in question. Wayãpí shamanism accusations are grounded on a
belief in *paye*, a belief in the existence of a quality, a power, a something or other which is effective. And we don't believe in shamanism.
That is all our periphrastic distinction of natural and supernatural was
trying to say.

III

The term *shaman* comes from a Tungus-Manchu word *šaman*, a noun
formed from the verb *ša-* (to know), hence *shaman* means 'he who
knows' (Diószegi 1974:638). Ioan Lewis gives the Mongolian word as
'one who is excited, moved, or raised' (1971:51). The *Oxford English
Dictionary* entry runs: 'Evidence seems to be wanting for the plausible
suggestion that the Mongolian word is an adoption of Chinese *sha
mên*, an ordained member of a Bhuddist fraternity, a. Skr. çramaṇa,
Pali *samana* Bhuddist monk or mendicant'. (This is probably an allusion to the philological dispute described by Eliade 1964:495–496.)

In some ways it is a pity that those who write in English (and
sometimes those who write in Spanish and Portuguese) about the
South American tropical forest use the Mongolian word instead of
Spanish and Portuguese *page* or *pajé*. Métraux suggests following the
example of the Indians:

> A leur exemple, nous appellerons *piai* l'agent du surnaturel dans
> les sociétés indigènes de l'Amérique du Sud tropicale: ce mot,
> d'origine tupi et carib, fait partie du vocabulaire des diverses
> langues parlées des Guyanes au Paraguay. Il est synonyme de
> terme sibérien *chaman* désignant tout individu qui, dans l'intérêt
> de la communauté, entretient par profession un commerce in-
> termittent avec les esprits ou en est possédé.   (Métraux 1967:81)

But if the following argument is worthwhile, then perhaps it is just as
well that *paye* is left more or less unscathed by use in our language.

Shamanism commonly gives rise to five lines of questioning:

(1) Definition: which in turn resolves into two main themes: (a) role
(functional, dysfunctional, healing, authority . . .) and (b) the nature
of the experience (ascent to the skies, possession . . .).

(2) How people become shamans: whether it is a calling or whether
anyone can become one, the procedures for becoming one . . .

(3) Are shamans people who are mentally unstable in some way?

(4) Are they effective?

(5) Is shamanism a 'rcligion'?

The first of these questions gets the most attention. Regarding definitions, many writers offer particular interpretations: Audrey Butt
stresses the shaman's legal role; Lévi-Strauss sees the shaman as a

psychoanalyst; Janet Siskind as a poet; Reichel-Dolmatoff as an intellectual; and so on. And a step back from these interpretations, there are further complexities in the evidence from the indigenous languages:

> Arriving at a broadly applicable definition of shamanism for lowland South America seems to be a particularly difficult task. This is in part due to local variation, especially when more than one category of specialist exists and is given lexical recognition.
>
> (Jackson 1975:324)

Many examples follow where the languages concerned have words that denote different roles or offices: the Jívaro distinguish between curing and bewitching shamans; the Cashinaua between herbalist and true shaman; among the Cubeo the herbal specialist can evolve into the true shaman; and so on into Golden Bough-ish obscurities: the Krahó do not distinguish their two types of shaman in terms of either task [i.e., curer or sorcerer] or moral connotation (so what do they do then?); the Tapirapé see shamans as necessary and good, yet all are eventually killed (all? always? still?). The more complex the picture the more interesting it becomes, but what will a definition of all this do?

Definitions are like oubliettes into which thriving ideas are dropped to end their days. A training in anthropology no more profound than watching a few John Ford movies would give people enough images of witch-doctors to make sure than when in the tropical forest they would not fail to be arrested by shamanism. Definitions do not help identify the phenomenon more easily or more precisely. Those who come across it, however definitionally astute they are, still have to try to understand it. Definitional ventures simply get in the way by trying to pen the matter within narrow enclosures of technicality.

Instead of a definition, I suggest that it might be useful to regard the notion of *paye* not primarily as a role or an office, but as a quality. No one, as far as I know, has been able to reduce *pajé*, *paye*, *piai*, and so on, into etymological components as can be done with *shaman*. We start and finish with the word itself. When the woman in the anecdote above said that the cause of her child's death was that / pạye òyụka /, I noted down 'pajé killed – a shaman killed the child'. Statements about shamans began to accumulate:

/ mòyo i-pạye /	the anaconda is a shaman
/ pèrɨrɨ i-pạye /	the angelim tree is a shaman
/ ạnyaŋ-pirèrë i-pạye /	the pau mulatto tree is a shaman
(lit. 'anyang-skin')	
/ kumạka i-pạye /	the sumauma tree is a shaman

As they stand these statements are puzzling. What on earth does it mean to attribute this office to these creatures and these trees? What does it mean to say that the anaconda is *a shaman*?

There is a clue in the negatives. If you see a bird you might ask: 'Is that a toucan?' and, if not, you would get the answer: '/ani, a'èrowa tukan /' (no, it is not a toucan). But if you ask: 'Is that man a shaman?' and if he is not, the answer is '/ani, nipayẹi /'. Compare the following:

/i-rọro/ swollen	/nirorọi/ not swollen
/i-pịraη/ red	/nipirãi/ not red
/aimè/ sharp	/nạimẹi/ not sharp, blunt

These adjectives resemble verbs in their declensions:

/i-aịwa/	tired (indefinite)
/eaịwa/	I
/neaịwa/	you singular
/yane-aịwa/	we inclusive
/orè-aịwa/ ·	we exclusive
/pè-aịwa/	you plural

hence blurring the distinction between adjective and verb, where 'tired' can be seen as a verbal phrase 'to be tired'.

Rather than translating /ni-payẹi/ as 'he is not a shaman', it would be better to give something like 'he is not shamanistic'. The shift of emphasis initially looks trivial, but allowing in this qualitative dimension dissolves all sorts of difficulties. Saying 'the anaconda is shamanistic' removes the obscurity of 'the anaconda is a shaman'. And instead of the original 'the tapir is a little shaman', I can now try 'the tapir is slightly shamanistic'. And when Yanuari says that he used to be a large shaman but now he is a tiny, tiny shaman (since that time he fell from a tree and broke his back), I understand that he used to have a lot of shamanism, but now he has only a little.

I suggest the following points:

(1) *Paye* primarily concerns a quality or attribute rather than a role or an office. The reason that the statements about the anaconda or the tree initially seemed opaque was that this priority had been reversed.

(2) If it is a quality rather than an office, then it admits of degrees. You can have a lot of it or a little of it. you can have some of it for a time and lose it completely. You are *either* a chief *or* you are not – that's an office – but you can be more or less shamanistic. Although there are no reports of any group where it is said that almost every adult was a chief, there are accounts (for example of the Jívaro and of the Emerillon) where we are told that numerous adults are shamans. This is puzzling until we think first of the quality.

(3) The attribution is not just one of static appearance: 'green', 'beautiful', 'tall'; nor just a transient state of being: 'out of breath', 'drowsy', 'angry'. It is also an attribute that describes a capacity to do something, like 'strong', 'knowledgeable', 'talented'.

It would be unhelpful to suggest that *paye* is strictly an adjective, but it is a useful start. Thinking of the word as representing a quality or attribute (adjectivally) allows the sense to move easily between those who possess it (noun) and what is done with it (verb). Rather than decide firmly which part of speech it is, this move allows us to put our neat distinctions of noun, adjective, and verb into abeyance.

Here I may well be going against the grain of grammatical interpretations competent in linguistic techniques. Against the considerable technical work in Tupian languages, the evidence I offer to back up my suggestion is only a scrap. Like finding a potsherd and inferring a civilization, I'm looking at this fragment and inferring an epistemology. Although it's a risky line to take it is consistent with the general theme, namely that the interpretative difficulty is not in confronting *different* categories and *different* distinctions, but in coming across a state of affairs where distinctions we expect to find are not made. Such a discrepancy can easily escape notice. Where the phenomenon lacks the form we expect, we can form it with our distinctions. Because it is fluid, we can make it run in our moulds. It will always appear to work according to our scheme since there is nothing intrinsic to the phenomenon which is going to present a *better* formed account, a *more* rigid one, than the one we have managed to impose on it. There is nothing intrinsic to the phenomenon that can speak back and correct the scheme.

Although my evidence is so slight, the same predicament has been faced elsewhere, and not with an unwritten language in this case, but with Greek, when translating the pre-Socratics.

The distinction among parts of speech is less pronounced in the Greek language than in the Latin and its Western successors. Accordingly it is often impossible for a translator to find in a modern language the precise equivalent of some word or idiom in the Greek. The difficulty indeed, is more than grammatical, it is ontological; for it concerns the *kind of being* which the different types of words are designed to indicate. Of particular interest are the three word-types of noun, adjective, and verb, together with the three modes of being for which they respectively stand – things, qualities, and events. The correlation is not absolute, to be sure; for we have to remind ourselves occasionally that an abstract noun such as 'justice' does not indicate a thing, and that the copula 'is' lacks the usual semantic properties of other verbs. But in general our contemporary Western languages keep a fairly steadfast distinction among the three types – nouns standing for things, adjectives standing for qualities, and verbs standing for actions and events.

Now in the thought of Heraclitus, abetted by the comparative fluidity of the Greek language, the linguistic distinction and correspondingly the ontological distinction are somewhat less firm. (Wheelwright 1959:13)

The writer goes on to discuss Fragment 126 (Diels) of Heraclitus which he translates: 'Cool things become warm, the warm grows cool; the moist dries, the parched becomes moist'. (G. S. Kirk gives: 'Cold things warm themselves, warm cools, moist dries, parched is made wet' 1954:149.)

> Is Heraclitus speaking here about things or about qualities? . . . The answer seems to be that scarcely any distinction was recognised between cool and warm things and the resident qualities of coolness and warmth. It was not until a century and a half later that Aristotle delineated the difference explicitly and showed what the intellectual penalty for ignoring it would be.
>
> (Wheelwright 1959:14)

Wheelwright suggests that if we want to understand Heraclitus we must exercise our 'negative capability'. The phrase is something of a cliché in English Literature. Wheelwright describes it as 'bracketing off our habitual ways of joining and distinguishing ideas wherever such ways differ from the writer's own' (16). (It is originally from a letter John Keats wrote to his brother George in 1817: 'I mean *negative capability*; that is, when a man is capable of being in uncertainties, mysteries, doubts, without any irritable reaching after fact and reason' 118 note 17.)

What Aristotle did to rescue us from the mystery of qualitative change and to spoil the opportunity for flexing our negative capability was to interpose a 'third something', in which both qualities can inhere. If 'warm cools' is too difficult for us, we only have to think of 'soup' and the mystery is over – warm *soup* becomes cold. We say 'yesterday it was cold but today it is hot', and when we're challenged as to what 'it' is, we say 'the weather', but what's that? Here the 'third thing' is becoming elusive. Wheelwright comments: 'The difference is not empirical, it is syntactical and epistemological. The preferred linguistic convention expresses a conceptual need' (34). The analytics of our language prevent us, like a fall from grace, from being able to see what it was like when they were not there. Aristotle is the angel set to guard the gate against our return. Our analytics, our 'irritable reaching after fact and reason', block our path and prevent us going further in that direction.

It comes back again to this fretful matter of distinctions. A specific technique that Wheelwright urges us to use when we bracket off our ways of thinking and enter into the thought of Heraclitus is to cultivate a 'readiness to think in terms of *both-and*, nor merely of *either-or*' (40). This of course is the problem of metaphor, the problem of the verb 'to be' (and the problem incidentally which is at the heart of Chapter V of Evans-Pritchard's *Nuer Religion*). Ricoeur summarizes as follows:

> From this conjunction of fiction and redescription I conclude that the 'place' of metaphor, its most intimate and ultimate abode, is neither the name, nor the sentence, nor even discourse, but the copula of the verb *to be*. The metaphorical 'is' at once signifies

both 'is not' and 'is like'. If this is really so, we are allowed to
speak of metaphorical truth, but in an equally 'tensive' sense of
the word 'truth'.   (Ricoeur 1978:7)

A tradition in our philosophy has for centuries regarded metaphor
as a scandal, and it still proves a major stumbling block for logic,
the philosophy of language, and semantics, not to mention how
the term was trivialized in Lévi-Straussian structural anthropology
where it was reduced to one side of an empty opposition
(metaphor/metonym). This is not a theme to follow here except to say
that metaphor is the most productive example of how we, in our
thought and language, escape the tyranny of logic and distinctions
and categories, and where we can see the processes of a more creative
mode.

The suggestion, then, is to loosen up our distinctions and show
more tolerance for both-and rather than either-or interpretations. I
can't say if thinking of *paye* in this way would be generally appropriate
in South America but there are hints that it might be. A good example,
outside Tupian languages, is found in the work of Stephen and
Christine Hugh-Jones on the Barasana. Even in these intensely detailed ethnographies, where the words 'shaman', 'shamanic', and
'shamanism' appear countless times and where the category
'shaman' is presented as one of a group of five categories central to
Barasana thought, there is not a Barasana term that is easily substituted for these words. There is a term *kumu* or *kumua* which is given
as 'shaman' (C. Hugh-Jones 1979:60, S. Hugh-Jones 1979:25). It appears there in Christine's book along with two other terms for shaman
which mean 'shamanisers of the beeswax gourd' and 'shamanisers of
tobacco'. But this is not the whole story:

> There are also grades of shamanic activity, the least demanding
> being shamanism of foods after minor life changes, and the most
> demanding being shamanism of the sacred beeswax and tobacco
> gourds during initiation.   (Christine Hugh-Jones 1979:62)
>
> In any one area, there are usually one or two shamans whose
> reputation for curing and for blowing surpasses that of all the
> rest. These men, known as *kumu* . . .
>
> Very few shamans have the necessary power and knowledge
> to officiate at this rite [the *He*]. Those who do are known as *kumu*
> or as *werea koa baseri masa*, the people who blow over the gourd of
> beeswax.   (Stephen Hugh-Jones 1979:36 and 120)

Clearly then *kumu* and 'people who blow over the beeswax and
tobacco gourds' are terms that represent a specially strong aspect of
shamanism, but it would be misleading to leave it that *kumu* simply
means 'shaman':

> Amongst the Barasana, there is no absolute difference between
> those men recognised as shamans and those who are not. At the
> lowest level, most adult men have some abilities as shamans and

will carry out some of the same functions as those men who have a widespread reputation for their powers and knowledge.

(Stephen Hugh-Jones 1979:32)

There are grades, or degrees, and presumably only the latter would be referred to as *kumu* or as those very powerful shamans who are called *yai* (jaguar) (124). But none of the terms mentioned so far seems to be suitable for all those other adult men who have some abilities in the matter. They are certainly not *kumu*, but are they or are they not shamans? The answer given in the ethnographies is that the essence of shamanism which informs terms such as *kumu* and *yai* is not given in a noun but in a verb: 'the act of shamanising, *base-* . . . ' (Christine Hugh-Jones 1979:62). 'The Barasana have a verb *base-* that covers the activities of shamans in general. I have translated this as "blow, blowing" as this action is a common feature of these activities' (Stephen Hugh-Jones 1979: 32 note 5).

'Blow, blowing' is a guess, then. *Base-* is a verb which means 'to shamanize' in all the impenetrability of the interloping Mongolian word. Shamanism in this example is doing something, or exercising a capacity to do something. Again, the least helpful starting point is 'shaman as role'.

Is there a philological connection between *base-* and *paye*? Phonetically it is a reasonable shift. But a threads and patches knowledge of Amerindian languages could guess forever about connections of this kind. There are no Amerindian equivalents of Sanskrit to help us towards an *Ur-sprache* and it is unlikely that Amazônia will have its Grimm's Law or its Verner's Law to show closer connections. 'The woods decay, the woods decay and fall.' There were no texts before Cabral and prehistory in Amazônia was fatally organic.

The point is not to deny that there can be specialist roles. Of course there can. The point is to loosen up the distinctions in our thought between the role (shaman), the quality (shamanism), the attribute (shamanistic), and the act (shamanizing), and to allow an easy passage between them. It requires flattening out those insistent salients of noun, adjective, and verb which have become so established in our thought, and allowing the conception of quality a proper freedom to move between them. This is not difficult to do if we retrace the steps.

It was Plato who first distinguished the noun and the verb, *onoma*, 'that of which some action or condition was predicated', and *rhema*, 'what was predicated of it': 'For this reason Greek adjectives which are formally akin to nouns (and were later grouped with them), were treated by Plato as *rhemata* since they could be used as predicates' (Robins 1951: 17–18). Aristotle continued to treat the adjective as a member of the verb class 'because it can fulfil a similar logical function as predicate, although there is no such thing as tense in the Greek adjective . . . ' (23). Robins suggests that in not isolating the adjective Aristotle failed to go far enough. But our problem lies in the opposite

direction: noticing that these grammatical distinctions have ontological and epistemological consequences that create difficulties for us.
When Edward Hussey is discussing the forces at work in Anaximander's *kosmoi*, forces that were later to be called 'the opposites' – the
hot, the cold, the wet, the dry – he notes: 'These were conceived of
neither precisely as substances nor precisely as qualities, these distinctions being post-Socratic' (1972:20). The noun / predicate distinction *is part of* the substance / quality distinction. Whereas from a strict
grammarian's point of view, Robins accuses Aristotle of not making
his distinctions firm enough, Hussey sees Aristotle's attempts to
interpret the pre-Socratics in his more precise terms as an example of
conceptual anachronism: being a victim of that interpretative pitfall
which imposes precision on a matter that was expressed vaguely.
And if Aristotle can stumble into that kind of anachronism when
looking back over a couple of centuries of his own language, the
dangers are far greater for our interpretative forays into the language
and thought of a more inaccessible, unwritten tradition.

These comments on Plato and Aristotle show how adjectives and
verbs are joined in the notion of *rhemata*, predicates. Hussey's point
suggests that if we look at the pre-Socratics we can loosen up the
noun / predicate distinction too. The key is in W. A. Heidel's essay
'Qualitative change in Pre-Socratic Philosophy' which 'had revol-
utionary implications when it first appeared in 1906' and which
'remains profoundly suggestive to this date' (Mourelatos 1974:5).

The main point of Heidel's essay is to challenge the textbook view
that pre-Socratic philosophy conceived reality as *one* in its underlying
arche (Thales said it was water, Anaximenes – air, Heraclitus – fire, for
example), and *many* in its modifications or alterations (Mourelatos
ibid.). This is not the point here. What is interesting for this argument
is the way he deals with the notion of quality:

> The question at issue is . . . whether primitive man conceived of
> qualities as abstract, or as material constituents or ingredients of
> things . . . When Shakespeare said 'Youth's a stuff will not
> endure', he used an expression that is true to primitive notions,
> as we meet them in such statements as that in *Proverbs* 27,22
> 'Though thou shouldest bray a fool in a mortar among wheat
> with a pestle, yet will not his foolishness depart from him'. Here
> folly is evidently thought of as an admixture, like the soul accord-
> ing to Epicurus, a *soma leptomeres par holon to athroisma paresparme-*
> *non* [Mourelatos 1974 gives this as a 'body of fine parts which is
> scattered throughout the whole aggregate (*athroisma*)'].
>
> (Heidel 1906:343)

This is followed by a fascinating footnote:

> It may not be out of place at this point to suggest that the notion of
> qualities 'inhering' in substances is probably a 'survival' of the
> conception of a quality, viewed as a physical constituent present

in an *athroisma* [a 'whole aggregate'] ... The primitive notion of a thing is that it 'contains' certain qualities, the point of view being purely physical. The logical or psychological view is that a quality is one of the 'meanings' of a 'thing', both 'thing' and 'meanings' being constructs growing out of certain interests directed to the realization of ends. On this view 'inherence' is meaningless and constitutes no problem. But in the transition from the physical to the psychological conception of qualities and things, a blending of the two points of view took place. The general stock of like 'stuff' of which a thing partakes in virtue of containing that quality, is converted into an Idea, half abstract and half concrete; and at once there arises the problem of relating the Ideas among themselves. This problem was to be solved only by a complete abandonment of the physical point of view with its implications.

(1906:346 note 28)

Coming in 1906, four years before Lévy-Bruhl's *Les Fonctions Mentales dans les sociétés inférieures* this is a useful direction to take. Like Lévy-Bruhl's work, this is trying to chart the distance between our thought and theirs, but unlike Lévy-Bruhl it covers the distance in such a way that we can cross it: by progressively dismantling our distinctions. This is a more productive line of inquiry than looking for a *different* kind of thought, a *pre*-logical mentality, a primitive or a savage mind.

By thinking of qualitative predicates *as if* they were substances, we can better understand the relation between the fool and his folly, that is, be better able to move between folly, the fool, foolish, and acting foolishly; between shamanism, the shaman, shamanistic, and shamanizing. The change in grammar leads to a change in thinking in the following way: thinking of shamanism primarily as a matter of role or office ('the shaman') makes it primarily a matter of defining exclusive boundaries between people – who is a shaman and who is not. As with all physical, logical, or semantic boundaries, the problem is how to decide what to include and what to exclude. I have given ethnographic illustrations of the kind of obscurity this leaves us with. Thinking of shamanism primarily as a quality or attribute allows another way in. The problem is not *difference* but *alteration*, not categories of people, but changes people undergo. This includes both moving from one quality to its opposite (from hot to cold, from being shamanistic to not being shamanistic), and the passage through states of a serial order, or better, degrees of intensity: being more or less shamanistic. And Heidel's suggestion that we should think of such a quality as a material constituent, an ingredient, is an image that makes this comprehensible. When appropriate we can make the transition between quality and role effortlessly: 'All aspects are within us, And who seems most kingly is the king.' The role follows from the quality.

Our indurated grammatical distinctions predispose an approach to *paye*:

as a role or office;

where an individual has certain knowledge (which others don't have) or certain powers (which others don't have);

which enables that individual to do certain things that have an effect on others.

Breaking up these distinctions suggests approaching *paye*:

as a quality;

which inheres in living things (there being no distinction between animate and inanimate);

in varying degrees.

Amongst human beings, different people can have a lot of it or a little of it, can have it for a time and lose it again, can have none of it at all, or be renowned as a specialist in its practice.

IMAGENS:
anyang, yarr, and *moyo*

And bogies, and serpents, and crows
Andrew Lang, 'Double Ballade of
Primitive Man'

In this chapter *paye* will be fleshed out with various related images all
of which have to do with the themes of illness, death, and birth
precautions ('the couvade'). First, this is the way the men talk about
being *paye*.

I

'We', the Brazilian Wayãpí have heard the Kamarara-ko, the French
Wayãpí, describe *paye* amongst their neighbours on the Oyapoque
known as the Emerillon. The Emerillon make it very easy to be *paye*.
They get drunk; they ingest tobacco juice; then they fall down in a
faint. Then other *paye* arrive and blow smoke on them. Then they see
everything. In contrast to this it is not easy for Wayãpí to be *paye*. It
takes a long time. When the Wayana are *paye* they clap their hands.
The Kamarara-ko have rattles /marari̱/. These are made of beads
nowadays. In the old days we had rattles too.

Moyo (anaconda) is *paye*, and it is moyo who teaches us to be *paye*.
When we are *paye* we have mirrors for our eyes and we see *moyo* not as
a snake but as a man. One person says 'I have often seen the snake but
never the man.' There are also men like us inside the various trees:
sumauma, angelim. These are *yarr*.

To be *paye* you've first got to be ill. While you're ill a *paye* Wayãpí
comes and blows smoke on you until you're better. From then on
moyo and tree *yarr* blow smoke on you for one month, or perhaps two,
until you're better. You must stay in your hammock as much as you
can. You mustn't get drunk. You mustn't have sex.

They ask: 'Are there any *paye*-people in your place?' No, I say,
none at all. 'Your people fuck a lot then.' Exaggerated giggling all
round.

It's very bad if infant children come near you, not that there is any danger to the children, but children are annoying. So are dogs. For this reason it is good to go and stay in a shelter away from the village. Then dogs and children will not come about you. If dogs come about you, *anyang* will kill you.

You stay in the shelter / tòkai / (c.f. Brazilian *tocaia*) for as long as possible:

   no game to eat – only inambu (a bird);
   no fish to eat – except trahirão and pirasisi; (or alternatively, most fish are all right to eat – certain ones such as surubim and piranha are not);
   no beiju (manioc bread) that's burnt – only white beiju – beiju made from tapioca is especially good;
   no carrying a gun when you are walking;
   no killing game.

When you are away in the shelter all sorts of / anyaŋ / come. Tapir, queixada, jaguar, armadillo, monkey, anteater, blue butterfly, urubu, eagle. They don't come as animals, they come as us. We ask: 'Who are you?' They answer: 'I'm tapir', 'I'm anteater'. That's the way we know who they are. They address us as 'grandchild'. We call them 'grandfather'. 'What's wrong, grandchild?' they ask. 'I'm ill. Blow smoke on me.' If you see *anyang* in your dreams you are slightly *paye*. (The sequence of this last point could be: 'If you are slightly *paye* you see *anyang* in your dreams.')

   Yarr come. They bring mirrors for your eyes. (One person said you have mirrors in your chest and back as well as in your eyes.) You can see *yarr*: sumauma, angelim, pau mulatto, / yapu-kuriwa /, and / wira-popemo / (all these are trees). *Takoro-yarr* (master of stone) too, a horrible person, and *moyo*. Women come too. We fuck them. They are young and beautiful with firm breasts. They have beads. If you wake in the morning with an ejaculation all over your loin-cloth you are no longer *paye*. The sperm should have gone into the woman to make her pregnant. The child stays with you, inside you. One man said: 'I have a lot of them inside me now. You also see that I don't wear beads. I don't want them. I have *anyang* beads inside me right now.' You sing when you are in the shelter, but only at night. If you sing during the day *anyang* might kill you. 'What do you sing?' 'I sing sumauma. I sing angelim'.

When you are *paye* you are given / ōpiwanë /. They are *anyang*. They are like pets. You have them inside you. 'I have / ɨg̈-ò / (caterpillar).' People who are not *paye* don't have any. Yanuari, the crippled man, has '/ pè'in, pè'iiiin /' (one, *one*, i.e., very very few). He lost the mirrors for his eyes after that fall from a tree when he broke his back.

Kasiripinar was given *ompiwan* only for a month. He lifted game and so lost his very quickly. After you have become *paye* you can go out and kill game but it has to be lifted and carried home by someone else. If you pick up game *paye* will finish. Also you mustn't walk too much if the sun is hot. If you get drunk you will lose your *ompiwan*. They will just go off. Your *ompiwan* finish when you die, but this is not always the case.

Some people at the Nipukú said that they were afraid of the abandoned village site at Kumakarɨğ (Agua Preta) beause Taèa, who was *paye*, died there, and his *ompiwan* are still there. Kaniyar, also *paye*, died in the now-abandoned settlement just across the water from the present site at Nipukú:

'/ iyɨ   èrōpi̧wanë   i-ka̧to /' said Kaniyar when he died.
I   my *ompiwan*   good

However, months later a man from another settlement, who is *paye*, arrived and said 'Kaniyar's *ompiwan* are still here', so he danced in a shelter and sent them away.

There was a spell at the Nipukú when there was a lot of illness about, coughs, fevers, an infectious skin complaint (called *coruba* by the Brazilians). This was when the tiny team of surveyors from the road had almost reached the Nipukú river, many miles downstream from the settlement. No one had visited the village for many weeks, not since a family had returned from the FUNAI post with the Nipukú's first chickens. Sirò had been off for a couple of days downstream on a fishing expedition, but he said he saw nothing of the Brazilians. The various causes suggested for the general malaise were:

(1) We had all brought it back after a visit to the post many months before. (2) Sirò brought it up from Ɨto-wasu – he got it from the Brazilians – he was lying when he said he didn't see them. (3) Sirò brought it – he got it from the Brazilians – it's true he didn't see them, but it got to him on the wind – he was close to them. (4) It came straight here on the wind from the Brazilians. (5) It's the hens that are responsible.

Then a visitor arrived. Of all the Wayápí he was the person most respected on account of *paye*. Commenting on the lingering illnesses he said that there were numerous *anyang* about. They were / ta̧poro /, maggots. It was the Aparai Indians from downstream on the Rio Jarí who had sent them. (The Wayana on the upper Parú and the Kamarara-ko on the Oyapoque have also sent *anyang* from time to time. *Paye* people can tell who has sent them because they ask them 'Who are you?' 'I'm Aparai', they answered this time.) Two days after his arrival he said that he had now driven them away at night in his dreams by blowing smoke on them. He also announced that there were lots of (or perhaps 'a great deal of') *moyo* in the water, a point frequently taken up and reiterated by others during and after his visit, although he did not claim to have taken any action against that. What was the nature of these maggots? *Anyang* maggots are *like* real maggots but they are not. They are / amo-ro /.

Yanuari, who used to be *paye* but lost the gift after he broke his back, has a chronic pain in his foot. It is *amoro* sent by *paye* Kamarara-ko. Sometimes shooting stars are said to be *amoro* on their way from one people to another. (Usually at the Nipukú they were said to be on their way from the Kamarara-ko in French Guiana over our heads to the Aparai downstream on the Jarí.)

A single shooting star is said to be a star dying or a star shedding its skin. You can find these skins in the forest. They are semi-transparent, crispy, spherical bladders about an inch across. I thought they were the seed of some plant.

/ ōpiwanë /, / amo-ro / and / anyaŋ / need translations. I have taken the form / ōpiwanë / from numerous examples where I have variously noted / ōpiwanë / and / ōpiwarë /. / -wanë / could be a 'people' suffix, though Wagley and Galvão give *piwara* in Tenetehara, a language closely related to Wayãpí, as 'spirits of animals' (1969: 104ff). / amo / means 'other', 'a different thing', / amo-ro / could be a way of saying, in the appropriate context, 'something of another kind'. But these are guesses. All three notions, together with the notion of / yarë /, shift around within the context of *paye*. At the time, I thought of this gamut of concepts as follows:

yarr: anthropomorphic entities which inhabit trees, rocks, water.

ompiwan: zoomorphic entities, usually insects of some kind, which are an indication of someone's state of *paye*. Owning *ompiwan* means that one has the power of *paye*.

amoro: a physical substance, like a sherd or a splinter, which can be directed against someone like firing a stone from a catapult. It can also take zoomorphic form like *ompiwan*.

anyang: Cognate terms are found in related languages and the translation in other ethnographies is usually given in a straightforward way as supernatural beings or spirits which inhabit the woods. Certainly when we are travelling and there is a sudden unexplained noise in the woods, someone might say '*anyang*', but I don't think the term refers to a specific being, in the manner of our word 'the devil'. I think it is elastic enough to include both entity and quality, as if it could bundle up in one term something like our words 'ghost' and 'ghostly'. *Anyang* can be both something and the quality of something; 'there are *anyang* about' and 'I have *anyang* beads inside me'.

Clearly *paye* and *anyang* overlap, but the second term shifts and changes. *Anyang* is certainly not a catch-all term for any invisible being. There are plenty of those around:

/ yurupari / is not *anyang*. The word refers to something dangerous and invisible that lives in the forest and that can attack us. At the end of a small spree, Kuyuri, who had retired to his house some time previously, startled the village by firing his shotgun. He had seen *yurupari* and shot the gun so that it would be afraid and go away. But then he hadn't exactly *seen* it. He'd seen it *inside*, like a dream. One of the explanations offered for Tora's death, described above, was that *yurupari* had killed him.

/ miyara-rowiyŭ / (literally, 'game-big', 'animals' chief') also live in the forest. The most obvious sense is something like 'monsters'. Someone said they were black, hairy men. Their beards fall down over their mouths and they have to lift up these beards to eat. They have lots of black hair all over them. They are not *anyang*.

/ tamòkò / (not / tamoko /), grandfather-people) is another dangerous being of the forest. Only two are left now. They live in the ground, away down. Their wives all died. Only men are still alive. / tamòkò / is not *anyang*.

Thunder gets anthropomorphic recognition as / tupan /. Tupan has lightning under his armpits. He lifts his arm and there's a flash. Tupan is not *anyang*.

Yanuari told a story about his elder brother, Mòyikosi, who had died some years previously. Once, when Mòyikosi was ill he met a person in his dreams called / Pè-tã-tõ /. This person made a point of saying, 'I'm not *anyang*. It's just me – Pè-tã-tõ.' He had blue-green beads on his wrist and he blew tobacco smoke on Mòyikosi who later became *paye* and could see *anyang*.

Anyang is clearly not a general term referring to all these invisible creatures and people.

When I asked, 'What is *anyang*?', a spontaneous answer was '/ takoro yarë anyan /', 'stone-*yarr* is *anyang*', and this was described as a horrible maleficent being with huge teeth. It was added that 'a long time ago *takoro-yarr* died' (this sounds like a myth fragment) and that it is only other *anyang* that are left nowadays. However, *anyang* you see when you are *paye* is not stone-*yarr*. You see *sumauma-yarr, angelim-yarr*. Tree-*yarr* are good.

/ kumaka-yarë òmòwɨyɨ	tòkai	pupè	karaɨğ	tòpe'a /
sumauma-yarr to cause to come down	shelter	inside	fever	in order to remove

You make *sumauma-yarr* come down into the shelter to take the fever away.

Leaving aside stone-*yarr, anyang* seems to refer to all those invisible creatures and things associated with *paye*. Pè-tã-tõ, in that dream, was a human being, therefore not *anyang*. 'Anyang come' refers to those normally invisible people with animal names. Also our *ompiwan* are *anyang*, as are *amoro* sent by other *paye* people. People like ourselves (Wayãpí, Wayana, Brazilians) can be *paye*, but we cannot be *anyang*.

Visible animals and trees can be *paye* because of the *yarr* that inhabit them, but the visible animals and trees are not *anyang*. The invisible *yarr* are, however, *anyang*. *Anyang* is the invisible part of *paye*.

Because these images are talked about so much, they are obviously 'vivid' in the sense of *lively*. But we would have to be careful how we attribute to Wayápí people a graphic or pictorial vividness, the imagistic precision, say, of a fairy-tale illustration of a unicorn or a gnome. Whenever we talk of devils and angels, of fairies and dragons, we so easily take for granted an immense history of representations from graven images to Arthur Rackham; but what does it mean to ask about a shared image, a collective representation (in the pictorial sense of the phrase) in a community that, apart from a handful of geometric designs, makes no images of anything whatsoever and whose access to images is almost non-existent? George Steiner mentions the impossible demands made by the notion of the Hebraic God of the Old Testament which declares itself as something which cannot be perceived, cannot be conceived, and which must not be represented. The Christian incorporation of this tradition relaxes these fierce exigencies in all sorts of ways, through 'God the Son', through 'the Holy Mother', and through the traditions of religious art which 'allowed scope for the pluralistic, pictorial needs of the psyche' (Steiner 1971: 36 38). But if the Mosaic God transcends images, requiring that the accompaniment of pictorial representation be dispensed with, what are we to make of notions where pictorial representation is not even a possibility? It is easier for us to think in terms of 20th century theological discussions than it is to try to understand a state of affairs where we would have to divest ourselves altogether of an imaginative life fed by pictures. How appropriate it is, then, that *anyang* refers to that which is, in the ordinary course of events, invisible, and that you only see *anyang* when you are *paye*.

'When you are *paye* you get mirrors / waròa / for your eyes.' Wearing small square mirrors on one's chest during a spree is not connected with *paye* – or rather people said it wasn't. If it is some kind of play-acting of *paye*, no one was willing to say so or make the connection in any way. They say they learned the custom from the Wayana and it is now part of a man's full dress for a spree, along with beads, a comb stuck in one's hair, and a long loin cloth. (Women don't wear mirrors.) I think there may well be notions about mirrors which I missed or which people didn't get round to revealing. When Kasiripinar returned from his trip to Belém I heard him describe a truck to his friends. He described how high it was, how the *yarr* (master) sat so high up inside it (just as tree-*yarr* do, actually), looking down at you, and how you had to climb up into it beside the driver. (Is there *yarr* inside it? was the first question he was asked when he begun his description.) I thought he might describe the interior with all the gadgets, or perhaps the driver at work with the steering wheel and the gears, but he went straight to talking of the driving mirror 'to see behind'. His audience gave one of those glottal gasps of astonishment.

It would be easy to improvise a little rhapsody here and say that mirrors are 'magical' or 'symbolic' items which suggest shamanism, hence men wear them on their chests (and one person did say that when you are *paye* you have them in your eyes, chest, and back), and that the reason one has mirrors for one's eyes is that one can 'see inside' as Kuyuri was said to have seen Yurupari. But such connections would be factitious. Nevertheless, I think 'mirrors for your eyes' does emphasize the change in vision that goes along with becoming *paye*, where we are allowed to see things not visible to us in the ordinary course of events. Actual mirrors need not have an intrinsic association with *paye*. What is curious is that the contrast between what is visible in the ordinary course of events and what is visible only to someone who is *paye* makes *paye* a visual watershed, giving an exclusive access to a way of seeing amongst people who have no pictorial images or representations.

Saying that you get mirrors for your eyes when you are *paye* does not make actual mirrors into *paye* objects. But there is an obscurity about identity and difference in other contexts. When *anyang* creatures blow smoke on you, tapir, queixada, jaguar, and so on, they come not as animals but as us. Does 'Tapir comes' mean 'a man calling himself by the name 'tapir' comes' or 'tapir comes in the form of a man?' Do the creatures we see in ordinary life have an intrinsic connection with those which appear in the contexts of *paye* and *anyang* or are they just used as emblems in a different looking-glass world? The anaconda is shamanstic, but did I shoot a shamanistic creature or just an ordinary creature? When Kasiripinar heard *moyo*'s whistle in Belém he said 'not *that* anaconda [the actual one] but the *other*'. He had often seen the snake but never the man. What is the nature of the connection between the snake and the man?

Initially this does not seem a difficult question. Children's stories that personify animals, and works such as *Animal Farm*, don't present us with a conceptual problem of identity and difference. In these fables animals stand for something other than that which they are in everyday existence. The simplest way to take it, then, is to say that there is no vital connection between the creatures we ordinarily see, and the *anyang* and *paye* creatures: 'Not *that* [visible] anaconda but the *other* [invisible *moyo*].' The connection is not some kind of shape changing, where creatures turn into something else. It is a figurative connection where real creatures are made to stand for *paye* and *anyang* beings. But while this distinction is clear to us it does not seem to be so clear from what they say and do.

As an example, there was a further unpleasant detail in the incident when I shot the anaconda (see p. 82 above). The wounded creature hid beneath a deep bank and we left it. Returning the same way a few hours later, we saw that the snake had disappeared. But it had regurgitated a partially digested *jacaré* (cayman, like a small alligator), which was lying in the shallow water. Back at the village, when Yanuari heard this part of the story he commented: 'Ha! *Moyo* was angry with his stool and ate it.' Explaining this, it was said that *jacaré* is anaconda's stool, hence the anaconda is *jacaré's yarr*, owner or master. Anaconda sits on *jacaré*, just as when we are *paye* we sit on a *jacaré* stool. These are typical of comments that refer to a large reservoir of mythy associations, including narratives about *moyo* and details about *paye*, which are revealed only through these fitful allusions.

There are two points here. First, looking for an interpretation *either* in terms of a vital connection where everyday creatures are the *paye*-beings in another form *or* in terms of a figurative connection where one only stands for the other, is pushing a logical insistence too far. What is required is a tolerance for ambiguity and vagueness where we will learn not to force an either-or question like this and to appreciate a 'both is and is not' answer. There is an association between animals and *paye*-beings. That association neither means that they are the 'same thing' nor that one just 'stands for' the other. There is no need to force a choice between literal and metaphorical, between actual and symbolic. We will have to do without such distinctions. Of course, logical insistence can produce a logical contradiction and force a 'not this but that' answer. I did that by pursuing the question about *which* anaconda we were hearing in the Belém street, forcing an impatient response, '*Not* those in the pit, but the *other*'. But what have I done in eliciting a response like this? I've scored a point for our logic, but I've violated the vagueness of their thought.

Calling it 'vagueness' is not a matter of poverty of detail. The examples given here, as well as those in the myths they tell, show an abundance of lively, intricate, and vivid images. By 'vagueness' I mean to indicate the failure of our logical typologies of discriminable kinds of relation – identity, difference, opposition, contrast, complementarity, symmetry, and so on – to give a plausible account of the imaginative associations that are described here. To force a distinction between literal and metaphorical, or between actual and symbolic, clarifies nothing. It is more profitable to approach these associations as irreducible. It's not a matter of explaining them, but of locating them. And what they are doing is connecting the phenomenal world to an imaginative background of mythy narratives and *paye* beliefs.

This is the second point. It seems that the everyday world is a fathomless source of associations with mythical narratives, some intricate, some fragmentary. There is a great deal of just-so stuff in these narratives which mention the origins of this or that, how we learned this or that, why this or that is the case; but to insist that the primary function of these narratives is to explain things would be contrived. The explanations are casual and random. The most obvious activity taking place is not so much explaining ('and *that*'s why the anaconda ate the *jacaré*') but reminding ('that incident reminds me of a mythy detail where *moyo* ate its stool'). Mnemonics are everywhere. There is a certain liana, quite abundant, which goes by the name of 'Japu's snot' (the *japu* is a bird). The connection is an incident in a narrative where Japu is found up a tree sobbing, its snot running down to the ground. Jacamin's back feathers are grey because Winame (*anambé, cotinga*) pushed him into the ashes of the fire when they had an argument. Winame has a purple throat because Jacamin pushed him and spilled pink kara-beer down his front. Tapir has a curly tail because it tried to climb up the chain of arrows that Armadillo made to the sky. The chain broke, Tapir fell, hence the curly tail (and Armadillo, who also fell, had his head pushed back into his shell). Toucan sings 'pinò kɨt kɨt kɨt'; when grandfather-people were stealing fire they wondered what to carry it in and Toucan sang. It means / pinò kɨrè / – a carrying basket / kɨrè / of bacaba leaves / pinò /. And so on. The allusion recalls a fragment of a fuller narrative of which everyone will know the salient points.

It is tempting to think of a 'set' of myths, a closed cycle, which, if one stayed long enough, one could exhaust. But it is not really like this. There certainly is an enormous number of stories, or rather the hidden reservoir is far more extensive than the parts of it I know. (It kept on appearing in unexpected places, on those occasions for instance when I'd suspect that a statement or a name was a mythy mnemonic and ask about it, or when a long story would be told incorporating two or three stories that other narrators had previously told separately.) But there is no closed cycle of myths. Sirò and Teyo knew more than anyone, but Waiwai knew a few that they didn't. There were many other people who could each recite a few, but everyone still listened attentively and asked questions when Sirò or Teyo told another. I suspect, though, that since there are no old people and since the numbers have dwindled so much, a great deal has been forgotten and lost.

The connections between the imaginative lore and the phenomenal world are made constantly, but that does not mean that the phenomena are confused with the lore. The existence of the actual anaconda animates the beliefs about *paye*-anaconda, but that does not mean that the anaconda we see *is paye*-anaconda. In an everyday context it clearly is not. (It is not seen in the form of a man; we are not in a *paye* state with mirrors for our eyes.) But since the invisible *paye* anaconda is equally real, this huge writhing emblem of it which we see makes a very forceful connection with the notion of *paye*. In this sense the anaconda *is paye*. Fiddling with the verb 'to be' is a way of maintaining that ambiguity about identity and difference. As I understand it, that vagueness is a characteristic that has to be accepted, not resolved into firmer schematisms.

When considering *paye* we must further suspend a moral distinction. *Paye* is neither good nor bad. This is much easier for us than doing without the logical distinction is/is not, the semantic distinction literal/metaphorical, or the grammatical distinction *onoma / rhema*. Since we hold on to our other distinctions so forcefully, it is odd that the moral one should be so easily slipped off. I suppose we are more comfortable with moral ambiguity and moral vagueness. *Paye* is a notion like 'force' or 'strength', like 'having power' or 'having influence', and however potent it may be, we easily allow of such a notion that it is neither inherently good nor inherently evil.

People who are *paye* are accredited with special knowledge and special powers of seeing. They can call game or see where it is. Those who first made contact with the Cuc Wayãpí knew where to go because they were *paye*. I never knew anyone claim to exercise the capacity in contexts such as these. I saw *paye* done only in connection with illness and death. *Paye* is both held to save lives and blamed for death. It is exercised by blowing smoke. A short *paye* session went like this:

Tenetí's infant daughter had been ill for some time. When the visitor who was *paye* arrived he was asked to do something about the child's illness. He asked a number of questions about symptoms and times, then asked Tenetí:

'What have you killed recently?'

'Nothing.' [But he had killed at least one toucan].

'What have you been eating?'

'Only sweet tubers, / yi-tïg /.' [But he has recently eaten *caititu*, a kind of peccary, and *trahirão*, a fish].

The visitor began to blow tobacco smoke on the child. He and Tenetí keep up a dialogue of statement and repetition, first the visitor making the statements 'May she . . . ' and Tenetí repeating, then the other way round.

'May she get well.' 'Yes, may she get well.'

'May she not cry.'

'May she drink her mother's milk' . . .

The visitor then announced:

'Tree-*yarr* have seen.'

'May they not see.'

'May she get well.' And so on.

It was a short session, five or ten minutes. The father held the child. The mother looked on but was not asked any questions and did not take any part.

Blowing tobacco smoke can just as well be maleficent. When Kasiripinar and I returned from our visit to Belém, he announced apropos of nothing in particular that, while there, he had been angry with the Brazilians. He would have liked to have blown smoke on them. Why? Because he saw them walking hand-in-hand and kissing in public. That had made him angry. Although he did not claim to be *paye*, 'blowing smoke' was a turn of phrase that illustrated his anger.

Those who are *paye* are specialists in causal explanations about illness; they know who is to blame. Those who are not *paye* 'don't see', 'don't know'. The curious aspect of this is that the person who is *paye* is the one most responsible for appealing to *paye* as the significant cause of illness and for finding other people to blame. The coughs and mycosis would have been left to the Brazilians, the wind, or the hens had not the *paye* visitor come along to say it was Aparai *paye* who were responsible.

Towards the end of my stay I decided that before returning to Britain I should try to visit the Oyapoque and see the Kamarara-ko. As it turned out, I couldn't, but when I first announced the plan at Nipukú, many people told me the names of those I must look out for, particularly those who were close relatives. When the man renowned for being *paye* heard of the plan he first said that if I go to the Oyapoque I must tell them not to send any more *anyang* here. 'When did they last send *anyang*?' I asked. 'They don't send *anyang* now. They don't know we're here. They think we're all dead.' This started off a crescendo of common opinion that I should not go to the Oyapoque at all.

Paye heals and saves, and also kills. A person who claims to be *paye* and who is accredited with the quality can be used and can be blamed. I saw only two tobacco-blowing sessions and I know of only one instance where an individual within the Brazilian Wayãpí was overtly accused of a person's death. It would therefore be rash to guess how *paye* accusations are related to tensions and rivalries within a settlement or to settlements breaking up and people moving away. But it seems improbable that an accusation could occur within a community and that community remain together. Accusations are best made from a distance.

As if inviting accusations, the best-known *paye* man lived apart from the settlements over on the east side. Just as those who are expert with *paye* are expert at making accusations, so this man's withdrawal would give *paye* more scope. For all its power to cure, *paye* is an anti-social business that deals with disruptions and death. Those most renowned for possession of the quality are the people most responsible for confirming and perpetuating it. In exercising its curing capacity they reaffirm its place as something to be blamed for misfortune. Furthermore, I would guess that in the ordinary course of things '*paye* killed' as an explanation of someone's death would go on to identify an accused person. There are a number of stories of killings in the past, almost all of them accusations against Cuc and Oyapoque Wayãpí killing one of 'us', which the FUNAI people took to be murder but which were *paye* accusations. In Wayãpí terms of blaming there is, of course, no difference between murder and *paye* killings.

II

When adults fall ill and die, if *paye* is going to be blamed for the misfortune, it is usually *paye* of other people that is said to be respon- sible. But illness and death of babies implicates not *paye* of people but of *yarr* and ultimately of *moyo* (anaconda). The sequence of causes may not be pushed as far as *moyo*. In explaining a particular death some people were satisfied with statements such as 'it just died' or 'it died of fever'. Others blamed the parents for negligence – 'letting the baby get too much sun'. Explanations that appeal to *yarr* and *moyo* involve the restrictions that parents of newborn children have to observe. If the parents break these rules *yarr* or *moyo* will harm the baby. Birth precautions are therefore precautions against *paye* of *yarr* and *moyo*.

Two words that appear in this context are / òyikoako / and / i'ŭ /. (/ ŭ / in this simplified transcription is the same as English 'ung' in 'sung'.) I found it difficult to translate / òyikoako / and simply used 'to couvade'. The word first appeared in answer to the question: 'Why does a man stay in his house when his child is newly born?' The answer was:

/ òyikoako	wakïriŋgwèrë	adyawïi	nòpòsikòi /
he couvades	child	therefore	doesn't work

Pierre Grenand told me by letter that this should be written / òyikoa- kowa /; that / -wa / belongs to the verb; and that it should be rendered 'ceux qui font le couvade'.

When I indicated that I didn't know the word, an old man who spoke no Portuguese said it meant 'not eating anything'. The best Portuguese speaker offered '*fica deitado na rede*', he stays lying down in his hammock; but 'to fast' and 'to stay in one's hammock' were descriptions of what was going on rather than translations of the term.

> Yamaira was a man of the most gentle and amiable demeanour who found questions baffling. When asked anything his usual response was a long, slow, silent smile, or else a languid bout of giggling. I had been treating his wife who was recovering from fever and I asked him at one point if she were up and about yet. 'No, she's staying in her hammock today.' 'Oh', I said ' /òyi-

koako/?' He thought this was enormously amusing. 'Yes, /òyi-koako poaŋ/ – she couvades the medicine.' One couvades something. Here as a joke it was the medicine, but in proper use one couvades the child.

/òyikoako/ only refers to staying in one's hammock at birth time, not to illness or laziness, and it only refers to men. For the first few days after the birth, the woman remains /ò-si/ (shy, withdrawn), and after that /ò'au kurinyonte/ (she just lies in her hammock). /ò-si/ also refers to a woman staying in her hammock while menstruating. It also refers to men when, for example, they are visiting another village:

> When you arrive you go directly to a house and stay there. You don't walk about. You are /ò-si/. When you are like this you don't laugh, you don't feel friendly. You might laugh in the house, but if you came out and went to join the circle of men sitting round the fire you would not say anything.

Asking if a man was /ò-si/ at the birth of his child received the answer: 'No, /òyikoako kurinyonte/, he just couvades.'

I thought it would be delightful if /òyikoako/ were related to /omoako/ 'causing something to be hot', which refers to a bird sitting on top of eggs, that is, an exact equivalent of the French *couver* from which the word *couvade* is derived. (/ako/ means hot and /mo/ is a particle meaning 'to cause to be' or 'to cause to do'.) I decided the two forms had nothing to do with each other, but Pierre Grenand wrote to say that the word were (a) /-u-kwaku/, *couver* and (b) /ye-kwaku/, *la couvade*, and that the terms were also used for hens.

Inactivity is the first feature. Fasting, or at least being careful about what one eats, is the second. Waiwai told a story about Tapir and his elder brother Kosiporo, the *quatipuru* of Amazônia or the *serelepe* in standard Brazilian Portuguese. Interestingly, von Ihering mentions that in folk traditions of Brazilian Amazônia nursemaids used to invoke the *serelepe* to make children sleep since it was thought to be the sleepiest of all the animals. Mothers used to say: 'Acutipuru, impresta-me teu sono, para minha criança tambem dormir' (von Inhering 1968: 632): '*Quatipuru,* lend me your sleep so that my child too can sleep.' Waiwai's story went:

> When they had children Kosiporo couvaded. He ate nothing at all. He didn't even eat beiju. So Kosiporo was small and Tapir was big. Tapir ate everything.
> '/nèro-miti ta'i̱rowa/' 'Your little father [i.e., father's brother] is huge', said Kosiporo to the child.
> '/nòyikoakòi/' 'He doesn't couvade.'
> 'So he goes away over there.'
> Tapir was stamping hard on the ground. Tòk, tòk, tòk . . .
> That's the way he walked about.
> 'Why does papa-miti stamp around and you don't?' the child asked Kosiporo.

'/ iyɨ ayikoa̱ko kato̱ /' 'I couvade properly.'

'So I don't stamp around,' he said to the child.

He finished the story by pointing out that the *quatipuru* has a very thin stomach.

So far, then, a woman is 'reserved' or 'shy' for some time after the birth, as she is during menstruation. But that passes after a time and she simply goes on resting in her hammock. All the while, on the other hand, the man is couvading. He is couvading the child, and the two principal aspects of this are fasting and not moving around, like the *quatipuru* who is both sleepy and thin.

/ i'ŭ / is best translated as 'soul'. It is indicated by the heart beat, located by placing one's hand firmly under the sternum, by the pulse in whatever part of the body it can be seen or felt, and by one's shadow. (One's breath is not part of this notion. Breath is the same word as wind.) I don't have a word for 'body' although Coudreau's word list of 1892 has / ètè / for *corps* and Pierre Grenand says that the word is / l-è-tèkè /. It would be useful to have my own confirmation of this since it would be a *living* body / soul distinction. I only have a clear *corpse* / soul distinction: / tea̱ngwèrë / and / ta̱ɨgwèrë /. The first 'stays in the ground', the second 'goes to the sky'. I think, therefore, that / ta̱-ɨgwèrë / is the dead soul and / i'ŭ / the living soul. Questions about the difference between them always got the answer that they were 'the same thing'. (I mentioned previously that the rainbow is *moyo*'s / i'ŭ /.)

While hearing about the prohibition on hunting which a father is under after the birth of his child, I asked if that also applied before the birth. 'No, he can kill everything. It's only snakes that a man mustn't kill. The child will then lose its skin and die.' But a young man whose wife was due to give birth in July was bitten by a *jararaca* in June. He killed it. 'That's all right. He killed it because he was angry. It's only if you kill a lot of snakes that it's bad.' This example would do well as a paradigm of what a 'rule' looks like.

When Kasiripinar was making a canoe beside one of the main paths out of the village, that young man who killed the snake made a new path for himself that skirted the place where the canoe was being made. If he saw the canoe it would break on firing – the Wayana say so. (They say they learned canoe making from the Wayana). I was out one day in that direction with Waiwai, whose wife was also pregnant, and he suggested that the two of us go and have a look at Kasiripinar's canoe. Kasiripinar's wife is Waiwai's brother's daughter. The two of them do not get on well. When Kasiripinar heard about this he said '/ pa'i / [mother's brother] wants my canoe to break'.

I found no other indications of restrictions on behaviour before the birth. Indeed during the time Apeyawar's wife was pregnant, he decided to take his family on a long trip to the FUNAI post. They were away for a month and arrived back four days before his wife gave birth.

When a woman goes into labour, her husband constructs a small shelter in a secluded spot on the edge of the village. The woman will remain in that shelter for about two months. The seclusion is necessary, they say, because it is dangerous for her to be near the river. *Moyo* is there and would kill the child by carrying off its *i'ung*. The women of the village will attend the birth, but the father does not. He remains in his hammock for three or four days 'until the umbilical cord drops off', eating 'only a little *beiju*'. After that time he will go and see the child.

The morning Siriyan saw his child for the first time, he came back into the village and set off with his second wife to cross the river to his garden. I suspect had Siriyan been a more popular figure and had he been more attached to another family group he would have been able to loll around and would not have had to go to his garden like this. But he was one of the Wayãpí / yanerowiyŭ /, literally 'our big', and vigorously maintained his reputation with loud speeches, haranguing the village every morning, shouting about laziness and about 'those who had no ears', for all the world like a hell-fire Presbyterian minister. This is a good example of how the notion of 'chief' in the tropical forest does not fit easily into our word. Although Siriyan is one of those referred to as 'our big', that does not entail everyone fetching and carrying for him. His fierceness leaves him an isolated character. So he had to go to his garden, which inconveniently was on the other side of the river. Before going across he covered himself from head to foot with urucú (red arnotto dye) 'so that *moyo* won't *see* him'. Later, when he had returned, he explained further that *moyo* doesn't like his *smell* in that condition and had he not put on urucú, *moyo* would have come and killed him (above p. 83).

After the birth there are no noticeable changes in rhythm. The mother remains in the shelter; the father takes no part in any specific activity. Siriyan's household was kept going by the activities of his other wife. His trips to the garden were not 'to work' but simply 'to get manioc'. Both parents are said to be eating very little at this time although there are no specific prohibitions on any foods (yet from the *paye* session described previously it appears that when something goes wrong with the child, certain foods can be blamed).

A curious association is that if couvading people eat game killed with a new shotgun, the shotgun will break the next time it is used. Anything shot with a bow and arrow does not come under this restriction. This notion about shotguns is 'what the Wayana say', and I would assume that it accompanied the introduction of shotguns by way of contact with the Cuc people. A similar association is that couvading people should not eat anything killed by a young man (about ten to fifteen years old) since the youngster will then have a lot of / pane / (bad luck). A person of that age has not 'finished', that is, finished growing up.

Bathing in the river is the most obvious prohibition during this time. The father goes to the edge of the water, fills calabashes, and carries them back to a secluded spot where husband and wife wash each other and the child. If the father were to bathe by himself, *moyo* would kill the child. The father would also get 'dizzy' and he would die. If a mother and child were to bathe in the river, the same thing would happen. It is sometimes put that *moyo* kills the *i'ung* of the child. The child's *i'ung* does not go to the sky but is taken off to *moyo*'s place. It was stressed that the Wayana don't know this and that Wayana women have been seen taking their children to the river and bathing the child and themselves.

After about two months the woman moves back into her house. The bathing prohibition still stands and the man still cannot go hunting. The day after one young woman moved back into her house her husband announced that he was going to join his brother and myself on a day's hunting. It was quite all right for him 'to hunt' as long as he did not kill anything. (/ atɨ ata / means 'I'm going hunting' but has to do for 'I'm going for a walk' too. What else does one 'go for a walk' for?) What took place was the most graphic example of the father taking care, in Métraux's words, of 'the infant's clinging soul' (1949: 374). / i'ŭ òmòwɨg̈ /, lifting up the soul, is done by blowing rhythmically towards the ground and making scooping gestures with the hand. The child's soul is lifted over impedimenta on the path, like fallen trees or streams. If the child's soul gets left behind in the forest it will not be able to find its way home and the child, back in the village, will cry incessantly. If there are any *paye* trees near the path (*sumauma, angelim, pau mulatto*) the father will be warned and he will make a detour through the woods to avoid them. If he passes close to the tree, *yarr* will take the soul of the child and the child will die. When crossing the river, the soul of the child has to be lifted both to help it across and to protect it from *moyo*.

> A young child about three or four years old is trotting around the village by itself, trips and falls and lies howling. Its mother runs over, picks it up, and begins blowing towards the spot where the child fell, making the characteristic scooping gestures with her free hand. She is lifting up the soul. She also blows on the head of the screaming child as she carries it off. A short time later, the mother leaves the child screaming in the house, and returns alone to the spot to repeat the process of blowing and scooping. The child will not settle down because its soul is still not attached to it properly.

When we travel through the woods with a child of that age, it will be carried or allowed to trot along by itself for a short time. Whenever we leave camp in the morning, or whenever we set off from a spot where we have stopped to rest, the mother will lift up the child's soul. It does appear to be the case that as time goes on, care of the child's soul is more of a burden on the mother. Six months after the birth, when the father is freely bathing in the river, the mother, leaving the child in the house with someone else, will briefly approach the side of the river and wash herself quickly by dipping in a calabash and pouring the water over herself. Also youngsters are always 'clinging to their mothers' during these months.

There is only one firm chronological indicator in the process of taking care of the child's soul: / òyikoako / proper (when the man stays in his hammock, does not even see the child, and eats 'only a little *beiju*') ends after a few days 'when the umbilical cord drops off'. It is during this period that the mother is described as / ò-si /. Beyond this, it is not clear how it is decided that on a certain day the secluded mother and child may move back into the house, or that a man may begin hunting again, or that the bathing prohibitions are over. It would be particularly interesting, for instance, to find out when a father, out walking when his wife and child are left at home, need no longer lift the child's soul since it is no longer clinging to him. (The soul may still leave *the child*, of course, if it trips and hurts itself.)

There is another vague indicator of the end of the whole business:

Yanuari said that Tenetí (the father of an infant) would be able to go fishing again 'when the child is walking'. Waiwai immediately interrupted with: 'That's wrong. Tenetí could kill fish now if his child did not have fever.'

There are two points here. First, the criterion is usefully vague, allowing a fair latitude of application – a child that trots about the village will still be carried during journeys. Second, as Peter Rivière points out, 'the duration and intensity of the couvade vary according to the condition of the child' (1974: 428). Couvade behaviour can be relaxed and then reactivated when it is considered appropriate to do so. The vagueness in the phrase 'when the child is walking' indicates how couvade behaviour is seen as a process that gradually, and fitfully, attenuates. 'Walking' indicates a stage in the child's development when the elaborate care taken to keep its body and soul together is no longer necessary.

The idea of 'the infant's clinging soul' is a useful way of looking at the evidence but one should note that, in everyday practical terms, an expression of the idea that the infant's soul clings to its mother does not arise. The child *does* cling to its mother. A woman would not go off for the day leaving the child behind in the village. When the father does so, his protective role becomes dramatically obvious in the various ways he protects the child's soul from dangers.

So many of the circumstances of birth, child care, and sex roles (women do the child care; women don't go hunting) conduce to making sure that birth restrictions are well-articulated from a male point of view. The father says he is taking care, and is seen to be taking care. All the commentaries I make come from talking to

Wayápí men. The word /òyikoạko/ which I translate 'to couvade' describes what men do, not what women do. But the bathing prohibitions show that both father and mother have to observe restrictions to protect the child from maleficent influences, and that protecting the child's soul is not exclusively the father's concern. A point that confirms this is that exposing the child to dangers can have dangerous repercussions for both father and mother. Both can get 'dizzy' and die if *moyo* gets hold of the child.

On the matter of adverse effects coming on careless parents, Roque Laraia gives examples from the Urubu where the Indians say: 'Anything can happen to a man who does not observe the restrictions.' He mentions a case where two men, as well as the husband, observed birth restrictions since they both had had sexual relations with the woman in the period before her pregnancy. It was safer for the two men to take part in the restrictions even though it meant making the adultery public and 'provoking the consequent wrath of the deceived husband.' In another case, an Indian, almost in tears, admitted to Laraia a few moments before his child died of meningitis that he had killed a *queixada* and asked 'tem remédio?' (have you a cure?, i.e., for himself) (Laraia 1972: 79–80). Here again it is the conversation of men that is reported. My predicament is the same. I don't have women's comments on birth and birth restrictions. Reports about childbirth given by Indian men to male anthropologists are bound to leave something out.

The image that has emerged is of a vital connection between parents and child where restrictions are imposed on what the parents do, so that they will not activate baleful influences that will harm the child (and that can also harm them). The vulnerability of the child is that its soul is not properly attached to it. The vital connection between parents and child is that the child's soul is still attached to the parents. Lévy-Bruhl puts it that the couvade is an example of mystical participation between father and child (1926: 259ff). One can take that a lot further. Given the participation, it makes sense to see the process as getting the soul separated from the parents and properly attached to the child. Just as death is expressed as a separation of the soul from the body, life entails an incorporation of the loose soul. It is striking how appropriate the chronological markers are: the dropping off of the umbilical cord (which joined the child to its mother), and walking (the end of clinging). When the child is walking it is integrally alive.

To summarize so far:

(1) Strictly speaking /òyikoạko/ refers to the restrictions on the father's behaviour immediately following the baby's birth until the umbilical cord drops off.

(2) /òyikoạko/ is the extreme example of a pattern of restrained

behaviour required of the father for a number of months following the birth.

(3) / òyikoako / does refer only to men, not to women, and if it is translated as 'couvade' it should be remembered that this is only one aspect of more extensive attitudes to caring for the child that involve both parents.

(4) As Peter Rivière points out, the ideas behind birth precautions are instances of a widespread general conception of the dual nature of human beings – body and soul, physical and spiritual.

(6) The clinging, physical and spiritual, attenuates until the child is integrally alive. Concurrently, the restrictions on the parents' behaviour attenuate.

III

What is it about couvade precautions that make them seen odd to us? I want to return to the notion of *paye* by way of hunting prohibitions and bathing prohibitions. These are digressions that take in a number of ethnographic bits and pieces. The unifying theme is to show how *yarr, moyo*, and *paye* are always there in the background.

Looking at the hunting prohibitions I want to show (a) how a particular detail – the *inambu*, a bird – is used to make a general statement and (b) that lists, in this case lists of prohibited species, are ragged and decidedly not systematic. They too are secondary justifications of general statements.

A man whose wife has recently had a child cannot kill game – only *inambu* (a bird resembling, but not related to, the European partridge). When one is learning to be *paye* one can only eat *inambu*. When one is ill, one should not eat game (because the blood in the game is bad for you), but one can eat *inambu*. There's no blood in it. When one's wife is ill one should only kill *inambu*. These statements all came up spontaneously in various contexts and the first step in finding out why this bird is chosen was to check a list of animals and birds to discover what exactly was and was not prohibited. But lists are not offered spontaneously. They are, though, extremely easy to produce by going through one's own catalogue of birds and animals and asking for a yes or no answer. This is obviously unsatisfactory and to make the matter more difficult, different people produce different lists. Finally my catalogue of animals and birds is limited and it also turns out that what counts as 'food' or 'game' varies according to circumstances.

> For example I was told, 'We do not eat *čacā* [a species of hawk]; we do not eat *sòcò* [a kind of heron]. But during journeys when there was nothing else available I saw young men eat both these birds. One person said: 'We do not eat male spider money.' Another commented: 'It is just he who says that. I eat them. If you cut out the musk gland it's all right.' (Females are preferred, however. It

is often difficult to sex a spider monkey while hunting it, and there is obvious satisfaction when it is discovered that a female has fallen.)

Asking what it would be all right to kill without harming the child, a short list went:

toucan, but not arara (macaw);
jacamin (trumpeter), but not jacu or mutum;
spider monkey, but not howler monkey;
cariacu (small deer), but not / sò'ò / (large deer).
Some say queixada is all right, others say no.
There is a similar disagreement about tapir.

Another list gave the effect that killing the animal would have on the child.

jaguar	pain
tamandua (anteater)	grasps tightly, makes the child cry
howler monkey	bites
jacu	fever
aracua	fever
large deer	fever
macaco-prego (monkey)	bites
electric eel	gives shock
large sloth	pain
'burnt' (three-toed) sloth	child won't walk
jacaré	child dies
anaconda	child dies
caititu (type of peccary)	child taken down hole
(queixada, the other peccary, does not take refuge in holes and therefore it's all right)	
'flying monkey'	child taken far away
aguti	pain
papagaio (parrot)	pain

Anaconda appears in that list because I asked. It does not count as food or game, just as jaguars and coatis, for instance, would never be killed for food. But the arbitrariness of the lists is matched by particular insistence on the *inambu*.

A morsel for structuralists: the various *inambus*, peculiarly amongst the forest birds, never take to the trees. They are always killed on the ground. *Jacamins*, which entered one list as safe for a couvading man to kill, may also be killed on the ground if the hunter has the opportunity; but since they often hear the hunter's approach before he can see them, and since they trot off through the woods very smartly, the best technique for hunting them is to run towards them making as much noise as possible as soon as one hears their loud alarm cries. This will startle them so much that instead of running off they will immediately take to the trees, giving the hunter a better chance of getting near them. *Mutuns, jacus,* and related species all take to the trees immediately when startled.

Although the *mutum* is the most prized game bird, the flesh of the *inambu* is considered particularly tasty. It is also exceptionally white. (My hands were once described by someone examining them curiously as 'white like *inambu* flesh'. In a discussion about eating prohibitions when ill, again initially put as 'we only eat *inambu'*, I asked about fish. I was told that *trahirāo,* the most commonly caught there, was all right but definitely not *pirara.* This is a red *peixe de coro* whose flesh when cooked remains tawny coloured and has quite a strong taste. / òyɨ / means 'cooked', or, as it is often put / òyɨ kato / 'cooked good'. The negative is / nòyɨi / and synonyms for that are / uwè wɨǧ / 'there is blood' and / wɨǧ nyi / 'blood still'. 'And sin not against the Lord in eating with the blood' (1 Samuel 14: 34). It is blood that makes hunting and eating dangerous.

The men never announced that they were going out to hunt something specific unless it was to follow up, say, pig tracks that had been seen the day before or unless they were to use some special technique such as making a jaguar trap. Saying 'in these circumstances we only kill *inambu'* indicates that it's pointless for a man to set off on a hunt and emphasizes the general point of couvade precautions: inactivity. Similarly, saying 'in these circumstances we only eat *inambu'* uses a particular image to make a general point: that in these circumstances we take care what we eat.

A similar example of an image making a general point: the people at Aroá exhausted their roças, moved over to the Capoeira side, and settled there for a time. There was bad feeling between the Aroá and Capoeira people and the reluctant hosts were very angry at the surreptitious raids made on their gardens by the Aroá people. 'But what will the Aroá people do if you do not give them manioc?' 'They can go and eat honey only.' At the Nipukú, asked what would happen if the roças were exhausted and nothing more had been planted, they say 'in these circumstances we just eat honey'. The unreality of the statement is like 'let them eat cake'. What happens, and indeed what happened to the Nipukú people some years ago, is that they go off into the forest and eat fruit – if they can find any – as did Waiwai and a few families when they moved off to a bacaba grove for a time. 'Just eating honey' indicates living off the wild and being hungry.

There is usually a hint here and there about the appropriateness of the various images. The main problem is to understand the way in which we are all surrounded by danger. Yanuari put it very well. Having been prompted to give a particularly long list of game that a couvading man should not kill, he went on:

EVERYTHING has *yarr*. You should not even work on building
your house [which we were doing at the time] because there is
/ǫwi-yąrë/ [master of *obim*, the leaf used for thatching]. He will
know and the child will get fever and die. *EVERYTHING* has *yarr*.
EVERYTHING is dangerous . . .

Hence the care required by parents of a newborn child and the general
point of the restrictions: that one should neither eat, nor hunt, nor
work.

Bathing precautions are a clearer example of the way we interact
with our surroundings and bring danger on ourselves. These restrictions are part of a congeries of ideas relating to menstruation,
blood, smell, and noise:

Examples have already been given. Rain and storms come because people make a noise in the river. Noise makes *moyo* angry
causing the rain to come. If a hunter washes off directly into the
river the blood of the game he has been carrying, *moyo* will get
angry, the man will get fever or get dizzy, and die. A menstruating woman must not bathe in the river because *moyo* will get
angry on account of the smell and kill her.

As regards this last example, the Indians pointed out that the
Brazilians must know this too since they say *'faz mal'* (it does
harm) for a menstruating woman to bathe. The Brazilians do
indeed say this but they don't say why. A FUNAI man emphasized the comparison in a different way. 'These Indians', he said,
'know that it does a woman harm to bathe when she's menstruating. But look at what they do. They stay in their hammocks. Our
women are not lazy. They don't bathe but they carry on with all
their work.'

The seclusion of the woman when she is giving birth is therefore explained as getting her away from the river where *moyo*
would do her harm. A man whose wife had lost her baby at birth
himself refused to bathe in the river because 'the smell hadn't
gone'. *'Moyo* does not like smell and if I bathe I'll get dizzy and
die.'

What kind of explanation would help here? We could try the theme
that liminal states are dangerous, but we would then have the odd
configuration that travelling through the woods, menstruating,
giving birth, and coming back from the hunt smeared with the blood
of an animal are liminal states. Perhaps they are, but the wider the
generalization is spread the emptier it becomes. Similarly pollution
looks like an easy generalization to draw everything together. But this
is not what they say and it would require another manoeuvre to
explain why shitting in the river is perfectly acceptable behaviour.
They are fastidious about smell and find farting offensive. (Kasiripinar yelled with disgust and retched slightly when he and I came
across a pasture of fresh cow pats near Serra do Navio; /inè/, stench is

used as an expletive and said with an emphatic sense of disgust.) The manoeuvre could be done of course, since losing blood is not comparable with other bodily secretions – sweat, excrement, urine, tears – even though 'smell' might be more appropriate to some of these: 'Primitive man did not need to wait for Harvey in order to be taught the significance of blood in relation to life . . . ' (Hastings 1909: 715).

As for blood smelling, the remains of game that has been skinned and gutted by the river are not thrown into the water because that would bring / pane / (bad luck) on the hunter. But if we're fishing and happen in the by-going to kill a *queixada* (peccary), it will be gutted on the spot and the intestines trailed in the water so that the blood will attract *trahirão* and piranha. The intestines are then deposited back in the woods. Bits of small birds and sometimes even chunks of raw meat from larger animals are used as the first bait of the day if nothing else is available. The first fish caught will then be used. Blood attracts creatures in the water in a way that excrement and sweat do not.

It seems better, then, to stay away from the abstract 'pollution' and stick to the specific examples of noise and smell.

We are in a living relationship with these causal agencies. Our actions make them angry; they 'see' or 'know'; and the maleficence of their anger is directed at us. The way to avoid the results of someone's anger is not to be seen and not to be known, either by noise or smell. To be safe one should not attract attention to oneself. Hence it wasn't a good idea for me to go to the Oyapoque since the Kamarara-ko would then know of the continuing existence of the Nipukú people and might start their *paye* again. Noise or smell in the water makes *moyo* angry, so the rains come or we fall ill. The best way of avoiding the attention of *moyo* and *yarr* is not to do anything at all, hence the inactivity of couvade restrictions.

Anger is a cardinal example of cause. Yaneyar (our master) is a remote being that has very little to do with the world at the present time, but in numerous myths about the origin of this or that he makes things happen because 'it is good that it be so'; he changes things because 'it's bad that they remain as they are'; or he causes something to take place 'because he got angry'. Toothache, mortality, taking speech away from the jaguar, and so on, all have their punch line: 'Then Yaneyar was angry'. Here are a few fragments from a sequence about sexual intercourse, child-birth, and related matters:

> Before, when children were born, they got up and walked straight away.
> They grew up quickly.
> Then women gave birth.
> 'Let me hold it', she said.
> 'All right,' said Yaneyar 'you'll hold the child for a long time.'

Now, when woman gives birth she has to hold the child for a
long time.
It doesn't know how to walk.

Before, when woman gave birth it didn't hurt.
Then woman gave birth.
'It didn't hurt,' she said. 'Make it hurt.'
'No,' said Yaneyar. 'That's not good. It's not good that it
should hurt.'
Then another . . .
Then another . . .
Then Yaneyar got angry.
'All right. Now when you give birth it will hurt.'
Now when woman gives birth it hurts a lot.

Before, our forebears didn't couvade.
/nòyikoakòi taimiŋgwèrë /
As soon as a baby was born the father went off to hunt.
He killed a lot of game.
He didn't couvade.
Then another . . .
Then another . . . Then they said: 'Why don't our children cry?'
'That's good', said Yaneyar. 'It's good that children don't cry.'
'No it's not', they said. 'It's good that our children cry.'
Yaneyar was angry then.
The men went off to hunt.
They killed a lot of game.
When they came back their children were dead.
They had died of crying.
'/ peyikoako   adyawïi   peiko /' said Yaneyar.
couvade   therefore   you do
So now when a child is born we don't go to hunt.
We don't kill anything.
If we don't couvade our child will cry.
It will be in a lot of pain.

Just as in the demotic use of our own language where the world is
represented in simple designs of snow and ink, so with them. States
of affairs are either good or bad. Nor is there, as far as I could find, a
large vocabulary to describe inner states, dispositions, or motivations. If motivations are referred to at all in the myths, then being
angry, being afraid, being ashamed, and wanting something, more or
less account for everything, just like those primitive reductions be-
haviourists use to explain our lives in terms of aggression, flight,
inhibition, and desire (as consumption and gratification).

If Yaneyar's anger in the mythy past accounts for much of our
permanent misfortune, particular misfortunes nowadays are the

result of the present anger of other people and of *yarr* and *moyo*. And *paye* is the vehicle by which that anger has its effect on us. All these notions allow causal explanations to be expressed in an idiom of living relations. Our misfortune is caused by the ill-disposition of others.

IV

As temporary landmarks, the previous chapters suggested that the discrepancy between our thought and theirs is that we don't believe in the existence of *yarr, moyo,* and so on, nor do we believe in the exitence of a quality or power called *paye*. There is no reason for trying to sidestep the disagreement. 'Obviously there are no *yarr'* is a wholly acceptable response on our part. It is not at all surprising or unusual to find ontological disagreements between people. We find them everywhere. Moreover the alleged existence of these extra entities is in itself a rather trivial matter. The significance of the disagreement will only emerge to the extent that we can find out what all these entities – the bogles and ghosties, the gods and spirits, the communists and subversives, the paranoid fantasies and the hebephrenic delusions – are supposed to be doing.

In this case what these entities indicate is that we are entering a state of affairs where our distinction animate / inanimate does not work. All those events and processes that make something happen and that make a difference are explained in terms of a living relation. Causes remain causes and have not been translated into conditions. Processes and events are explained in terms of responsibility and blame, that is, in terms of relations between living things. Misfortune and illness, danger and death, are brought upon us because others are angry. *Yarr, moyo,* and the other creatures are a vivid technique by which this state of affairs is enunciated. Given that stone, earth, water, are living, the entities are images of them as living things.

The entities lead us towards the living relation, and the most vivid example of that relation in action is *paye*, the quality that involves human beings in actual day-to-day relations with that living reality, illustrating a morality that says not so much 'be good' but 'be quiet', since the anger of others is the most fearful force that can be directed against us.

When discussing the extremes of causal reasoning one can so easily make others appear stranger than they are by awarding them a spurious rationality. For example, if it is apparently puzzling why the Indians will go on approaching Brazilians even though they know that the Brazilians bring fatal illnesses, we could so easily say: 'The answer is that they think that it's not the illness that kills but only *anyang* sent by enemy *paye* that kills.' Our generalization neatly places them within a simple husk of reasoning that makes them look peculiarly different from ourselves. But they know perfectly well that illness kills, and attributing our generalization to them does not locate any significant difference between us and them. The causal state ments are not associated with a different rationality or a different logic. The mistake we make is to abstract extreme examples, present them as typical, and assert that they disclose a mode of thought and action different from ours.

If Wayãpí people lived a thoroughly 'alien mode of thought and action' it would be impossible to make any attempt at translating at all. The nonsense notion of an 'untranslatable language' is useful in reminding us that it is only through translations that we recognize what we have encountered as a language in the first place. Similarly, that I have been able to offer comprehensible translations of what Wayãpí people say and do (and that these have been examples *in extremis*) makes the notion of an 'alien mode of thought and action' into something like a little technicality of grammar.

Given that we can and do translate (and leaving aside the question of the adequacy of the translations offered in any instance), the interesting question is how to appreciate the conditions of these possibilities of mutual comprehension. How did we manage to find a way in? And how is it possible to offer these translations, especially of those extreme examples? At various points I suggested that the imaginative effort required of us is to abandon various cherished distinctions: the logical distinction between 'is' and 'is not'; the grammatical distinction between *onoma* and *rhema*; the semantic distinction between literal and metaphorical. These examples require a more radical effort than the more usual 'understanding native cat egories' sort of thing where, for example, if we were looking at the pre-Socratic notion of *nous* or the Anglo-Saxon notion of *modege þ anc* we would have to see that our notions of 'mind' and 'will' which we discriminate are bound together in these notions. The benefit of such exercises is that the indigenous integral reveals the tension between our discriminations, reminding us of a relation we might have overlooked between our own distinguished concepts. Problems like these are familiar and are usually discussed in terms of categories that overlap or in terms of conceptual grids that have to be redrawn. But the question I am referring to is not just one of readjusting the boundaries of particular conceptual items. The three examples given (logical, grammatical, and semantic) are used as 'polar expressions' (see Lloyd 1966: 90ff) and the peculiar difficulty of doing without polarities like those is that there is no single term to substitute for them. If one says, for example, that the literal/metaphorical distinction does not get us very far, that is not to say that all linguistic expression is metaphorical (or literal). Asking us to abandon the distinction requires us to redesign the initial question without using these words.

These exercises may be tricky but we can get on with them because there are familiar precedents close to home. As soon as we turn away from the insistence of logic and its endless distinctions we can find, in our poetry and literature, boundless examples of the fluid possibilities of our language and thought. Those, then, are part of the conditions that allow us to understand the fluidity of the language and thought of others. But the animate/inanimate distinction is a little more obdurate. How does it come about that we can find translations that allow us to illustrate the thought of others 'as if' we had emulsified that basic oppositional distinction that seems so comprehensively to inform our world? Are there aspects of our lives that would be conveyed by Tylor's ancient diagnosis of 'animism'?

Of course there are. We can understand Tylor's disjunctive way of putting it, where others are said to be 'animists', precisely because to a degree we are 'animists' too. But we will not see this if we insist on diagnostic descriptions that obscure the compatibilities between us and them. Those various writers on the philosophy of cause, cited above, repeatedly pointed out how our causal formulae were wholeheartedly 'animistic'. The habits of our language then are a most vivid example of 'as if'. It is 'as if' we and they use the same habits of language but whereas they mean what they say, it is 'as if' we don't.

And we can come even closer. The examples of illness, death, shamanism, and the couvade, are examples *in extremis*. They are the instances that strike us as most extravagant. But the point made at the end of chapter 4 was that as we move away from animism as a diagnosis we can begin to see it as a matter of degree. Animism refers to an idiom of describing relationships between human beings and the world around them, incorporating in its most exaggerated expressions powers and beings that we do not agree exist. This is the bizarre extremity where *paye* human beings and *paye* entities are blamed for the deaths of others and where those humans accused can even be put to death in revenge. But this idiom can also ebb into mere figures of speech and offhand conventional responses: merely a 'manner of speaking' of no real consequence. And this lower ebb, as Collingwood and the other writers mentioned above show, obviously implicates us.

Causal reasoning discloses a continuum of intensities that varies through different degrees of vividness, conviction, and consistency of response to the animateness of what surrounds us. Just as it is inappropriate to make a terminal diagnosis of Wayãpí people as living within a carapace of animism, so it is misleading to assume that we live outside that. Our distinction animate / inanimate and our divisions into animal, vegetable, and mineral stand on the sidelines of our lives for most of the time. We appeal to them when we are challenged and we assume that they inform our responses to the world, as indeed they do – when it comes to a matter of appeal. But for the most part we too live through changing processes where our sense of the animacy of what surrounds us swells and shrinks. Our distinctions and divisions and categories appear immutable fixtures when examined in isolation from our everyday lives, but there is not as much fit between them and our everyday responses as we might assume. We can well tease Wordsworth, as Aldous Huxley does (1929), when as a boy in the Lake District:

I heard among the solitary hills
Low breathings coming after me, and sounds
Of undistinguishable motion, steps
Almost as silent as the turf they trod . . .
(The Prelude 1805–6, I:329–32)

and when a 'huge cliff' in a moonlit night made him aware of 'unknown modes of being', 'huge and mighty forms, that do not live / Like living men . . . ' (406ff). But have we not all been aware of *something* like that? Surely we can recognize our own intimations of the animacy of objects.

Wayãpí notions of *paye, yarr,* and *moyo* are similarly by-standing in the ordinary course of events, becoming a precedent for responses in those critical situations: birth, illness, death. These intensities do seem extravagant to us, but they are so only in terms of extent and degree. They do not disclose a radically incompatible mode of being in the world. All those 'different forms of life' arguments reveal the same morbidity: elaborating factitious designs of difference between ourselves and others out of a few lurid bits and pieces. There is no guarantee that doing fieldwork will rescue us from these gentle forms of academic foolishness, but it does offer an opportunity to be with others and to plunge into their circle of understanding and believing (I borrow the phrase from Paul Ricoeur). Living with those people and sharing their lives reveal the import of an extensive area of emotional and moral experience: the exchange of kindness and concern, worries and fears, interest and pleasure, selfishness and spite, good and bad temper, laughter and despair. All that turns the notion of a separate reality into a bauble. The equivalents and parallels, the concordances and analogues between their lives and ours, apart from that obvious membrane of technological and ecological difference that marks their experience so differently from ours, all declare a massive communion of moral responses to one another and to the world we live in. If we fail to appreciate that, it is because we clutter the way with our endless abstractions and distinctions, enthralled as we are by our obstinate logic and under the spell . . .

Of that false secondary power by which,
In weakness, we create distinctions, then
Deem that our puny boundaries are things
Which we perceive, and not which we have made.
(The Prelude 1805–6, II:220–24)

PARENTESCO:
a formal puzzle

He lived in a cave by the seas,
He lived upon oysters and foes,
But his list of forbidden degrees,
An extensive morality shows.
Andrew Lang, 'Double Ballade of
Primitive Man'

So often we can subdue odd aspects of the language and thought of others by yoking them to our distinctions. Our impositions will be seen to work as long as there is no protest from the phenomena; and even when there is, we may not be listening. The following puzzle starts from a point where a set of relationship terms can be seen to work within a distinction of ours as long as some slight anomalies are ignored. But as more evidence is taken into account, it becomes clear that the anomalies have to be taken seriously, and that, in so doing, the initial organizing distinction has to be abandoned. Visualizing the interconnections between the terms then requires seeing the set as an integral design without the simplifying device of an imposed duality.

The puzzle appeared by accident. The formal features of Wayãpí relationship terminology seemed straightforward and they were to have been presented in a few pages of technical drudgery. They revealed the principles of what Louis Dumont called a 'Dravidian terminology' and what Rodney Needham described as a 'two line prescriptive terminology'. Peter Rivière had pointed out that the principles of a two line prescriptive terminology constituted a 'structural feature' found throughout Lowland South America (Rivière n.d.). Buchler and Selby described Dravidian terminologies as 'simplicity itself' (or to be fair, as seeming to be simple), but their own breathtaking blunder in describing them as 'patrilineal systems associated with matrilateral cross-cousin marriage' (1968:135) warns how brittle simplicity can be.

The argument here is built on the original work of Dumont and

Needham. It was helped by discussions with N. J. Allen, whose paper on 'tetradic' principles (Allen 1986) anticipates most of the ideas presented here. The solution offered solves not only the original puzzle but also a more difficult one presented in another case: Bernard Arcand's account of Cuiva relationship vocabulary (1977). I would not have seen a solution to the puzzle without the insights offered in the work of these four people.

Having listed Wayãpí relationship terms, I followed Dumont's diagram in his original article (1953). To simplify the matter for the moment, the terms appeared in a box diagram of this type. For the sake of brevity:

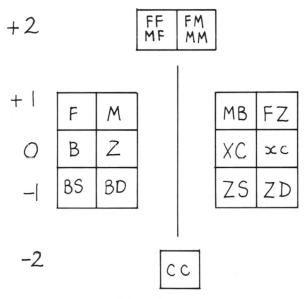

xc stands for male bilateral cross-cousin, i.e. MBS=FZS
xc for female bilateral cross-cousin, i.e. MBD=FZD
z stands for sister
cc for children's children.

Figure 1.

But there is an awkwardness in this diagram since +1 level is of two marriage pairs whereas 0 and −1 levels are of sibling pairs. According to another conventional diagram, I had presented the terms within a schematism of this kind:

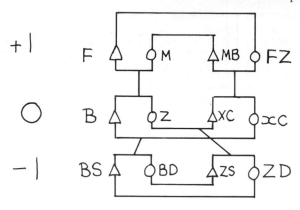

Figure 2.

The answer seemed to be a simple shift to a diagram of sibling pairs using either the box type or the twigs and branches type:

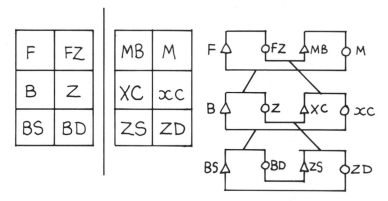

Figure 3.

Looking back over the literature where these conventions had been used, an anomaly appeared. Needham's work on 'two line prescriptive' terminologies used box diagrams to show the two 'lines' exchanging women. Thus, for example, Garo terms (a matrilineal case), and Manggarai terms (a patrilineal case), were displayed within the following form:

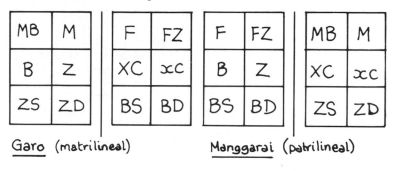

Garo (matrilineal)   Manggarai (patrilineal)

(cf. Needham 1966:145,151)

Figure 4.

To make the presentation here as simple as possible I have kept the 'lines' (MB, B, ZS; F, XC, S, and so on) as Needham presented them, but I have arranged the terms in sibling pairs which Needham's original diagram did not. Twigs and branches equivalents are obvious and can be constructed mentally.

The puzzle is: How is one to present the principles of a terminology where there is no principle of unilineal descent? There is a patrilineal descent format, and a matrilineal descent format. But what of a 'cognatic' format? Dumont's original format is diagrammatically obtuse: the relation represented between 0 and +1 is not the same as the relation represented between 0 and −1, but both other solutions (the Garo and Manggarai patterns) write a unilineal principle into the presentation, which in the case of Wayãpí terminology, and in the case of so many other Dravidian terminologies, is not there. The solution I had adopted was a patrilineal format, and that would not do.

The inadequacies of the diagrams reflect inadequacies in the ideas they represent. I will argue that Dumont's distinction 'kin/affine' is superfluous and that Needham's characterization of this configuration of principles as 'two line prescription' is misleading. The aim is to find an adequate diagrammatic representation of this bundle of formal features.

I refer to the configuration as 'Dravidian' because Dumont's 1953 article was the first clear explanation of these features. The name has nothing to do with Murdock's attempts (1949) to classify 'kinship systems' according to the features exhibited by the various cousin terms he came across – Hawaiian, Iroquois, Sudanese, and so on. That activity would be harmless trifling had it not led to mistakes. Presumably as a result of Dumont's work, 'Dravidian' had to be included in this collection and the attempt to do so led to a widespread confusion. A popular introductory textbook called *Kin Groups and Social Structure* attempts to explain the difference between an 'Iroquois *system*' and a 'Dravidian *system*' (Keesing 1975:111) and of course ends in a muddle. The tag 'Iroquois' referred to certain features of cousin terms. 'Dravidian' referred to a configuration of formal principles underlying a full relationship vocabulary. The comparison is like trying to show the differences and similarities between an aquiline nose and a mesomorph. However, readers who find that the word 'Dravidian' raises Murdock's spectral classifications should use some other term, but *not* one such as '*two line* prescription' that imputes features to that bundle which are not there.

The formal exercise looks at the relations among fifteen Wayāpí words. Making clear the principles that relate these words reveals nothing whatsoever about the daily life of the Wayāpí. Nothing in the principles I present has any necessary correlation with semantic connotations or moral attitudes associated with the terms. For example, time and again in the stories they tell, when a Wayāpí meets a mythical person, that person will be addressed as / tamu /, roughly 'grandfather', and the Wayāpí will be addressed in turn as / è-parë /, 'grandchild'. It is said that in the old days, when the people from Aroá first travelled north and met the people from Kumakarɨ̈g, having no established relations to refer to, they said 'let us call each other / tairò /', roughly, 'brother-in-law', i.e., MBS = FZS. There are obvious reasons for these usages, explicable through interpretative exercises, but they do not *necessarily* follow from the principles that relate the terms, in the sense that, in transformational grammar for example, rules at a deep level are said to 'generate' surface patterns. Hence the temptation to go on from the formal exercise to grandiose implications about structures of the mind, or even to go on to more modest views about rules for the conduct of people in their daily lives, should be resisted. In those senses there is no necessary engagement between the formal exercise and the interpretative one. They are separate activities. In Buck Mulligan's wheedling voice: 'When I makes tea I makes tea, as old mother Grogan said. And when I makes water I makes water.'

But there *is* a relation between the formal exercise and the rest of this essay. It is like that of a pictorial representation of a prose theme. It is the same story as before told on a quite different scale and in a quite different idiom. Aldous Huxley mentions the idea of novels within novels, like the quaker holding the box of oats in the Quaker Oats packet, all telling the same story but at different removes: 'At about the tenth remove you might have a novelist telling your story in algebraic symbols or in terms of variation in blood pressure, pulse, secretion of ductless glands and reaction times' (1955:298). What follows, then, is an allegory in algebraic language and geometric devices which illustrates our general predicament with regard to others. It is a series of pictures of what happens to an indigenous phenomenon when it is emancipated from our distinctions, the move in this case being represented by a shift from two-dimensional pictures to a three-dimensional one.

To summarize the steps of the argument to be presented:

(1) It is odd that there is no adequate convention that can represent diagrammatically the principles of such a 'simple' configuration of fifteen terms.

(2) Examining previous diagrams reveals some superfluous ideas about these terminologies.

(3) An apparent awkwardness in the way the Cuiva of Colombia use their Dravidian vocabulary is resolved.

(4) This leads to the final diagram representing the 15 terms.

II

The accompanying diagram (p. 148) presents Wayãpí relationship vocabulary in a box diagram. Were it done out in a twigs and branches diagram it would show (a) marriage pairs, not sibling pairs, and (b) a patrilineal format, thus:

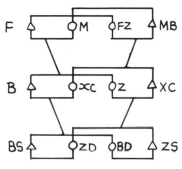

Figure 5.

This is another inadequate pattern but the solution will be provided later.

Where appropriate in the main diagram, the reference term is placed first with the vocative term below in parenthesis. A fuller gloss on each term will be found in the appendix which also indicates difficulties in isolating a neat reference and vocative distinction at ego's genealogical level and below. There are five other terms I deal with here because of their peculiarities. These are: /a'o/, tạ'aŋga/, /ya-pò/, sè-mu/, and /yè-pè/.

The marriage rule is that a man marries a / pa'i rayỉrë / and a woman a / pa'i ra'ỉrë /, i.e., term 6 + term 12, and term 6 + term 11, literally, MB + D and MB + S. In certain cases the rule might be expressed as / pipi mèmỉrë /, term 5 + 11a and 12a, literally FZ + C, but in general

	(1) / (3) / (7)-(11)	(2) / (4) / (9)-(13)	(5) / (8)-(12)	(1) / (6) / (10)-(14)
2nd Asc.	(1) tamòi (tamu)	(2) i-yarɨi (sa'i)		(1) tamòi (tamu)
1st Asc.	(3) to (papa) F.	(4) i-yɨğ (mama) M.	(5) i-yaye i-tẹia (obsolete) (pipi) FZ.	(6) tatɨu (pa'i) MB.
0	(7a) tèkè'ɨrë (kakanyɨ) eB. - - - - (7b) i-momini (m.s.) i-kɨwɨrë (w.s.) yB.	(9a) èrèkwarë (m.s.) (9b) tõ'i (w.s.) FZD. MBD.	(8a) nyanya eZ. - - - - (8b) i-kunyaŋ (m.s.) i-kɨpɨ'ɨrë (w.s.) yZ.	(10a) tairò'ɨrë (tairò) (m.s.) (10b) i-mèn (w.s.) FZS. MBS.
1st Desc.	(11) ta'ɨrë (m.s.) (11a) i-mèmɨrë (w.s.) S.	(13) ta'ɨrë tatɨğ (m.s.) (tatɨğ) kunyaŋtai pɨ-sɨ (w.s.) ZD. (m.s.) BD. (w.s.)	(12) tayɨrë (m.s.) (12a) i-mèmɨrë (w.s.) D.	(14) tanyowèn (kwani) ZS. (m.s.) BS. (w.s.)
2nd Desc.		(15) i-parɨ èmiŋyariroŋ (obsolete)		

m.s. = man speaking.
w.s. = woman speaking.

Figure 6.

the formulations are 'the same'. Questions as to whether a man could marry a D, FZ, or ZD always got the emphatic response that this was 'no good at all'

The most common form of jocular abuse is to describe someone as being like an animal of some kind, like a monkey, like a tapir. From the Brazilian frontiersmen they have met, they have picked up a phrase from the pidgin Portuguese used by those men when they talk to Indians. The phrase is *tamanho cachorro*, 'like a dog', and it was in vogue at Nipukú in its Portuguese form as an expression of derision and disgust. A hunter caught in the forest at nightfall had to sleep on the ground. This was considered amusing, and mildly humiliating for the man concerned. He had to sleep *tamanho cachorro*. A nine-year-old mentally retarded child often sat on the ground of the village plaza not taking the trouble to squat or to find a piece of wood to sit on. This was mocked and described as *tamanho cachorro*.

Asking why it was bad for a man to have sexual relations with women in those prohibited categories (and with a mother), the most vivid reponse was '*tamanho cachorro*', said with some vehemence and an expression of disgust. In one myth, 'The Origin of the Moon', where a man is discovered having a sexual affair with his sister, the reason given for his leaving the village is that he is ashamed, / ònyi-mò-siǫka /. It is said that if a man and his sister copulate, their dead souls, / taïǧwèrë /, will not go to 'Yaneyar's place' in the sky but will stay wandering the earth. These wandering spirits of incestuous couples are considered maleficent. One Indian explained that he would not have sex with his sister's daughter [the girl in question being his MeZDD and FDD] because it was very dangerous, / i-pòyï-tè /, to do so. He referred to the supernatural sanction.

I did not find a word that I'd translate as 'incest' but the idea of sexual relations between close kin is described with derision and disgust, and the offender is said to suffer shame and to expose him or herself to the danger of supernatural sanctions.

All women in the category MBD = FZD are / èrèkwarë /, potential or actual wife to the man speaking. But the distinction between sex and marriage is clear. 'Yes, she was his wife, / èrèkwarë /, [i.e. in the category "wife" to him], but they did not marry, / noèrèkòi /, they only copulated, / omèno kurinyonte /.' This is the relationship described as / im-ï'a /, lover. These relationships are supposed to be secret. / wèrèko /, to marry, refers to a process that involves discussion between the fathers or other male relatives of the couple, obligations of the young man towards his WF, public cohabitation, and cooperation between partners.

The marriage rule is expressed firmly, but a casual glance at genealogies reveals that in a large proportion of marriages, the man and woman are not in the prescribed category. When this is questioned it is said that such marriages do take place, and that they are 'good' in those circumstances when a man does not have a / pa'i rayɨrë / to marry. I have instances of marriages of men to women in all the categories of the relationship terminology with the exception of / sa'i / (+2 level), and / mama /, but by far the most common solution is marriage with a / tatɨg̈ /, ZD, although it should be said immediately that I have no recorded instance of a marriage with an actual ZD.

/ a'o / and / ta̱'anga /: / a'o / can be suffixed to all terms presented in the relationship diagram (except +2 and −2 genealogical levels). For instance / tayɨrë a'o / is variously explained: 'not a real daughter'; "daughter" is just what one says'; 'another daughter'; 'a far-off daughter'; 'she calls me / papa miti /'; and so on. Thus the question: 'Did X marry his / tayɨrë / (daughter)?' would get the reply: 'No, she was / tayɨrë a'o /.'

/ a'o / in some other contexts is, like / miti /, a diminutive suffix. When attached to a word ending in / −a / the addition is simply / -'o /, thus / papa'o /, / mama'o /.

/ ta̱'anga / means image, imitation, likeness, or drawing. It is the word used for a photograph. / apɨa ra̱'anga / means a cowardly or weak man. It is also used to explain apparent anomalies in the way people address one another. A typical case is presented here.

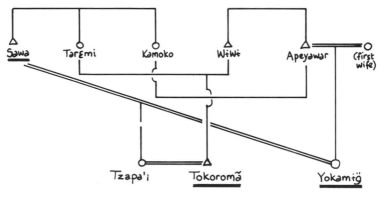

Figure 7.

Sawa has married a classificatory ZD, but it was said that she was not a / tatɨg / but a /ta̱tɨg a'o /. When Tokoroma marries his MBD, his WM is a classificatory sister; but, he explains, Yokamɨg̈ is / pipi ra̱'anga /, that is, *like* a / pipi / (FZ); a reasonable statement since he has married her daughter.

/ ya-pò /, / sè-mu /, and / yè-pè / are not originally Wayãpì words. Discussing these introduced terms it was usually said that 'this is what the Wayana say', but a number of people explained that it was Sarapó who taught them how to use the words. The image of an isolated Aparai, expelled, they say, by his own people, becoming a Kamarara-ko Wayãpí by adoption, and teaching the Brazilian Wayãpí how to use Wayana relationship terms, is bizarre. However it took place, the result is the following.

/ya-pò/. Hurault (1961) records the Wayana terms *papak* and *yapo* without discrimination under the specification 'father and father's classificatory brother'. Waiwai explained that in Wayana use, *papa* referred to one's real father and that *yapo* was like /papa miti/ in Wayãpí, that is, FB, real or classificatory.

In Wayãpí usage /ya-pò/ is exclusively a form of address between men; it is reciprocal; and it takes the place of a relationship that would formerly have been expressed as F/S, or more precisely /papa'o/ (or papa miti/) and /ta'ɨrë a'o/. Which was formerly the classificatory father and which the son is easily checked by looking at what a man calls the sister of his /ya-pò/ since this remains unchanged.

The term is used in the following circumstances. When a man marries a classificatory ZD he is marrying a classificatory son's wife. The men then address each other as /ya-pò/. 'He married my wife therefore I call him /ya-pò/' is the usual explanation. Children of one's /ya-pò/ will be children or grandchildren as appropriate. If it is the former 'son' who is speaking he will regard any issue from the marriage as his 'children' since they are from his 'wife'. A female child he will refer to as /èrayɨrë/, my daughter, and will address her as /si'ŭ/. If male, the child will be /èra'ɨrë/, my son, and will usually be addressed as /ya-pò/.

There seems to be no inherent moral connotation in the use of the term. Although it is true that most of the /ya-pò/ relationships are indeed between adult men who have no particularly close ties with one another, a number of such relationships are extremely close, where, for example, two men who are /ya-pò/ to one another share the same house, and do everything together.

/sè-mu/. This is a reciprocal vocative form used only between men. It was first explained as being a /kakanyɨ a'o/, another brother, a distant brother. One person explained that a man does not say /kakanyɨ/ to another when his mother was not a 'real mother' but only a mother 'from far away'. Making the same point, another glossed the word as /òɨg'ɨrë mèmɨrë/, that is, 'another mother's child' (see term 4 in the lexicon in the appendix) and added that it was a mother 'from another place'. What the word is indicating is a 'brother' whose genealogical connection is unknown.

The word does not appear in Hurault's lists either for the Oyampi of the Oyapoque or for the Oayana (Hurault 1961, 1962), yet many

individuals said it was a Wayana word. Yasito, who talked about
these matters with unusual care, said that was not so and that it was a
/ tamo-ko / (grandfather-people) word. One interesting gloss suggested that it was generally held to be 'the same' as the Brazilian *compa-
nheiro*, companion, friend.

There are not very many / sè-mu / relationships. At Nipukú only
Sirò and Kasiripin called each other by this term, Sirò being the only
surviving member of a settlement to the south, and Kasiripin marrying into the Nipukú group from Capoeira. It is a device to indicate
distancing and formality. During one colossal fight between Siriyan
and two of his sister's sons, both of whom were actually married to his
daughters, he said in one of his furious outbursts that these men were
no longer / kwani-ko / (ZS) but / sè-mu kurinyonte / – merely / sè-mu /.

/ yè-pè /. I was unable to discover a clear rationale for the use of this
term. Although it does not appear on Hurault's lists, the Wayápí say it
is a Wayana word. The explanation always given is that it means
/ anyimoripa /, my friend, and that it is 'the same' as the Brazilian
amigo. Sarapó is said to have taught them how to use the term.

It is a vocative form used reciprocally. I didn't hear women calling
each other / yè-pè / but Teyo calls the entire Waiwai family, wives and
children included, by this term and is responded to in kind. Most
commonly it is an address form between men although it is said 'we
call / yè-pè /'s sister / yè-pè / too'. Everyone who uses the term can, if
pressed, produce the term previously used and explain the obscured
relationship. In many cases it was said that 'I could call him / kwani /
(or / èmomini / and so on) but Sarapó said that / yè-pè / was better'.

Some typical examples: Kasiripinar used to call Mikoto / papa miti /.
Then Mikoto said 'let's call each other / yè-pè /'. But nowadays since
Mikoto married a girl that was a possible wife for Kasiripinar they call
each other / ya-pò /. Waiwai said of Teyo: 'Teyo is not my / kwani / (ZS)
because his mother was a / kunyaŋ a'o / and not a / kunyaŋ / therefore I call him / yè-pè /.' Kasiripinar calls all Anisu's brothers / pa'i /
(MB) and is in turn called / kwani / (ZS). But why, since he calls Anisu
/ yè-pè /, does he not address the other brothers in the same way?
'Because it is not good to have a large number of / yè-pè /.' He went on
to say that calling someone / yè-pè / was / anyimorara-ti kurinyonte /,
just joking or playing. The verb / onyimorara / is related to / anyimori
pa /, a friend.

There is an element of fashion in the use of this term as there is in
the adoption of all things Wayana:

> Tsako and I always address each other as / tairò / but towards the
> end of my stay he suggested that we call each other *kono* 'as the
> Wayana do'. (Hurault 1961 confirms this as the equivalent.)
> Tsako is justly proud that he has travelled widely and is good at
> languages.

Furthermore it is clear that /yè-pè/ is only introduced in instances where the relationship conventionally expressed in Wayãpì is not very clearly marked in the first place, that is, where someone is not a 'real' B, ZS, MB, and so on. Also, if a firm relationship does emerge, /yè-pè/ will disappear and be replaced by a more suitable term. Thus, if a man marries another's sister the men will always, from then on, call each other /tairò/.

III

To arrive at the formal features of the terminology I shall go by way of the Cuiva of Colombia, an example that shows how the principles underlying terminologies of this kind can be reduced to relations among four positions. It turns out that there are *two* (and only two) possible configurations of these four positions. One of these configurations is well known. The other is an interesting surprise. Noticing that there are *two* possible ways of reducing a Dravidian terminology solves the puzzle of how to represent them diagrammatically without writing in a unilineal principle.

There should be no doubt that there is a problem with the traditional diagrams. If I presented a terminology in the following way:

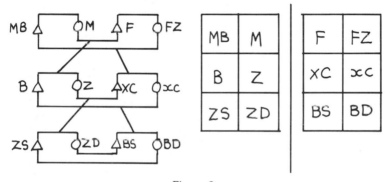

Figure 8.

and went on to say that there is a patrilineal principle at work here, then it would be correct to say that the diagram is inadequate. The diagram represents a matrilineal schematism. Similarly, it is not an adequate defence of traditional diagrams of Dravidian terminologies to argue that we use a patrilineal format but manage to remind ourselves when we look at it that we are not supposed to be representing patrilineality. If there is no principle of unilineality to be represented then it should not be represented.

But first, inadequate though it is, a presentation of Cuiva relationship terms in patrilineal format, man speaking. The terms are taken from Bernard Arcand's paper (1977).

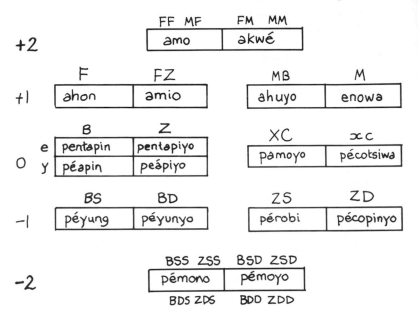

Figure 9.

This is a straightforward Dravidian terminology: five genealogical levels with the distinction between what Dumont called kin and affine maintained only at levels O, +1, and −1. There is a distinction of age in the B / Z position, terms that distinguish eB / yB and eZ / yZ, but this distinction does not affect the relations with other positions and can be left out in the final configuration. It is needed for the first step, though. Marriage is with *pécotsiwa*, the term being reciprocal between persons of different sex. There is another term for the position when it is woman speaking, but it is sufficient to work with man speaking.

The first interesting feature is this: looking at +2 and −2:

> ... an adult man would consider a baby as being his *pémono* and would see himself as the *amo* of that child; but as soon as the child comes to the age of about 10, he and the older man would simply call each other either *pentapin-péapin* [eB / yB] or *pamoyo-pamoyo* [XC / XC].   (Arcand 1977:25)

What happens is that the terms on +2 and −2 disappear by being folded on to 0. This kind of equation across alternate genealogical levels is familiar enough but the way it's done is curious. For a male ego, the children of his *péyung* and *pecopinyo* (BS and ZD) become his *pamoyo* and *pécotsiwa* (XC and xc), while the children of his *pérobi* and *péyunyo* (ZS and BD) become his *péapin* and *péapiyo* (B and Z).

Having folded in +2 and −2 in such an economical way, the same thing is done to +1 and −1. First of all Cuiva sometimes use composite relationship terms made up of one term from +1 together with one term from −1. Thus a male ego might call his *péyung* (BS) *'péyung-ahuyo'* (BS-MB), or he might call his *pécopinyo* (ZD) *'pécopinyo-amio'* (ZD-FZ). But such composite terms are rarely heard. More commonly one term is used, *either* a term referring to +1 *or* a term referring to −1. That is, taking a male ego and looking at all his male relatives in both adjacent levels (+1 and −1) he will call them all *either ahon* (F) *or pérobi* (ZS) and *either ahuyo* (MB) *or péyung* (BS), and the corresponding terms for women on these levels. The choice as to whether the person is to be called *either ahon or pérobi* is determined by that person's age in relation to ego. In terms of sibling categories, the Cuiva themselves explain that the pair of terms *ahuyo* and *enowa* (MB and M) are 'like' the pair of terms *péyung* and *péyunyo* (BS and BD) and that *ahon* and *amio* (F and FZ) are 'like' *pérobi* and *pécopinyo* (ZS and ZD).

The criterion of relative age being used in this way makes the phrase 'genealogical level' more appropriate than the word 'generation'. Peter Rivière explains: 'Frequently generation and genealogical level coincide, but not always. Thus ego's FyB may be the same age as ego in which case ego and this man belong to the same generation but different genealogical levels, while ego's F belongs to the same genealogical level as his younger brother but different generations.' (Rivière 1969:67 note 1)

Starting with a straightforward Dravidian terminology, we impose on it the principle of equating alternate genealogical levels. 0, +2, and −2 are equated. +1 and −1 are equated. We are therefore left with *two* genealogical levels and *four* sibling categories. This obviously suggests a similar sort of arrangement of principles as found in the classic case of Kariera terminology.

But this leads to Bernard Arcand's first problem. Dumont had explained that the difference between a Kariera terminology and a Dravidian terminology was that in the Kariera one we can discover what he called a 'holistic' formula where we can see a wholesale division into 'moieties' (in scare quotes), an image rather like Needham's 'two lines', and it is the establishment of marriage between these two metaphorical or figurative moieties that is fundamental. And in the Kariera case, if the marriage relationship is going to be established in this way between the 'moieties' this *demands* or *requires* (*'exige'* Dumont wrote) that the distinction between sibling categories on 0, +1, and −1 (a distinction that we can call kin/affine) be carried into the +2 and −2 levels (Dumont 1970:285). That is to say, if the principle of equating alternate genealogical levels is to work, we can't get away with one category distinguished by sex into two terms at +2 and −2 (*amo / akwe*, and *pémono / pémoyo*). We have to produce two sibling categories and four terms like those at 0. This is exactly what the Cuiva do, producing composite terms, *amo-pentapin, akwé-penta-piyo, amo-pamoyo, akwé-cotsiwa* on the +2 (and the same on −2, *pémono-péapin* etc.), then dropping the *amo / akwé* (and the *pémo / pémoyo*) leaving four terms in two sibling categories. This was the sort of arrangement that led Dumont to talk about 'global dualism', a dichotomy running right through all the genealogical levels – again the compelling image of dualism and two lines.

Bernard Arcand notices that there is something we can call 'dualism' in the Cuiva example.

> Every Ego makes, *at least within his own generation,* [my emphasis] a very sharp distinction between the category of marriageable individuals (*pamoyo / pécotsiwa*) and the category of those who are not marriageable (*péapin / péapiyo*); and these two categories are linked together by a relation of inter-marriage.

He then goes on:

> What is more difficult is to find out how this simple opposition is part of a broader dualism which runs through all genealogical levels. In other words, which are the two 'halves' of Cuiva society which are linked together in a relation of inter-marriage?
>
> (Arcand 1977:28–29)

Notice the proliferation of scare quotes. They are not really moieties, not really halves, (and not really lines), partly because the terms are 'analytic' and do not refer to 'real groups of people', but partly I think because there is a hesitancy about how this duality is perceived.

My answer to Arcand's question is that it is misleading to think of these terminologies as revealing a 'broader dualism'; that phrases such as 'global dualism' and 'two line prescription' are unhelpful; and that there is a more illuminating way of thinking about these terminologies that does not depend *fundamentally* on dichotomies like 'kin / affine', 'marriageable / unmarriageable', 'two lines exchanging women' and so on. (Not *fundamentally*, although distinctions like these can be 'globally' imposed in some particular cases.) The simplest, most economical set of principles underlying Dravidian terminologies in general and these alternative level arrangements in particular is a configuration of relations between *four* categories.

Just as I use 'Dravidian' as a convenient device to label a bundle of relational principles, so I am going to use 'Kariera'. There is a crucial distinction between the four terms that refer to Kariera marriage classes (usually written Palyeri, Banaka, Burung, and Karimera) and the full relationship vocabulary which can be given genealogical specification, *mama, kaga* (F, MB) and so on. Kariera relationship vocabulary does not produce the complete folding in to make it exactly equivalent to the marriage classes. But I need a word to label the formal features, and formally the Kariera show these principles at work.

There are two ways of folding in a Dravidian terminology.

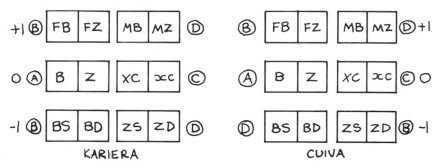

Figure 10.

For these diagrams to be read either from male ego or female ego points of view it is best to write not S/D (to go along with ZS/ZD) but BS/BD to balance ZS/ZD. Reading up to +1 no adjustment is required, but for formal consistency I write FB and MZ in place of F and M. I haven't learned the more adequate convention of relative sex notation used by N. J. Allen (1986) – PosG, and so on.

There are now only four sibling categories left, A, B, C, and D, but the equation between the alternate levels is different. Notice that both diagrams are at the moment in patrilineal format. We have written an extra principle of unilineality into the diagrams. What is interesting is that even if we chose a matrilineal format, the equations would be exactly the same.

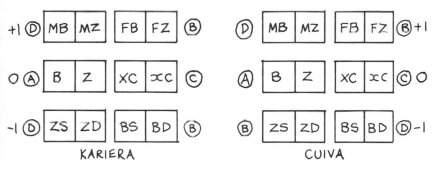

Figure 11.

Again in the Kariera case +1 and −1 fold over directly whereas in the Cuiva case there is the same odd twist. But whichever presentation we use the results are identical. This is why Dumont said in another context that he was exorcising 'the spell of underlying descent' (1966:231). A unilineal descent principle is superfluous to explain the configuration. Why, then, do we go on representing 'lines' that are not there?

The Cuiva example forces us to take on the problem since neither of the representations suggested above is adequate. We cannot just say the categories 'cross over', since it is not clear what is being crossed over. It certainly is not crossing over 'lines'. Bernard Arcand got into difficulties with his diagrams and offered two possible schematisms, one showing 'male to female to male lines of descent' and another showing 'male to male and female to female lines of descent'. But going back to the four sibling categories, there are diagrams that show at a glance the two and only two possibilities of arranging them. These are set out in the attached figures (p.159).

It can be seen from these diagrams that in the Kariera case one can produce 'two lines'. Men are going to be *either* ABAB *or* CDCD, while women will always be *either* ADAD *or* CBCB. But this cannot appear in the Cuiva case. A man's 'descent line' is ADCBA and a woman's the reverse, ABCDA. One can also read off these diagrams the typical equations described above, either the Kariera way (FB = BS) or the Cuiva way (FB = ZS) and so on.

There are two ways of folding in a Dravidian terminology. The Kariera case has been known all along. The Cuiva case has not. Because it is so complete, in that we cannot be misled into a misconceived dualism, I find the Cuiva solution more satisfying from the point of view of balance and design. But as formal solutions there is nothing to choose between the two.

There are two lessons from the Cuiva evidence: (1) It should have been possible to predict a Cuiva configuration but no one saw it until Bernard Arcand produced his work. It would be reasonable to guess that there must be other examples hidden away in ethnographic reports of lesser quality. The most obvious place to look is the Mundugumor 'ropes' but the ethnography in Margaret Mead's *Sex and Temperament* is too slight (Mead 1935:176ff).

(2) Understanding the Cuiva example in this way reflects back on our way of thinking about Dravidian terminologies in general. By 'our way of thinking about terminologies' I mean precisely our diagrams. The diagrams *are* the way we think about terminologies, the pages of prose that surround them being merely their glosses. Many of the controversies and disagreements in this field are the result of inadequate diagrammatic representation. For example, Dumont's solution to the confusion about the Aranda (1966) is in his diagram, and the previous misleading statements about the nature of Aranda marriage classes which he illustrates were the result of what various writers said, having gazed at and fiddled with their misleading diagrams.

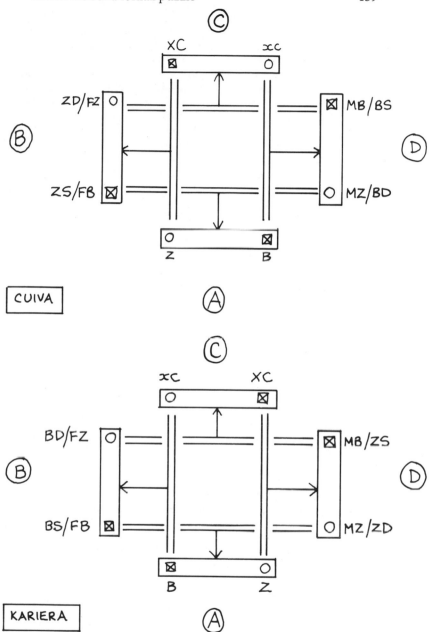

Figure 12.

So far the diagrams of the folded-in terminology are easy. They represent what Dumont called 'the lack of linear genealogical time and the presence of circular genealogical time' (1966:239). (Time, here, is an image of how the terms are related. It would be a blunder to take this as evidence of picturesque Kariera notions of 'time'.) The difficulty is finding an adequate representation of the complete set of terms where we return to the 'linear genealogical time' of the five successive genealogical levels. The difficulty is to find something that is simple and visually convincing. What we have to do is to imagine a representation of either the Cuiva diagram or the Kariera diagram (and from this point I will stick to the Cuiva solution) in three dimensions with the A/C level above the B/D level, thus:

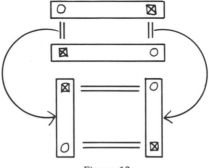

Figure 13.

This represents the formal relation between *either* the +1 level and the 0 level, *or* the 0 level and the −1 level of a complete Dravidian terminology. The minimal genealogical specifications could be written in as required. Holding on to this image as the informing principle of Dravidian terminologies shows that it is impossible to produce 'two lines' crossing genealogical levels, nor a kin/affine distinction that is consistently reflected in 'two halves'. The kin/affine or marriage-able/unmarriageable distinction, as Bernard Arcand said (empha-sized in the quotation above), only makes sense as the opposition of sibling categories at ego's own genealogical level; but it does not split the scheme into two, into two lines, or into a general distinction between kin and affine. Dualism of this kind is not therefore a *necess-ary* feature of the scheme but only one that may be added on as an extra, as, for example, the Piaroa do (see Kaplan 1975). Dualism cannot, however, be induced in Cuiva terminology.

It is awkward to represent the relation between three levels (be-tween +1, 0, −1) all at once on a flat surface. The only adequate representation is a three-dimensional one, thinking of each relation-ship term as the corner of a cube. There is nothing eccentric in using three dimensions. I think the diagram attached here (p. 162) is easier to understand than the three-dimensional one in Dumont's original article (1953).

The figure shows the principle represented in the preceding figure, the relation between two levels, working down through the three central levels of a Dravidian terminology. A point to notice is that I have chosen to represent the configuration in such a way that if $+1$ were equated with -1 according to this diagram Cuiva equations would result. Illustrating the other formal possibility requires the necessary adjustments, for example, placing the FB term above the BS term and so on.

A final comment on five-level Dravidian terminologies: Dumont pointed out that in order to produce 'circular genealogical time' rather than 'linear genealogical time', there have to be two opposed sibling categories at the $+2$ and -2 levels so that they can be equated and the circle completed. The reason such a distinction is superfluous in a full, five-level Dravidian terminology, where there are usually just two terms at the $+2$ level (one for men and one for women) and two or even one at the -2 level, is that in terms of minimal genealogical specifications and in terms of ego's point of view, the four terms we could produce to form the sibling categories, FF + MM and MF + FM, are all parents' parents. Similarly, at -2, all the specifications are children's children regardless of the link they go through.

The final diagram is the proper kind of schematic representation for Wayãpí relationship vocabulary. The answer to the question, 'What does this tell us about the Wayãpí or the Cuiva?' has to be, 'Next to nothing as far as I can see'. It tells us about ourselves. Bernard Arcand opens his essay with some critical comments on previous attempts to relate 'kinship domains' to other domains, but concludes by doing just that. He says that the 'logical principle' lying at the back of Cuiva relationship vocabulary is reflected in other aspects of Cuiva culture. Briefly it is that a member of one class is obtained from its opposite class. Wet food is obtained in dry places, dry food in wet places, and so on. Similarly the 'logic' of the 'kinship terminology' is that males are produced by females and females are produced by males because of the 'lines of descent' generated by the terminology. Regarding the food, the animals, and the other ethnographic details I can only say that they sound intriguing and I'd like to hear more about the matter. But his conclusions about the 'logic' of the relationship terms is not helpful. There is no evidence that Cuiva say that men are produced from women and women are produced from men. Arcand thinks they might, and if they did it would be an intriguing statement. But there is no basis for that kind of reasoning in the principles of the relationship vocabulary. There is no evidence of such 'lines of descent' and no need to invoke them. Such lines are no more than

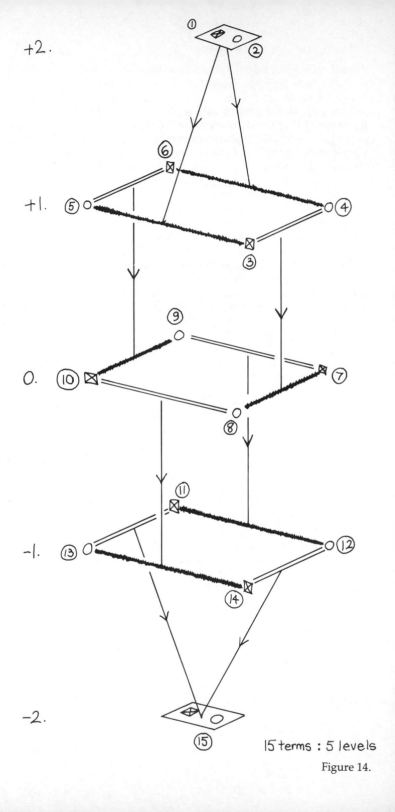

+2.

+1.

0.

−1.

−2.

15 terms : 5 levels

Figure 14.

diagrammatic phantoms. The terminology results from a simple fold-ing-in of Dravidian principles.

He concludes with the question: 'Assuming there were other logi-cal possibilities available to them, why have the Cuiva choosen this particular logical form?' (Arcand 1977:33). I suggest that there were only two possibilities; that both possibilities are equally plausible; and that there is no reason why the choice of one should be any more mysterious than the other. The mystery is that the Cuiva solution has not been recognized before and Bernard Arcand should be thanked for finding it.

The justification of an exercise like this is not that it reveals some-thing about Wayãpí culture. It is to show how our distinctions, our moieties, our lines, those 'things which we have made' are so easily imposed on others and are seen to work because the protests against their ordered discipline are so faint. This particular example also shows how difficult it can be to remove distinctions in those cases where they are already in place.

CLAREIRA:
a clearing

Fallentis semita vitae
(The untrodden paths of life)
Horace, *Epistles*, Book I,
xviii: 102.

There is no end to these weird hypostases. Using the strategies of anthropology we can go on creating differences between ourselves and others by inventing substances and essences and principles that we then say are not our things but theirs. We say they have sibs and phratries, totems and taboos; we say they have clans and Crow-Omaha systems, other logics and other minds. Like Pascal we might frighten ourselves contemplating space or like Augustine we might be baffled by the notion of time, but we encompass *their* ideas of time and space with an insouciant analysis. As a result of a chosen idiom others are made to appear to us objects to be contemplated or commodities to be trafficked. We say: 'Amongst the So-and-so's this is the case . . . ' or 'The Such-and-such case shows that . . . ', turning our backs on our previous hosts and referring to them as the teaching doctor describes a patient.

Ethnographies produce that kind of terminal judgement found in biographies and obituaries: those simplified, self-contained descriptions which allow others to say, 'and *that's* what the person was'. Such accounts aim at being a list of qualities and final judgements, but they are really disguised accounts of relationships. She may have been that person's lover, I may have been a friend, a third person no more than a neighbour, and all three of us may agree that the subject was, say, smug and arrogant. But though the particular details (lover, friend, neighbour) have been submerged in the judgement, what we are agreeing about is still the general quality of our relationship with that individual. It is surely an unnecessary terminus to say we have described that *person*. However firm the agreement between the three of us and however often it is reinforced, our common judgements cannot deny to that person other possible relationships of an alternative quality where we and our judgements would be irrelevant.

Should we just keep our biography open-ended, waiting for the accumulation of as many different accounts as possible, waiting for some general outline of agreement to emerge? This would certainly be more tolerant, but the predicament is more than a matter of appreciating *different* interpretations, as in the Rashomon tale, where we might be hoping that each account could complement the others and add further dimensions to a growing story. It is not just a matter of the accumulation of knowledge. The difficulty lies in finding a way to reveal as fully as possible the relational nature of our judgements and to be aware of how much we implicate ourselves into our descriptions of others. In Martin Buber's elliptical terms, it would be a move from the world of 'I – It' to the world of 'I – Thou':

> The primary connexion of man with the world of *It* is comprised in *experiencing*, which continually reconstitutes the world, and *using*, which leads the world to its manifold aim, the sustaining, relieving, and equipping of human life. . . . The development of the ability to experience and use comes about mostly through the decrease of man's power to enter into relation . . .
>
> (Buber 1959:38–39)

The most worthwhile audience for my ethnography should be those friends in the Amazon forest I am writing about, and the most adequate idiom would be a dialogue where they entered the account as 'Thou'. That is a fanciful state of affairs, not yet a serious possibility, but it does set a course away from a diagnostic idiom towards a relational one. I find such a move hindered by three aspects of anthropological work which I describe under the headings 'katabasis', 'details', and 'vocabularies'. These headings pick up themes mentioned in chapter 1.

KATABASIS: 'THE RETURN'

Looking at the motives for doing fieldwork, it is curious that regardless of the quality of being there, regardless of whether one likes being there or loathes being there, the common achievement is realized in the return. The fulfilment of being there is in coming back again, just as in Xenophon's *Anabasis Kyrou* (the 'up-country march') the climax is the *katabasis*, the return, when in 400 BC those 10,000 Greeks fought their way through Kurdistan and Armenia, savage lands to them, and got to the Black Sea. 'Thálassa, thálassa', they cried: 'The sea, the sea'. That meant ships and an easy trip home, 'on their backs' as they put it. Fieldworkers will be familiar with the feeling when they at last get to the airport. What was it all for, then?

A section of *Tristes Tropiques* (Lévi-Strauss 1955) contrasts the sensibilities and apprehensions of travellers with those of anthropologists. Travelling, together with the popular appetite for travel books, is said to be bogus since the real purpose of doing it and talking about it is dissembled. Mere travel does not really search out significant myster-

ies or interesting themes. It is not an intellectual or scientific endeav-
our. It is more accurately described as a 'Quest for Power' (*Quête pour
pouvoir*), and, the argument goes on, analogies can be drawn between
this and primitive initiation rites. Just as young men amongst certain
North American Indian peoples gained prestige by submitting themselves to ordeals, painful initiation rites, and dangerous journeys, so
our travellers and explorers gain prestige through recounting their
adventures in newspaper articles and bestsellers, no matter how
feeble these accounts may actually be. The argument is presented so
attractively; but the purpose of it is to imply that fieldwork, as distinct
from mere travel, is free from that counterfeit. This is not a conclusion
that can be taken seriously. Certainly ethnographies and travel books
tend to follow different conventions, and certainly the two genres
tend to appeal to different readerships, but the quest for power is
certainly not a feature that distinguishes the second from the first.

Well away from fieldwork and anthropology, let me suggest a
peculiarly vivid illustration of the quest for power. An enthusiastic
review by Richard Gott (*The Guardian* 9 October 1981) of a book of
photographs taken by Susan Meiselas in Nicaragua during the Sand-
inista revolution described it as the work of someone now 'at the top
of her profession' and also as 'an extraordinary achievement depicting the banality of war'. The reviewer had been 'waiting im-
patiently' for publication of the book, having enjoyed her previous
one which had been on 'strippers in New England'.

It would be silly to suggest that taking photographs of war is a
duplicitous activity. Similarly there is no question as to the value of
such work in alerting the outside world about what was going on. But
in the context of this kind of review there is an odd tenor to the
judgements that are invited. In this case I am being asked to appreciate that depicting the banality of war is an extraordinary achievement
that affords people the means to get to the top of their profession.
Suddenly, like the flip-over in catastrophe theory, the reviewer in-
vites me to leave off considering the suffering of those torn by a brutal
conflict and to turn to appreciating the glamour of someone's success.
Once that move is made 'Nicaraguans' becomes no more than a
diacritical device or a totemic emblem, like the lists of tribal names in
The Golden Bough, devoid of specificity and context. Any shell-
shocked human frames would do. I am to gaze at their suffering as at
an object for contemplation, arranged for me by a clever hand, whose
talent I am asked to applaud. It is an odd reflection of how strangers
can be used.

Those of us implicated in anthropological fieldwork might claim
that we do not trespass in this way. The commitment to our hosts is
there. We don't only observe; we participate in their lives. We learn
the language and we stay for long spells. But in this case too the point
of being there is the return. Coming home accomplishes the intent.

Like Xenophon's companions we have a bit of plunder, described through a vague synecdoche as one's 'material'. With this to take back, the value of the experience can then be realized in the conference halls and the journals and the other professional exchanges, where, being academia, reputation is more important than the strangers who are its pretext. Here too the strangers are used as objects which we display on our return for our own self-exaltation.

DETAILS

Looking at a block of library shelves filled with the publications of the Bureau of American Ethnology, I am excited by the promise of all sorts of exotic mysteries. It is a wonderful collection to look at. Although the books share a uniform cover, the spines are of random thickness, from massive handbooks to the slim transcription of a song. But though they appear to represent the lives of people, how little one learns of lives. These publications are the result of an implacable resolution to catalogue and classify. It was said of those writers of Franz Boas's time that they were mere collectors of facts and had little theory to inform their work. But what is the difference now? What 'theory' offers is no more than techniques for arranging these facts into systems and structures of varying degrees of complexity and obscurity. The puzzle is why should these followers of Mr Gradgrind, whether in Boas's time or today, want to collect these details in the first place?

I share a community of interest in the minutiae of detail about Wayãpí people with no more than three or four outsiders who have been there and who know the place with an intense intimacy. Extending the interest, I know of two individuals who lived and worked with the Kamarara-ko in French Guiana, and they would also give their thorough attention to every ethnographic detail I could present, in the same way that I am fascinated by anything they tell me. Amongst that half dozen, some of us are friends with many Brazilian Wayãpí, and all of us have some grasp of the language. Shared friends and a shared language bring us together. But as the circle of interest grows and extends throughout the tropical forest, so the significance of the minutiae begins to fade. The shared intimacy is not there to give life to the displayed details. We fall back on themes, like residence patterns, relationship terminologies, cosmological notions, and hope to catch the broader interest in that way.

As the living relation is obscured, the strangers become transformed into named curios. They become fictitious objects, with no human context or human specificity. The tribal name presented with such positivistic confidence has no more substance than the grin on the Cheshire cat. Those names, which keep on accumulating as more ethnographies are published, are just colourful tags in an exotic indexing device – the social organization of the Notobotocudo, kin-

ship among the Quidquidcana, the religion of the Gorgotoqui. Martin
Buber, more passionately this time, puts it like this:

> Man travels over the surface of things and experiences them. He
> extracts knowledge about their constitution from them; he wins
> an experience from them. He experiences what belongs to the
> things.
>
> But the world is not presented to man by experiences alone.
> These present him only with a world composed of *It* and *He* and
> *She* and *It* again.
>
> ... Inner things or outer things, what are they but things and
> things! (1959:5)

The name's the thing. When someone who knows little about the
anthropology of South America asks me to name the people I stayed
with, I find myself reluctant to do so and uneasy if I have to state it.
Amongst those university students I have taught over a number of
years hardly any of them can say the name 'Wayãpí' so rarely have
they heard it said. I am pleased when I find that anonymity maintained. On those occasions in this country when I hear the name said
by someone else I am embarrassed. As far as I know I am the only
person in Britain who has seen these people and if someone else
makes a statement about what 'they' are like, or what 'they' do, or
what 'they' have, I feel I am responsible for what's said. I want to
protect my friends from becoming the objects of sociological car-
icatures such as 'Wayãpí social structure' or 'amongst the Wayãpí it is
believed that ... '. I would be ashamed if they became a name in
anthropological debate. On those few occasions in this country when
I have heard the name said I feel that my interlocutor and I have
become actors playing at understanding in a make-believe show.
What's Hecuba to him or he to Hecuba? The living relation disappears
and we take our parts in a dumb show.

In the preceding essay the name 'Wayãpí' has little importance.
Allowing it to fade in an academic context releases it into its proper
place for its proper function: namely Brazil, where the name is used to
give news of these people to others who are concerned about them,
to tell of incidents that have taken place, and to report on their
present circumstances. 'Last year a subsidiary of the multinational
conglomerate XYZ petitioned the Brazilian government for the right
to exploit resources of tantalite ore in land belonging to the Wayãpí.'
There the name is doing its work. It is not a cipher for indexing a
catalogue of academic abstractions, as those names 'Dravidian', 'Kariera', and 'Cuiva' were, perhaps insensitively, used in the previous
chapter.

VOCABULARIES

Those involved in any one of the various branches of human studies
usually feel that their own discipline deserves precedence over the

others. I feel an urgency about anthropology because it places fieldwork at the centre of its tradition thereby involving practitioners
directly with living people. The subject matter of, say, literary criticism or philosophy, history or archaeology, is already intellectualized
to an extent, but the grounding consideration in anthropology is not
texts, or ideas, or dead people. Anthropology is based on a living
relation between us and them. After a spell doing fieldwork, we are
expected to intellectualize the experience into general themes. Were
ethnography crafty enough, we could use anecdotes as epiphanies,
as Stephen Daedalus wanted to do; but without the accompanying
literary talent the results would be awful. We make the path safer by
finding questions we agree are interesting and procedures we agree
are fruitful and go off in single file following each other through. We
show that we have agreed on the appropriate questions and procedures by using a shared vocabulary. The quality of that vocabulary
discloses the quality of our relation with those we describe within it.
Trivialize the vocabulary and we trivialize the relation.

The vocabulary of structuralism, for example, was a disastrous
murrain that laid the discipline low during the 1960s with still prominent results. It was an astonishingly limited argot, reducing its working terms to the words 'transformation', 'mediation', 'opposition',
'metaphor and metonym', and a few metaphysical flourishes such as
'structure and event'. The principal inadequacy of this fashion was
not that the grandiose claims about revealing 'fundamental structures
of the mind' were bogus (serious though that was) but that devotees
used the vocabulary so unreflectively without a check on its prov-
enance. Lévi-Strauss always gave his sources, and it seems to me that
followers could not have made the fetishes they did of, for example,
'transformation' or 'metaphor and metonym' had they considered the
original sources: in these examples D'Arcy Wentworth Thompson on
the one hand and Jakobson and Halle on the other. e.e. cummings
heard the coarseness underlying assumptions that people very close
to us make about strangers, that coarseness being revealed in the
words they use:

> dem
> gud
> am
> lidl yelluh bas
> tuds weer goin

duhSIVILEYzum

(cummings 1969:52)

Anthropologists, in their turn, go and structuralize 'em by arranging
their lives within a minimal vocabulary. Is that the best we can do?

If we made sense of our own lives and the lives of those close to us
in terms of systems and structures, in terms of transformations and
mediations and oppositions, in terms of ritual this and symbolic that,

of metaphorical this and metonymical that, then there would be a way of relating the descriptions we offer of those strangers to something we understand. There are certainly occasional pieces written about ourselves in this language: about table etiquette, about fashions in clothes, about the ceiling of the Sistine Chapel, about mushrooms, or Picasso; and I suppose as Sunday journalism, they are very clever. But it's hard to find a sustained attempt to offer a comprehensive commentary in this language which would inform our daily lives. Turned on ourselves, what emerges are these offhand comments that while away the afternoon. But when turned on the strangers not a corner of their lives, from settlement patterns to eschatology, escapes the caricature of that language. Words that we use for marginal notes and throw-away observations about ourselves are used to totalize the lives of strangers with the result that ethnographies written in that idiom transform those peoples into curios, into disembodied *objets trouvés*; things to be owned and traded, displayed and valued, praised and depreciated, depending on the fashions and the company one keeps.

As a named fashion, structuralism has apparently gone out of date. People now declare their mental tastes under a variety of other labels – transactionalists, ethnoscientists, kinship specialists, marxists, post-structuralists – and make up derogatory labels for those identified as having interests inimical to theirs – collectivists, symbolists, subjectivists. In a different context, a century ago, Giuseppe Verdi described a similar slew of -isms as 'devilish pedantries':

> I've no idea how we are going to escape from this musical ferment. Some want to be melodists like Bellini, some harmonists like Meyerbeer. I don't want to be one or the other, and I want the younger composers of today not to think about being melodists, harmonists, realists, idealists, futurists or any of these other devilish pedantries. Melody and harmony should only be tools for music-making in the hands of the artist; and, if ever the day comes in which people no longer talk of melody, harmony, German and Italian schools, the past, the future etc. etc., then perhaps the kingdom of art will begin.   (Osborne 1971:196)

The various branches of human studies are still packed with such pedantries. But the divisions between these collectivities are hardly more than choices between one vocabulary and another. Furthermore, declaring that a piece of work belongs to a particular -ism does nothing to establish its value. Maurice Bloch states that much of what is called 'Marxist anthropology' is 'barbarously phrased' (1983:v) before going on to defend it. If that is so, whether or not it is 'Marxist' is neither here nor there. A marxist heart may be one that's in the right place and a marxist awareness of the imperfections of social conditions may be commendably acute, but if marxist prose is teeming with undisciplined squads of production it is not going to produce particularly illuminating commentaries on the world around us. If the prose is barbarously phrased it is bad work, and that's that.

To complain about bad style is risky since it concentrates judgement on my own. 'Le style c'est l'homme même', said Buffon, but Voltaire thought Buffon's style was execrable and d'Alembert called him 'the great phrase-mongerer'. Even so, even if I am hung like Deacon Brodie on a gibbet of my own design, the concern is worthwhile. Barbarous prose is an identifiable crisis in much more than 'Marxist anthropology'. Some thirty years ago, C. Wright Mills referred to 'a serious crisis in literacy' (1959: 217) involving the social sciences. The phrase was borrowed from Edmund Wilson who wrote in the original piece:

> As for my experience with articles by experts in anthropology and sociology, it has led me to conclude that the requirement, in my ideal university, of having the papers in every department passed by a professor of English might result in revolutionizing these subjects – if indeed the second of them survived at all.
>
> (Wilson 1957:123)

Well, that was before the gimcrack antics of deconstruction spread through the English schools, where writing obscurely is seen as both necessary and virtuous. I wonder what he'd have said about that.

This is a dangerous theme to negotiate since it is so charged with moral feeling. And properly so, since there is so much at stake. One of the dangers is that of appearing like some pompous gentleman from the Shires sounding off about 'proper English'. On a more serious level, nerves are still taut. Robert Burchfield says that Colin McCabe was 'right – or partially right' when he asserted that 'the eighteenth-century grammars, and more importantly the views of language and class which underpinned them, continue to terrorize English speech' (*The Listener* 12 August 1982:13–14). Burchfield goes on: 'But if McCabe's post-structuralist views were to prevail, some new and even more unacceptable views of language and class would place grave restrictions on (that is, terrorize) English speech' (1986:3).

I think we can get away from jeremiads about literacy crises, which at any rate appear to be as old as literacy itself. It is not a question of 'getting it right'. It is not a question of, for instance, cleaning up sexism in one's speech by avoiding expressions such as 'mastering the native language'. Though particular efforts like that are important, they assume an eventual state of grace: 'I once was lost but now am found'. But it is not a matter of proscribing and prescribing vocabulary.

If I get tired, not just of a vocabulary that indicates a passing fashion ('transformation', 'mediation'), but one that consists of worn-out semaphore postures ('theory', 'analysis'), and if I avoid these words, I am not 'taking words away'. I'm doing the opposite. I'm suggesting a self-conscious effort to enrich everyday vocabulary by looking at the invigorating resources of literary traditions, etymologies, and the connections amongst different languages. In short, a query about style is not a prissy demand that people 'speak correctly' but a request for the latitude to be allowed to speak originally.

> Interesting philosophy is never an examination of the pros and cons of a thesis, but implicitly or explicitly, a contest between an entrenched vocabulary which has become a nuisance and a half-formed new vocabulary which vaguely promises great things.
>
> (Rorty 1986:4)

Literacy concerns and literary concerns are indissolubly involved one with the other, and there is a refreshing emphasis in recent years on paying attention to ethnographic texts as literary texts (e.g., J. Clifford and G. Marcus 1986). Clifford Geertz refers to some dangers in this approach, amongst them, that it may turn into endless struggles about the meanings of words, as in certain varieties of linguistic philosophy: 'What is Culture?'; 'Does Kinship exist?'; 'Do Institutions think?' Another danger, according to Geertz, is that in attending to style and genre, one runs the risk of aestheticism:

> ... the possibility that both ethnographers and their audience may come to believe that the value of writing about tattooing or witchcraft exhausts itself in the pleasures of the text. Anthropology as a good read.   (Geertz 1988:142)

Geertz sees such risks as worth running. I cannot see them as risks at all. The first refers to those 'barren logomachies' (as Matthew Arnold referred to some of Plato's discussions) where cherished abstractions are defended by hanging on to fetish words ('culture', 'kinship', 'relations of production') and insisting on their definition. But this is the *least* obvious peculiarity of any kind of 'literary' approach, and one of the *most* obvious peculiarities of traditional social studies. And as for the second, if the choice is between anthropology as a good read and anthropology as a bad read, as 'barbarously phrased', or as plain boring, the alternatives there can hardly be said to present us with a difficult decision.

What is offered in a 'literary approach' is not a polemical alternative to, but an enrichment of what is already going on. Here are some suggestions:

(a) A quotation from Wordsworth can be as appropriate in anthropology as a quotation from Lévi-Strauss. There is no reason to suppose that there is a class of quotations called 'anthropological' that is conventionally acceptable in laying out an argument, and a class of quotations called 'literary' that is seen as some sort of frivolous habit of embellishment.

(b) When Renato Rosaldo looks at Le Roy Ladurie's *Montaillou* and at Evans-Pritchard's *The Nuer* he sees them as modern versions of 'the pastoral' (1986). That term refers us to a mode that goes back as far as Theocritus and the original 'Daphnis and Chloe':

> Smooth life the herdsman, and his snow-white herd
> To triumphs and to sacrificial rites
> Devoted . . .

(Wordsworth The Prelude 1805–6, VIII:316–18)

It is such a vivid *topos*, so rich in association, that using it in this way throws a genuinely original light on to these two books. There is no need to see that kind of originality as a threat to the more usual commentaries that worry as to whether the one might belong to the *Annales* school and the other to 'structural-functionalism'. Why not embrace the originality of the association?

(c) It is refreshing that words like *topoi* and 'tropes' become current (although those who use them might be more aware that they are not interchangeable). The point is not that such terms introduce a new jargon, but that they indicate such productive parallels to ethnography by introducing the vividness and variety of literary examples.

(d) Those examples also focus on an particular concern with language. I would suggest, for example, that Lienhardt's *Divinity and Experience* is a more interesting piece of work than Evans-Pritchard's *Nuer Religion* because of a more subtle and more inventive choice of words. That mysterious vocabulary in Evans-Pritchard's book (hierological, polyonymous, henotheistic, *numen* and *nomen*, theophany, theriomorphic) fits well with the general theme: interpreting Nuer religion through the terms and experiences of a theological vocabulary and a theological awareness. More interesting, though, are Lienhardt's choices amongst ordinary words: 'emblems', 'images', and the resurrection of the etymology of 'passions', as well as numerous reminders that everyday words of ours such as 'mind', 'self', 'memory' can stand in the way of understanding others. Both books can be contrasted with Bateson's *Naven* where, like a medical researcher or zoologist, he goes to Greek for quasi-technical terms and nonce-words: 'ethos and eidos', 'symmetrical and complementary schismogenesis'. Is that because 'scientific' terms were necessary for a vocabulary to be respectable in 1936? I. A. Richards would have called such discussions 'practical criticism'. There is nothing exclusively 'literary' about them and they can only enrich, not threaten, current habits of judgement.

To summarize, I'm suggesting three efforts: first of all to put aside as far as possible the quest for power and to emphasize an extraversion to the up-country march as worthwhile in itself without these ulterior glances in the direction of the return. Secondly, to appreciate that no compendium of details is worthwhile without adequate reflection on why these details have been collected in the first place. While maintaining an extraverted curiosity towards what is going on up in the Himalayas or along the banks of the Nile, one should be scrupulously inquisitive as to the locus and motives of that curiosity. And thirdly, instead of covering one's tracks with a borrowed vocabulary, to use a diction that reflects the private effort to find the right word from the full resources of our languages.

Anthropology is said to be a moral education. Students are told that it corrects 'ethnocentric bias', that it educates towards a tolerance for other ways of life, and especially towards an understanding of primitive societies and dispossessed minorities. Even further, it is said that knowledge of others allows us to reflect better on ourselves:

Learn of the green world what can be thy place
In scaled invention or true artistry.
Pull down thy vanity,
          Paquin pull down!
The green casque has outdone your elegance.

(Pound 1948:LXXXI)

Paquin was a Parisian dress designer. If elegant salons and the sophisticated tastes of the privileged and influential parts of our world are representative of our culture, there is much to learn from the green world. The critic and broadcaster J. W. Lambert, a gourmet, apparently, as well as an expert on classical music and a literary editor of *The Sunday Times*, wrote a piece in that paper describing the Wagrani (or Auca) of Ecuador, then in their final resistance against the insidious encroachment of missionaries, as 'a bunch of scrabbling murderers little above, indeed in many ways below, the level of the beasts with whom they shared the forest' (Lambert 1980). A vulnerable group of Amerindians was here prominently described by a well-known critic on a full page spread in one of Britain's leading newspapers in words that could have been used by Gobineau or Goebbels, and there was not a hint of repercussion. Perhaps it needs to be emphasized that this outlook is standard. It certainly has a long history. Going back a century, admirers of the novels of Anthony Trollope may be surprised to learn that after a visit to Australia he wrote of the Aborigines:

Of the Australian black man we may certainly say that he has to go. That he should perish without unnecessary suffering should be the aim of all those who are concerned in the matter. But no good can be done by giving to the aboriginal a character which he does not deserve, or by speaking of the treatment which he receives in language which the facts do not warrant.

(Trollope 1873:76)

In 1537 Alessandro Farnese, known as Pope Paul III, issued the Bull *Veritas Ipsa* which declared that American Indians were true men, not beasts. Beyond his efforts, four and a half centuries of enlightenment and progress have clearly made little impression on this brutish aspect of our awareness. It's a moral ignorance long decayed and one can nose it today in the most priviliged corridors.

It is difficult to claim confidently that anthropology can educate this awareness, not only because it is so deeply ingrained outside the discipline, but because it has not entirely vanished within. What is judged good work by academic standards may reveal nothing about moral dispositions. In a commentary on the work of Céline, George Steiner takes up a theme prominent for instance in the thought of Ruskin and Sartre that a good work of art could not be produced by a morally repulsive sensibility. Céline, praised as a genius of prose but revealing an 'infernal sociology' including a particularly vehement streak of anti-semitism, gives the lie to that 'serene assumption'. Making the point in a less extreme context Steiner refers to:

> . . . that dissociation between professional zeal and true accuracy of spirit, between the humanities and the humane, that marks so much of present academic work . . .   (1972:49).

Well-phrased and technically competent work may shelter all sorts of unattractive presuppositions. Even further, there is no guarantee that actually doing anthropological fieldwork will alter a distaste for allowing strangers to come close. Extensive familiarity with other peoples can just as well confirm the prejudgements and confirm the old despair. At the end of a book that claims to discover the nature of 'primitive thought' by using evidence from developmental psychology, a writer who has carried out fieldwork with various peoples says:

> It is thoroughly sensible to love one's own society and to dedicate oneself to its interests in preference to those of other societies, to prefer the company of those of one's own kind to that of strangers . . .   (Hallpike 1979:495)

'One's own kind' is such an arresting phrase. I notice that I would not care to start charting the differences between 'my own kind' and 'strangers' by quantifying lexicons, by testing verbal skills, by measuring conceptual astuteness, or by assaying degrees of cognitive development. Nor are these the grounds on which I judge the quality of other people's company. I also remember how much I'd prefer the company of so many Wayãpí friends, strangers in this context, to that of many of 'my own kind' however these may be identified by marks of caste or place or speech. 'Strangers' to me suggests people I should welcome, 'for thereby some have entertained angels unawares'.

Anthropology's professional zeal in gathering facts about strangers makes it seem as if it is on their side, but that depends on what the knowledge is for. 'Knowledge kindles calentures in some.' The activity may be no more than a fervid display for self-interested, professional ends. Writing of those who have worked with Indians in the Amazon forest, Roberto da Matta describes the anthropologist as the person who:

> . . . constrói seu prestígio e faz sua carreira sobre os ombros do miserável grupo tribal que estuda.

(. . . builds up his prestige and makes his career on the backs of the miserable tribal group that he studies.)   (Da Matta 1972)
It is a devastating observation, and unless it can be ameliorated there is no place in such a state of affairs for any claim to moral relevance.

The peculiarity of anthropology amongst other human studies lies in its role as intercessor for the strangers. Interceding in a practical way, protecting their lives and their land, requires the commitment of being there, making oneself available to them on a daily basis with antibiotics and hypodermic at hand, prepared to take their part in facing the violence and greed that our way of life throws towards them (the prospectors and desperadoes, mineral explorations and road schemes), and prepared to argue for their interests in the offices of bureaucratic authorities. Without that commitment, the most sincere efforts at part-time, far-away help through conference resolutions, newspaper articles, and letters to heads of governments is of very limited help. You do what you can at the time. From outside the subject, it would be inappropriate to make too much of accusing the anthropological community of failing to do enough for these peoples since there may be so little opportunity to do something effective. From within the subject, claims to be politically active should be considered in terms of how far the commitment to being there can be followed through.

The conditions of dominion – imperial, colonial, economic, or material – that made anthropology possible in the first place, still obtain. However sensitive we may be to these conditions we cannot carry on the activity pretending that it has been deodorized of them. While anyone involved can recognize these preconditions and can go on to repudiate them (taking the side of the strangers, fighting for them against the forces of possession, oppression, and manipulation that accompany our economic, political, and religious ways of life), we cannot repudiate the state of affairs that allows us access to their lives in a way that they do not have access to ours. We have access to comparisons and alternatives, to history and documents, to means of communication and diverse audiences. And of course we return home and write about *them*. In other words we have power, which is more than authoritarian and more than materialistic. It is epistemological. And we cannot repudiate that.

It is easy to appreciate the political and material dimensions of the relationship between us and them, easy to see that what is being done to the indigenous peoples in Amazônia is appalling. Although proposing and implementing alternatives to the abuses perpetrated by our world on theirs (alternatives other than 'hands off' and 'get out') is very much more difficult, appreciating the problem is pretty straightforward. But it is uncomfortable to have to face up to this business of 'knowing more than they do'. There is no point in side stepping the problem by saying that their botanical taxonomies are richly detailed, that their practical skills are breathtaking, and that the wisdom they reveal about the value of human relationships and family life is admirable. Be that as it may, they do *not* know us as we know them.

I think there is a way of appreciating this without being pompous or paternalistic. It is somewhat as we appreciate the literature and philosophy of the past: 'Someone said: "The dead writers are remote from us because we *know* so much more than they did." Precisely, and they are that which we know' (Eliot 1953:25). They are that which we know, and though remote from us in the Amazon woods, they are alive, and we can take part in a living relationship with them. And 'that which we know' in this case becomes uniquely precious, far removed from any taint of bookish pedantry.

We can use that knowledge to intercede for the strangers within the moral climate that prevails in our world. Practically, up to now, that has done little to protect them. Those peoples we write about are involved with us through conditions of contact that were deadly in the past and that remain precarious today. For them the involvement is overwhelming. But most of the time our world remains ignorant of its part, unaware of what it did, and unaware of what it is doing. When that involvement is brought to its notice, we find strangers being referred to in that brutal language illustrated above where any question of a relationship with them is treated with indifference or even derision. But it seems to me that it is through our responses to strangers that we disclose our deepest human dispositions. Even though a concern like that may fail, here and now, to do anything much for them, it is not a modest programme, nor is it cloistered, nor antiquarian. It reveals an aspect of human studies that can properly be described as a moral education. It insists on declaring that we are indeed involved with strangers and begins to query the nature of that relationship by asking: What is it that lies between us and them and what is it that we cross in our encounters with others?

Once, when travelling alone from the Nipukú to the FUNAI post, I came across a *desmatamento* team (see p. 40) on the banks of the Rio Felício. They were dressed in ragged shorts and I saw that their hunters went out barefoot. In so many aspects of their material life the gap between these people and the Indians is hardly apparent. But in the manners and attitudes nurtured by that, the difference is enormous. I saw them as hardened people, tanned and calloused by the indignity of being hopelessly poor in a huge acquisitive society. When I walked into their camp my arrival produced a silent, tense suspicion so unlike my first meeting with the Indians. I don't know what they thought I was, in a grubby loin-cloth and T-shirt, and filthy with mud. Obviously I was not an Indian since I had a rucksack and rifle, a beard and the wrong kind of long hair. I greeted them in Portuguese which broke the stillness. The *empreiteiro* (the boss) quickly appeared from the shelter. He was an older man, neatly dressed. He gave me a kindly greeting and offered me beans and coffee; wonderful luxuries which I accepted. I was offered a place to put my hammock but I declined that, being anxious to get on. I explained something of my presence and was interrogated as to whether there were *índios bravos* in the woods ahead. All road teams are nervous about unknown *índios bravos*. Suddenly the *empreiteiro* summed up the interview. 'Ah! I see. *O senhor e amador dos índios.*' He used the formal address *'o senhor'*. *Amador* means amateur. It can also translate the Spanish *aficionado*, a fan. It also means lover. I was frightened for a moment that things were turning ugly since I heard an echo of that violent celluloid American expression: 'injun lover'. He didn't mean that, but even if he had it would have been a description to be proud of.

> *el problema es este* this is the difficulty –
> *lo que se pierde* what gets lost
> *no es lo que se pierde en traducion sino*
> is not what gets lost in translation but more
> what gets lost in language itself *lo que se pierde*
> *en el hecho en la lengua,*
> *en la palabra misma.*
>   Alastair Reid, 'What Gets Lost / *Lo Que Se Pierde*'

'What we learned from the Wayana'.

I have noted the following bits and pieces of material culture as coming from the Wayana:

The technique for making canoes.

Hanging square mirrors round their necks.

Certain songs about 'papai do ceu', Portuguese for 'daddy in the sky'.

The design of one kind of wooden stool.

A leg design painted on in genipa dye consisting of / pira-kang-wèrë / (fish bone) and / pana-pè-pòkwèrë / (butterfly wings) (the solid triangles).

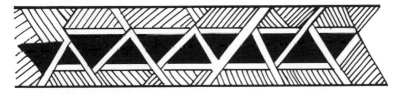

A useful technique in thatching (shown in a second but tedious to describe). As each leaf of / owi / (obim) is bent over, a long string of / yo / cut from / naya / (inajá) is quickly wrapped round to hold the leaf in place. Formerly each leaf of owi had to be tied separately. They say this type of thatch is called / mararia / in Wayana.

Mentioned as having been learned from the Kamarara-ko are:

The / asikaro-pòka /, an ingenious sugar-cane squeezer. Two varieties of banana (to add to their own ten varities), / pakòaka'ïg / which tastes vaguely of oranges, and / pakò-raporo / which smells slightly of the cacao fruit, hence the name, /raporo/ meaning cacao.

Making caxiri (manioc beer) in small, roughly hewn 'canoes'. Formerly caxiri was made in huge clay pots which are not made any more.

As well as these items, it was on the Cuc that they found their main supply of axes, machetes, knives, manufactured red cloth, and beads.

They say that in the old days, before they had axes and machetes, they had only / tapɨina / s. This is the current word for a temporary shelter, the kind of thing we would build when travelling, covering it with a quick thatch of / wasei / (açaí), / pinò / (bacaba), or / moromoro / (a palm leaf similar to açaí but covered with spikes). / tapɨina / however is a new word learned from the French Wayãpí. The old word was / tòyǫpa / (cf. Brazilian Portuguese *tejupá*). They now build three kinds of house:

(1) ɨwɨ-ǫ̀ / (old word)

/ okạ-wɨrɨ / (Kamarara-ko word)

This has an earth floor and open sides

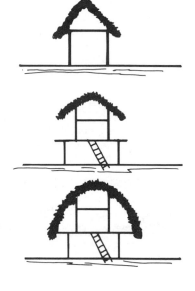

(2) / òkạpɨṣèṣè /, now the most common type at the Nipukú, built on stilts with a raised floor of slats cut from the açaí palm. The sides are usually left open though slatted walls can be made.

(3) / wamɨg̈ /, also on stilts, but the thatch comes down to the floor. The gable ends are also slatted to give complete privacy.

It would be very difficult to build the last two kinds without axes or machetes, but since they have an old word for the first kind, and since it is really no more than a large, carefully built tapɨina with proper thatching, I think the statement about them living only in shelters is a mythy elaboration. Interestingly, in myths, when the jaguar or anaconda 'comes to the house' it is the word / òkạ-wɨrɨ / which is used, not / ɨwɨ-ò /. Perhaps many of the stories they now tell were taught to them by the Cuc and Oyapoque Wayãpí.

The following is a short lexicon of 'old words' and their equivalents in use today. I will leave the implications of this list to those who know more than I about the comparative linguistics of the Amazon area. I am sure there will be inaccuracies here, but I offer what I was told. From the little I know, it seems that the new words sometimes show Carib influence while the old words are closer to the Tupí terms found in the writings of the chroniclers, in Lingua Geral, and in Brazilian Portuguese dialects.

	old word	kamarara-ko word
farinha, manioc flour	o'i	kwakɨ
chibé, manioc porridge	siwè	meyotɨkwarë
caxiri, manioc beer	* kasiri	parakasi
tucupí, hot spiced manioc juice	* minga'o	? takaka
tapioca, white sediment	* tɨpɨ'ò	? takaka
sugar cane	kan	asikaro
jerimum, pumpkin	nyèrōmo	asikara
tobacco	pètɨu	makurè
large calabash	kawasu	mòròtoko
house	ɨwɨ'ò	òka-wɨrɨ
shelter, tejupá	toyọpa	tapɨina
cage (for bird or animal)	kurạrë	pari
knife	kɨsè	marịa
machete	kɨsè-wasu, sa	sa
spoon	* séré	sèrèti
shotgun	* mòka	wɨrakausa
man	* apịa	kwaima'è
woman	* waimingwèrë	? waimi
old	* ka'a koa	tamusi
hen	sapoka	masakara
wild duck	ɨpè	ārāpono
jejú, species of fish	yoyo	warapạ
poraque, electric eel	* pɨrakè	ariminŭ
also	nyawinawa	
trahirão, species of fish	tarè'ɨrë	? tare'ɨ
also	tairosọ	
saúva, (leaf cutting ant)	* asa'ɨğ	ɨa
maçaranduba, bully tree	* masarandɨ	ɨwɨ
a wild tree with leaves like the cultivated banana	sòròró ka'a-rò (otter leaves)	
three	mosapɨ	moapɨ
only	* kurinyon	kèrenyon
rice	(no word)	arèsi

Kamararo-ko words tend to be used more. Asterisks indicate old words which are still in most common use.

Wayãpí relationship terms

Certain words in Tupi-Guaraní languages take what Ayron dal Igna Rodriguez (personal communication) has called 'relational prefixes'. The best known instance is what Métraux refers to as the 'well-known' t— r variation (e.g. 'tata', fire, becomes 'uruwu-rata', the urubu's fire). There is no advantage in abstracting the root morpheme (here 'ata') since it never appears without a prefix of some kind. In all cases when the word stands unqualified, it is given with the 't' prefix. Examples are given in the following lexicon. In the gloss terms are given minimal genealogical specifications.

(1) tamu
    (tamòi: FF, MF, MBF, FZF
    èramòi – my grandfather
    nèramòi – your grandfather
    tamo-ko – 'grandfather people'
    Myths are often described as taking place in / tamoko-rèmè /,
    i.e. 'the time of grandfather people'.

(2) sa'i
    (i-yarɨi): MM, FM, MBM, FZM
    èyatɨi – my grandmother
    sa'i-ko – 'grandmother people'

(3) papa (to): F, FB
    èro – my father
    nèro – your father
    papa miti – FB (/ miti / is a diminutive – for use see below).

(4) mama (i-yɨğ): M, MZ
    èɨğ – my mother
    nèɨğ – your mother
    e'i òɨğ-pè – 'he said to his mother'
    i-yɨğ'ɨrë – / mama miti / or / mam'o / (see / a'o / below)
               'another mother', 'distant mother'

(5) pipi
    (i-yayè, i-teia): FZ, MBW, WM
    The descriptive form / papa kuyaŋ /, literally 'father's sister'
    is often used. It is not common to hear the reference form
    either in conversation or in myth telling.

(6) pa'i

> (tatɨu): MB, FZH, WF
> The reference form should not be confused with (13) / tatɨg /.
> eratɨu – my / pa'i /.
> Description: mama-kɨwɨrë – literally, 'mother's (younger) brother'.

(7) kakanyɨ: eB

> There is a reference form – / tèkè ɨrë / – hence / nèrèkè'ɨrë /, 'your elder brother', but the term is also used in the series:
> > tèkè'ɨrë, mɨtèpòr, miti, sakɨre
> terms which carry the sense of 'elder', 'middle', 'small', and 'infant' (see below).

(7a) i'momini (m.s.), i-kɨwɨrë (w.s.): yB.

> / i-kɨwɨrë / (w.s.) is a reference form. Both men and women use the vocative / èmomini / when addressing an adult yB. A child is addressed as / mimi / and when mature / toko / (cf. 11.) The old term of address / sọi / is not now used.

(8) nyạnya: eZ

> i-kunyaŋ (m.s.): yZ
> i-kɨpɨ'ɨrë (w.s.): yZ
> / nyạnya / is vocative only. The general word for 'sisters' is / i-kunyaŋ / but this is also the vocative form used by both men and women. / i-kɨpɨ'ɨrë / is referential only.
> Within the household a child is addressed as / si'ŭ / and when mature either as / ya'ɨg / (Nipukú) or / mã'si / (Capocira). / ya'ɨg / is said to be a term of address introduced from the / kamarạra-ko /.

(9) èrèkwạrë (m.s.): W, BW, FZD, MBD

> An obsolete form, possibly an original referential term, is / ewewarë /.
> The category is usually described as:
> > / pa'i rayɨrë /, literally FZD
> > or / pipi mèmɨrë /, literally MBD
> A man will confidently describe the woman he is actually married to as / èrèrèkwạrë / but prefers one of the above periphrases to refer to other women in the category.

(9a) tõ'i (w.s.): FZD, MBD, HZ

> One form only found.

(10) tairò (m.s.) (tairò'ɨrë): FZS, MBS, WB

> Reference forms: èrairò'ɨrë (my 'tairo')
> > nèrairö'ɨrë (your 'tairo').

(10b) i-mèn (w.s.): H, FZS, MBS

> While a woman will easily describe a man as / nyanya-mèn /, literally eZH, considerable embarassment is shown in using the term / è-mèn /, my husband, especially if the man is only

categorically so. The usual periphrases are the parallels of
(9a), i.e., /pa'i-ra'ɨrë/, MBD, or /pipi-mèmɨrë/, FZD.
The term seems to be related to the verb /o-meno/, to
copulate.
In the old days a woman might have used the term
/sèkunyaŋ/ to address a HB. One person said that a man
might have used the same word for addressing a BW.
/Si'ŭ-ro/ or /ya'ɨg̈-ro/, literally 'child's father' is a form of
direct address from W to H, but such forms are seldom used.

(11) ta'ɨrë (m.s.): S
(12) tayɨrë (m.s.): D
  /ta'ɨrɨŋ/ means small
  /ta'ɨrë/ is also the word for sperm.
(11a) i-mèmɨrë (w.s.) S and D
and   Sex is distinguished by adding /kwạima'è̥ (Nipukú) or /apɨa/
(12a) (Capoeira), that is, 'man', or /wạimi/, 'woman'.
  Address within the household is the same as that for (7) and
  (8):
    /mimi/ or /ya'ɨg̈/ (infant son)
    /toko/ (when mature)
    /si'ŭ/ (infant daughter)
    /masi/ (when mature, Capoeira)
    /ya'ɨg̈/ (when mature, Nipukú)
  The general term for 'children' or 'young people' is
  o-kɨrɨŋgwèrë.
(13) tatɨg̈ (m.s.), kụnyaŋ-tại (w.s.) (ta'ɨrë tatɨg̈): ZD (m.s.), BD
(w.s.)
  The reference form is seldom heard. At the Nipukú both
  /tatɨg̈/ and /kunyaŋ-tai/ have been replaced by one term:
  /pĩ-sĩ/, said to be a term taught to them by the /kamarara-
  ko/. Some men speakers at the Nipukú do still use /tatɨg/. It
  is said that /tatɨg/ and /kunyaŋ-tai/ are terms not known by
  the /kamarạra-ko/.
(14) kwani (tanyowè̥n): ZS (m.s.), BS (w.s.)
  The referential form is rarely heard.
(15) i-parë
  The single term covers all specifications at the 2nd
  descending genealogical level.
  /sa'i-ko/, 'grandmother-people' are said to have used the
  term   /èmiŋyarịoŋ/.
  In the myths supernatural beings usually refer to Wayāpí
  characters as /è-parë/, my grandchild, and the Wayāpí
  responds /tamu/, grandfather.
There is a set of four qualifiers:
  tèkè'ɨirë (/tɨker/ when qualifying a female term), mɨtèpòr,
  miti, sakɨre.

/ tèkè'ɨrë / is the referential form of the vocative / kakanyɨ /.
Thus:

> nèrèkè'ɨrë – your eB
> papa-rèkè'ɨrë – FeB

but / papa tèkè'ɨrë / means 'eldest father' in a series which can
include any two or all of the above terms.
/ mɨtèpòr / means 'middle', e.g.:

> ɨwɨ mɨtèpòr – the middle of the earth, as opposed to,
> ɨwɨ pò-pɨ   – the end of the earth.

/ miti / is a general diminutive with wide application,
e.g. / ɨğ miti /, a tiny stream.
/ sakɨre / refers to a human infant.
These qualifiers can be attached, when required, to the
vocative terms and the composite term can be used either
vocatively or referentially. They are used to distinguish
amongst a group of individuals in the same category by
relative age.

However, / papa-miti / and / mama-miti / are also used
without reference to relative age to describe genealogically
distant fathers and mothers.

References

Allen, N. J. (1986) 'Tetradic Theory: An Approach to Kinship.'
JASO: Journal of the Anthropological Society of Oxford vol. 17, no.
2, 87–109.
Arcand, Bernard (1977) 'The Logic of Kinship, an example from the
Cuiva.' *Actes du XLIIᵉ Congrès International des Américanistes* Vol.
2, 19–34.
Ardener, Edwin (1971) 'Introductory Essay' in *Social Anthropology
and Language* A.S.A. Monograph 10. ix-cii. London: Tavistock.
Augustine (1961) *Confessions* trans. R. S. Pine-Coffin. Penguin
Books.
Bates, H. W. (1863) (1930) *The Naturalist on the River Amazons*
London: Everyman's Library.
Bateson, Gregory (1936) (1958) *Naven* Stanford University Press.
Black, Max (1958) 'Making something happen' in Sidney Hook (ed)
Determinism and Freedom in the Age of Modern Science 15–30. New
York University Press.
  (1969) 'Some Troubles with Whorfianism' in Sidney Hook (ed)
Language and Philosophy 30–35. New York University Press.
Bloch, Maurice (1983) *Marxism and Anthropology* Oxford: Clarendon
Press.
Bodin, M. (1825) 'Précis de la Relation encore inédite d'un Voyage
chez les Oyampis, à la source de la rivière Oyapock, par M.
Bodin.' *Bulletin de la Société de Géographie* vol. 4, 50–61.
Bourne, Richard (1978) *Assault on the Amazon* London: Victor
Gollancz Ltd.
Buber, Martin (1937) (1959) *I and Thou* trans. Ronald Gregor Smith.
Edinburgh: T. and T. Clark.
Buchler, I. R. and Selby, H. A. (1968) *Kinship and Social
Organization: An Introduction to Theory and Method* New York:
Macmillan.
Burchfield, Robert (1986) *The English Language* Oxford University
Press.
Clifford, J. and Marcus, G. E. (eds) (1986) *Writing Culture: The
Poetics and Politics of Ethnography* University of California Press.

Collingwood, R. G. (1938) 'On the so-called idea of causation.' *Proceedings of the Aristotelian Society* N.S. vol. XXXVIII, 85–112.

Cooper, John M. (1946) 'The Araucanians' in Julian H. Steward (ed) *Handbook of South American Indians* vol. 2, 687–760. Bureau of American Ethnology Bulletin 143: Washington.

Coudreau, Henri (1892) *Vocabulaires méthodiques des langues Ouyana, Aparai, Oyampi, Émérillon* Paris: Bibliothèque Linguistique Américaine XV.

(1893) *Chez nos Indiens* Paris.

Cowell, Adrian (1973) (1976) *The Tribe that Hides from Man* Abacus.

Crevaux, J. (1883) *Voyages dans l'Amérique du Sud* Paris.

Cummings, e.e. (1960) (1969) *Selected poems 1923–1958* London: Faber and Faber.

Da Matta, Roberto (1972) 'Contracapa' to R. Cardoso de Oliveira *A Sociologia de Brasil Indígena* Rio de Janeiro.

De Bauve, Adam (1833) 'Voyage dans l'intérieur de la Guyane, par MM. Adam de Bauve et P. Ferré.' *Bulletin de la Société de Géographie* no. 126, vol. 20, 210–27 and 265–83.

(1834)'Voyage dans l'intérieur de la Guyane, par MM. Adam de Bauve et P. Ferré.' *Bulletin de la Société de Géographie* 2nd series, vol. 1, 105–17 and 165–78.

Diaz de Aguiar, Braz (1942) 'Trabalhos da Comissão Brasileira Demarcadora de Limites – Primeira Divisão – nas Fronteiras da Venezuela e Guianas Britânica e Neerlandesa, de 1930 a 1940.' *IX Congresso Brasileiro de Geografia, Anais* vol. II, 202–375. Rio de Janeiro.

Diószegi, Vilmos (1974) 'Shamanism.' *Encyclopaedia Britannica* 15th Edition vol. 16.

Douglas, Mary (1980) *Evans-Pritchard* Fontana.

Dumont, Louis (1953) 'The Dravidian kinship terminology as an expression of marriage.' *Man* vol. 53 art. 54.

(1966) 'Descent or intermarriage?: a relational view of Australian section systems.' *Southwestern Journal of Anthropology* vol. 22 pp. 231–50.

(1970) 'Sur le vocabulaire de parenté Kariera' in Jean Pouillon and Pierre Maranda (eds) *Échanges et Communications* vol. 1, 272–86. Paris, the Hague: Mouton.

Eliade, Mircea (1964) *Shamanism* trans. W. R. Trask. London.

Eliot, T. S. (1919) (1953) *Selected Prose* Penguin Books.

Evans-Pritchard, E. E. (1937) *Witchcraft, Oracles and Magic among the Azande* Oxford: Clarendon Press.

(1956) *Nuer Religion* Oxford: Clarendon Press.

Farabee, W. C. (1917) 'The Amazon Expedition: The Tapajos.' *The Museum Journal* vol. 8, 126–44. University Museum, Philadelphia.

Findhorn Community (1976) *The Findhorn Garden* London: Turnstone Books.

Flew, Antony (et al) (1979) *A Dictionary of Philosophy* London: Pan Books.

Gadamer, Hans-Georg (1976) *Philosophical Hermeneutics* trans. and ed. D. E. Linge. University of California Press.

Galvão, Eduardo (1960) 'Áreas Culturais Indígenas do Brasil: 1900–1959.' *Boletim do Museu Paraense Emílio Goeldi* N. S. Antropologia No. 8, Belém, Pará.

Gillen, John (1948) 'Tribes of the Guianas and the Left Amazon Tributaries' in Julian H. Steward (ed) *Handbook of South American Indians* vol. 3, 799–860. Washington: Smithsonian Institution.

Goodland, R. J. A. and Irwin, H. S. (1975) *Amazon Jungle: Green Hell to Red Desert?* Amsterdam: Elsevier.

Grenand, Pierre (1972) *Les Relations intertribales en Haute. Guyane de XVIII° siècle a nos jours* Mémoire de maitrise, Paris V. Paris: Institut d'Ethnologie.

(1978) 'Histoire des Amerindiens.' *Atlas des Departments d'Outre-Mer. La Guyane* Planche 17, 3–4. Paris: CNRS/ORSTOM.

(1980) *Introduction a l'Étude de l'Univers Wayãpí* Paris: SELAF.

Hallpike, C. R. (1979) *The Foundations of Primitive Thought* Oxford: Clarendon Press.

Hampshire, Stuart (1959) *Thought and Action* London: Chatto and Windus.

Hart, H. L. A. and Honoré, A. M. (1959) (1985) *Causation and the Law* Oxford: Clarendon Press.

Hastings, James (ed) (1909) *Encyclopaedia of Religion and Ethics* vol. 2. Edinburgh and New York.

Heidel, W. A. (1906) 'Qualitative Change in Pre-Socratic Philosophy.' *Archiv fur Geschichte der Philosophie* Band 19 (Neue Folge 12 Band) 333–79.

Hemming, John (1978) *Red Gold: The conquest of the Brazilian Indians* London: Macmillan.

Hertz, R. (1907) (1960) *Death and the Right Hand* trans. R. and C. Needham. London: Cohen and West.

Hugh-Jones, Christine (1979) *From the Milk River: Spatial and Temporal processes in Northwest Amazonia* Cambridge University Press.

Hugh-Jones, Stephen (1979) *The Palm and the Pleiades: Initiation and Cosmology in Northwest Amazonia* Cambridge University Press.

Hurault, Jean (1961) 'Les Indiens Oayana de la Guyane Française.' *Journal de la Société des Américanistes de Paris* N.S. L. 135–83.

(1962) 'Les Indiens Oyampi de la Guyane Française.' *Journal de la Société des Américanistes de Paris* N.S. LI. 65–82.

(1963) 'Les Indiens de Guyane Française. *Nieuwe West-Indische Gids* vol. 42, 81–186.

Hussey, Edward (1972) *The Presocratics* London: Duckworth.

Huxley, Aldous (1929) 'Wordsworth in the Tropics' in *Do what you will* 113–29. London: Chatto and Windus.

(1928) (1955) *Point Counter Point* Penguin Books.

Jackson, Jean (1975) 'Recent Ethnography of Indigenous Northern Lowland South America.' *Annual Review of Anthropology* vol. 4, 307–40.

Kahn, Charles H. (1960) (1974) 'Anaximander's Fragment: The Universe governed by Law' in Alexander Mourelatos (ed) *The Pre-Socratics* 99–117. Anchor Books.

Kaplan, Joanna Overing (1975) *The Piaroa: A People of the Orinoco Basin* Oxford: Clarendon Press.

Keesing, Roger M. (1975) *Kin Groups and Social Structure* Holt, Rinehart and Winston.

Kirchhoff, Paul (1948) 'The Caribbean Lowland tribes' in Julian H. Steward (ed) *Handbook of South American Indians* vol. 4, 219–29. Washington: Smithsonian Institution.

Kirk, G. S. (1954) *Heraclitus: The Cosmic Fragments* Cambridge University Press.

Labat, Jean Baptiste (1730) *Voyage du Chevalier des Marchais en Guinée, Isles Voisines, et à Cayenne, fait en 1725, 1726, et 1727* four volumes. Paris.

Lambert, J. W. (1980) 'Close encounters in the jungle.' *The Sunday Times* 17 February 1980, 42.

Laraia, Roque de B. (1972) *Organização Social dos Tupi Comtemporâneos* Brasília.

Laraia, Roque and Da Matta, Roberto (1967) *Índios e Castanheiros* Sao Paulo: Difusora Européia do Livro.

Leach, Edmund (1954) *Political Systems of Highland Burma* London: G. Bell and Sons.

(1966) *Rethinking Anthropology* University of London: Athlone Press.

Leprieur, M. (1834) 'Voyage dans la Guyane Centrale.' *Bulletin de la Société de Géographie* 2nd series vol. 1, 201–29.

Lévi-Strauss, Claude (1955) *Tristes Tropiques* Paris: Plon.

(1963) 'Responses à quelques questions.' *Esprit* no. 322 vol. 31, 628–53.

(1970) *The Raw and the Cooked* London: Jonathan Cape.

(1974) *Tristes Tropiques* trans. J. and D. Weightman. New York; Atheneum.

Lévy-Bruhl, Lucien (1926) *How Natives Think* trans. L. A. Clare. London: George Allen and Unwin.

Lewis, I. M. (1971) *Ecstatic Religion* Penguin Books.

Lienhardt, Godfrey (1954) 'Modes of Thought' in

E. E. Evans-Pritchard et al. *The Institutions of Primitive Society* 95–107. Oxford: Basil Blackwell.

(1961) *Divinity and Experience* Oxford: Clarendon Press.

Lloyd, G. E. R. (1966) *Polarity and Analogy* Cambridge University Press.

Louch, A. R. (1966) *Explanation and Human Action* Oxford: Basil Blackwell.

Malinowski, B. (1948) *Magic, Science, and Religion and other Essays* Glencoe Ill.: The Free Press.

Maybury-Lewis, David (1974) 'Preface' to paperback edition of *Akwe-Shavante Society* 7 pages, no page numbers. Oxford University Press.

Mead, Margaret (1935) *Sex and Temperament in Three Primitive Societies* London: Routledge and Kegan Paul.

Métraux, Alfred (1927) 'Les Migrations historiques des Tupí-Guarani.' *Journal de la Société des Américanistes de Paris* N.S. vol. 19, 1–45.

(1949) 'The Couvade' in Julian H. Steward (ed) *Handbook of South American Indians* vol. 5, 369–74. Washington: Smithsonian Institution.

(1967) *Religion et magies indiennes d'Amérique du Sud* Paris: Éditions Gallimard.

Mills, C. Wright (1959) *The Sociological Imagination* New York: Oxford University Press.

Monod, Jaques (1977) *Chance and Necessity* Collins: Fount Paperbacks.

Montaigne, M. de (1595) (1962) *Essais* Paris: Éditions Garnier Frères.

Mourelatos, Alexander P.D. (ed) (1974) *The Pre-Socratics* 'Editor's Introduction.' 1–19. Anchor Books.

Murdock, George Peter (1949) *Social Structure* New York: Macmillan.

Murra, John (1948) 'The Cayapa and Colorado' in Julian H. Steward (ed) *Handbook of South American Indians* vol. 4, 277–91. Washington: Smithsonian Institution.

Needham, Rodney (1966) 'Terminology and Alliance 1: Garo, Manggarai.' *Sociologus* 16, 141–57.

(1972) *Belief, Language, and Experience* Oxford: Basil Blackwell.

(1976) 'Skulls and Causality.' *Man* N.S.11, 71–88.

O'Brien, Conor Cruise (1967) 'Politics and the Morality of Scholarship' in Max Black (ed) *The Morality of Scholarship* 57–74. Cornell University Press.

Okely, Judith (1975) 'The Self and Scientism.' *Journal of the Anthropological Society of Oxford* vol. 6, no. 3, 171–88.

Oliveira, Roberto Cardoso de (1964) *O Índio e o Mundo dos Brancos* São Paulo: Difusora Européia do Livro.

Osborne, Charles (ed) (1971) *Letters of Giuseppe Verdi* London: Victor Gollancz.

Pound, Ezra (1934) (1948) *The Cantos of Ezra Pound* New York: New Directions Book.

Pratt, Mary Louise (1986) 'Fieldwork in Common Places' in J. Clifford and G. Marcus (eds) *Writing Culture* 27–50. University of California Press.

Quine, Willard van Orman (1953) (1963) *From a Logical Point of View* New York: Harper Torchbooks.

Ralegh, Walter (1596) (1928) *The Discoverie of the large and bewtiful Empire of Guiana* edited by V. T. Harlow. London: Argonaut Press.

Reichel-Dolmatoff, G. (1975) *The Shaman and the Jaguar* Philadelphia: Temple University Press.

Ribeiro, Darcy (1970) (1977) *Os Índios e a Civilização* Petrópolis: Editora Vozes.

Richards, I. A. (1932) *Mencius on the Mind* London: Kegan Paul, Trench, Trubner and Co. Ltd.

Ricks, Christopher (1980) 'Prefatory Note' in L. Michaels and C. Ricks (eds) *The State of the Language* xi–xii. University of California Press.

Ricoeur, Paul (1977) 'Construing and constructing.' *Times Literary Supplement* 25 February 1977, 216.

(1975) (1978) *The Rule of Metaphor* trans. R. Czerny. London and Henley: Routledge and Kegan Paul.

Righter, William (1977) 'The 'Philosophical Critic' in David Newton-de Molina (ed) *The Literary Criticism of T. S. Eliot*, 111–38. University of London: Athlone Press.

Rivière, Peter G. (1963) *An Ethnographic Survey of the Indians on the Divide of the Guianese and Amazonian River Systems* Unpublished B. Litt. thesis. University of Oxford.

(1969) *Marriage among the Trio* Oxford: Clarendon Press.

(1974) 'The Couvade: a problem reborn.' *Man* N.S.9, 423–35.

n.d. 'The Lowland South America Culture Area: towards a structural definition'.

Robins, R. H. (1951) *Ancient and Mediaeval Grammatical Theory in Europe* London: G. Bell and Sons.

Rosaldo, Renato (1986) 'From the Door of His Tent: The Fieldworker and the Inquisitor' in J. Clifford and G. Marcus (eds) *Writing Culture* 77–97. University of California Press.

Rorty, Richard (1986) 'The Contingency of Language.' *London Review of Books* vol. 8, no. 7, 3–6.

Rosie, George (1978) *The Ludwig Initiative* Edinburgh: Mainstream Publishing Company.

Rüe, E. Aubert de la (1950) 'Quelques observations sur les Oyampi de l'Oyapock.' *Journal de la Société des Américanistes de Paris* N.S. XXXIX, 85–96.

Sahlins, Marshall (1974) *Stone Age Economics* London: Tavistock.

Sausse, André (1951) *Populations Primitives du Maroni* Paris.

Schulz-Kampfhenkel, O. (1940) *Riddle of Hell's Jungle* trans. V. M. Macdonald. London: Hurst and Blackett.

Seymour, M. C. (ed) (1968) *Mandeville's Travels* Oxford University Press.

Shapiro, Judith (1972) *Sex Roles and Social Structure among the Yanomamo Indians of Northern Brazil* Ph.D. Columbia University: University Microfilms, Ann Arbor, Michigan.

Spruce, Richard (1908) *Notes of a Botanist on the Amazon and the Andes* edited and condensed by A. R. Wallace. 2 vols. London: Macmillan.

Steiner, George (1971) *In Bluebeard's Castle* London: Faber and Faber.

(1972) *Extraterritorial* London: Faber and Faber.

Thomas, Keith (1984) *Man and the Natural World* Penguin Books.

Thoreau, H. D. (1854) (1937) *Walden and other writings of Henry David Thoreau* New York: The Modern Library.

Toulmin, Stephen (1953) *The Philosophy of Science* London: Hutchinson's University Library.

Trollope, Anthony (1873) *Australia and New Zealand* vol. 1. London.

Turnbull, Colin (1966) *Wayward Servants: The two worlds of the African Pygmies* London: Eyre and Spottiswoode.

Tylor, E. B. (1871) (1903) *Primitive Culture* vol. 2. London: John Murray.

Von Ihering, Rodolpho (1968) *Dictionário dos Animais do Brasil* São Paulo: Editôra Universidade de Brasília.

Wagley, Charles (1953) (1976) *Amazon Town* Oxford University Press.

(1977) *Welcome of Tears* Oxford University Press.

Wagley, C. and Galvão, E. (1949) (1969) *The Tenetehara Indians of Brazil* New York.

Waismann, F. (1968) *How I see Philosophy* edited by R. Harré. London: Macmillan.

Wallace, Alfred R. (1853) *A Narrative of Travels on the Amazon and Rio Negro* London: Reeve and Co.

Wheelwright, Philip (1959) *Heraclitus* Princeton University Press.

Whorf, B. L. (1956) *Language, Thought, and Reality* edited by J. B. Carroll. M.I.T. Press.

Williams, Raymond (1976) *Keywords* Fontana, Croom Helm.

Wilson, Edmund (1957) *A Piece of my Mind* London: W. H. Allen.

Winch, Peter (1964) (1970) 'Understanding a Primitive Society' in Bryan Wilson (ed) *Rationality* 78–111. Oxford: Basil Blackwell.

INDEX

Note. Portuguese and Wayãpí terms are printed in italics; names of Wayãpí are printed in **bold type**